FONT. THE SOURCEBOOK

FONT. THE SOURCEBOOK

**black dog
publishing**

london uk

CONTENTS

INTRODUCTION 10

THE DEVELOPMENT OF WRITING 14

PRINTING AND PROCESS 42

LETTERS 58

PUBLIC TYPE 80

MOVE TO THE MODERN 92

MECHANISATION 114

ART AND STYLE 136

THE DIGITAL AGE 164

CONCLUSION 198

FIRST THINGS FIRST

THE MECHANICS OF TYPE 206

FONT RESOURCE 212

INTRODUCTION

The story of typography just is the story of human communication. Across space and time and throughout all of recorded history, the way that humans have chosen to record stories, theories and all manner of public declaration has been informed by the technologies and designs surrounding the field of typography. Font. The Sourcebook tells the story of the printed word, and how the form of that word has influenced—and been influenced by—the content of history, politics, technological invention and artistic innovation throughout the entirety of human culture. This volume is divided into two main parts: the first is a narrative unpacking the story of type, the various technological markers that chart its development and the multitude of creative interventions that have driven its evolution. The second part of Font. The Sourcebook is a resource of some of the most noteworthy typefaces in use today, exploring distinctive aspects of their origin and design, and analysing their place in the wider history of type.

The opening chapter of the book begins with the first set of formal marks made for the purpose of communication, journeying through the emergence of hieroglyphs, Egyptian papyri and Greek scrolls to arrive at the format of the printed book still more or less in use today. Chapter two describes the mechanics of early printing methods, and how those practices were upset by the intervention of one German goldsmith, Johann Gutenberg, foregrounding the practice of printing from moveable type that would revolutionise the way written matter was produced and distributed for generations to come. "Letters" takes a closer look at the changing letterform and the course of events that led to the diversification of typefaces available to typesetters and designers, introducing the classification systems

that emerged to contain the proliferation of new design conventions. Chapter four takes us into the nineteenth century, with its bold display types transforming public space into a platform for the new typography to take hold, complete with daring letterforms and eye-catching innovations in layout and composition. "Move to the Modern" charts the end of the manuscript tradition, ushering in the age of the printed book in earnest and spinning the tales of the early typesetters and typographers who cemented its dominance at the heart of the public word. Chapter six describes the changing technology of the printing industry, from the Stanhope to the Albion to the advent of the steam powered press, and how these developments in the print workshop altered the look and feel of letterforms on the page. "Art and Style" looks at the various aesthetic movements that have influenced type design across the twentieth century, including Art Nouveau, Bauhaus, Constructivism and Futurism. The private press movement is also discussed here in relation to the rise of particular printing conventions and standards, engendered by different schools of aesthetic theory. And finally, chapter eight unpacks the events leading up to the dawn of the digital age, and how typography became synonymous with graphic design through the advent of software programs used today to forge some of the most innovative and important typographical work of the twenty-first century.

The story of type is periodically interrupted with comment and analysis by some of today's most important typographers, graphic designers, critics and theoreticians. London-based graphic designer David Pearson discusses the inspirations and machinations behind his work for Penguin's Great Ideas series, offering a first look at the never-before-seen covers of series three. Chairman of the Type Directors Club, Alex W White, gives counsel on how to farm inspiration from the larger visual world in order to fuel the most effective use of type, one that is both beautiful and meaningful. Will Hill offers up an interesting analysis of type revivals, explaining the technological necessity for the re-invention of some of history's most enduring typefaces, and the aesthetic ambition behind some of the more curious historical revivals. Pentagram's Domenic Lippa answers questions about the nature of good typographical practice, sound approaches in graphic design and ideas about the future of font in the digital age. A visual essay by Ed Fella explores the relationship between fine art and typography, depicting the mark of the artist on an underlying template—the 'mailer'—common to commercial graphic design. Teal Triggs interviews Sybille Hagmann in "Great Women Typographers—Where are They?", exploring the role of women in typography and giving insight into why they have historically had a low-profile in the industry, followed by a prescriptive analysis into how to better equip younger practitioners for a greater measure of success in the future. Renowned typographer Peter Bil'ak gives a fascinating account of the type family, how they work in relation to one another, and how to parse the emergence of new font 'superfamilies'. The cutting edge graphic design studio, Experimental Jetset, discuss their motivations and ambitions for what they take to be good graphic design practice and how that practice is informed by the changing demands of culture. Finally, Sam Winston's visual essay explores the space between content and form, and how that space can platform all manner of typographic challenges while also acting as fertile ground for artistic experimentation.

The second section of Font. The Sourcebook is a reference resource for designers, students and artists with a specific interest in the shape of letterforms and the ambition underlying their creation. 50 of the most interesting and innovative typefaces in use today are profiled in these pages, with a short history on their origin, their inspiration and the designer who brought them to life. Every typeface entry is illustrated with an extensive library, alongside a type example highlighting the most interesting aspect of the font's design.

Font. The Sourcebook is designed to be a resource for those interested in the story of type, that is, the story of visual communication across different moments in time and different aesthetic periods. The changing shapes of letterforms is explored against the backdrop of changing technologies, social mores and artistic movements, culminating in a complete look at the ever-evolving ways that humans have created form and meaning using the written word, and how that meaning has been imparted to the world through the changing forms of visual communication.

1 THE DEVELOPMENT OF WRITING

THE DEVELOPMENT OF WRITING

Typefaces are forms of letters, together with the associated punctuation and odd miasma of symbols that form the basis for communication on the printed page. Letters did not appear fully formed, but rather they gradually evolved over millennia through various communication systems. Even today, with the 26 character Western alphabet, Cyrillic, Oriental pictograms, the Greek alphabet, there are many different forms of written communication. In each culture and communication system there is a historical pedigree that has informed the way that letterforms appear today.

The Western alphabet in use today—that in which this book is printed—probably originated in the eastern corner of the Mediterranean some two millennia ago. In *The Alphabet*, David Diringer asserts that all alphabetic systems in use across the world today are derived from this invention, and that "the inventor or the inventors are to be ranged among the greatest benefactors of mankind… only the Syro-Palestinian Semites produced a genius who created alphabetic writing, from which have descended all past and present alphabets".[1]

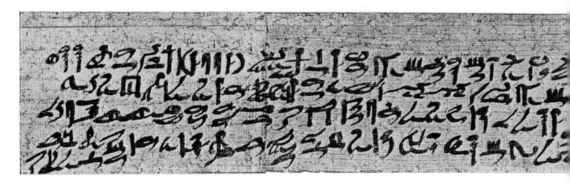

1 The *Papyrus Prisse* from Middle Kingdom in Egypt is commonly regarded as the oldest book in the world, dating to 2000 BC.

2, 3 An example of early Japanese printing from the year 770 by Empress Shotoku. Buddhist charms are printed in Sanskrit and in Chinese.

Writing is both functional and decorative, and from the earliest times the creators of written works have strived to form their letters and symbols in the most aesthetically pleasing way. At one end of the scale simple records of taxes and payments can be elegant if functional, whilst devotional works such as medieval illuminated manuscripts, Egyptian papyri or Chinese scrolls demonstrate an awe and reverence to their respective deities in the finesse of their production. Language in anything other than an oral tradition must be transmuted into a series of symbols that can be universally recognised and decoded by others. These may be the hieroglyphs of Ancient Egypt, Classical Greek or the modern alphabet. Each symbol acts as a signifier that indicates meaning or parts of a meaningful whole. Without this common understanding there can be no communication over distance and time, and the existence of maintained records defines man's ability, in Rousseau's words, to live a life that is anything other than "nasty, brutish and short". It is no coincidence then, that the great library at Alexandria is sometimes added to the list of the seven wonders of the ancient world.

The Alexandrian library was, however, not the first such collection of the written word known to civilisation. In the seventh century before Christ, Ashurbanipal—one of the last great monarchs of the Assyrian Empire—wrote about learning of "the wisdom of Nabu, the entire art of writing on clay tablets… I received the revelation of the wise Adapa, the hidden treasure of the art of writing… I considered the heavens with the learned masters… I read the beautiful clay tablets from Sumer and the obscure Akkadian writing which is hard to master. I had the joy of the reading of inscriptions on stone from the time before the flood…".[2] Ashurbanipal was perhaps the first recorded bibliophile, with an insatiable appetite for adding new works to his collection. He sent envoys out to scour the known world for the Sumerian and Babylonian texts that, even by his day, were regarded as ancient artefacts. These were far removed from modern books and even from the papyrus scrolls and parchment codices of the Alexandrian library, consisting of clay tablets, cylinders and octagonal columns into which pictograms, shapes

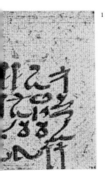

1

2

3

and symbols (some known as cuneiform writing) had been pressed whilst the clay was still wet.

The scribes who were the artificers of these, the earliest documents, and the creators of the first lettering systems were "the cohesive force that helped preserve and enrich one of mankind's very earliest civilisations throughout its long historical career… with the deployment of the first practical system of writing—an innovation which obviously lent societal mores a permanence and continuity heretofore lacking—the scribe emerged early as a central figure in the workings of Mesopotamia".[3] Armed with a system of rendering markings on damp clay, it was perhaps inevitable that the tablet writer should come to occupy a dominant position in his multifarious roles as temple attendant, commercial recorder, theologian and scholar. This role would appear to be very little different from that occupied by the residents of the medieval scriptoria.

There is, then, a similar link with the Egyptian scribe with his palette of inks and brushes. Like the rubricated bookmakers of Medieval Europe, he used black ink for the text and red to delineate titles and section beginnings. Early Egyptian scrolls were written in pictograms of hieroglyphics, or in their simplified form, hieratics, in vertical columns divided by black ruled lines. Illustrations run along the top and bottom of the scroll providing a separate, but corresponding, interpretation to the text. Later on, hieratic texts would come to be written horizontally, from right to left but still arranged in columns. Here the continuous frieze has been abandoned and the pictures populate the columns to which they refer. These visual commentaries, unframed and integrated into the text, persist stylistically through Greek and Roman manuscripts into Medieval and modern books, thus forming one of the most enduring traditions persistent in book design.

Egyptian papyri were also principally written in demotic and Coptic, but there are also papyri written in other languages and scripts: Aramaic, Greek and Latin, Persian, Arabic and Syriac. In the fourth century, when Alexander the

4

4 The earliest form of writing known is called cuneiform writing. The marks were created using a blunt reed into wet clay, and the first known examples are from the Sumerians, around 3000 BC.

Great completed the conquest of Egypt, he established Alexandria as the cultural pivot of the Hellenised world. Ptolemy II, in particular, continued to develop the collection, reputed to have grown to some one million scrolls, including the 200,000 scrolls looted from the great Library of Pergamum and given to Cleopatra by Mark Anthony as a wedding gift. Scribes copied any text that was brought into the city, transmuting Egyptian texts into classical culture and preserving the great Homeric odes with unusual perspicacity.

Greek scrolls were written in columns in a manner that would seem incongruous to the modern typographer, with neither punctuation nor spaces between the words. Instead, breaks were indicted by adding a subscripting line know as the 'paragraphos', or by inserting a small blank space. Such conventions continued to be frequently employed right up to the eleventh century.

Titles were inserted, if at all, at the end of the text in a sort of colophon, as they had been in earlier Egyptian scrolls.

5

6

5 Example of early forms of Akkadien writing.

6 Egyptian hieratic script, Papyrus, circa 1600 BC.

This practice would persist right through to the medieval period and into the earliest printed books. Style was often determined regionally with the scribe choosing his own column width dependant upon the writing material available and the nature of the text to be copied. In poetic works, for example, column width was dictated by the length of the individual lines. This multi-columnar approach into which illustrations could be applied persists into the European tradition of illuminated (and then early printed) Bibles, with their finely decorative initials, miniatures and text demarked by verses and chapters.

For informal and non-literary writing, a more fluent and casual types of script could be employed. These were known as cursive or demotic hands and they run through the history of book-making as counter to the constrained letterforms of more formal hands, emerging in printed books as italic.

Those restrained letters are perhaps best exemplified by the Latin alphabet, and in particular the angular use to which it was put with chiselled inscriptions on columns and the like. The Romans based their alphabet on that of their Etruscan neighbours, though its antecedents were in common with those of the Greeks, the Phoenicians and the Egyptian hieroglyphs and hieratics. Until well into the Christian period, Roman writing was executed in majuscules, or in capital letters only. But these formal capitals, relatively common in architecture, are rare in surviving manuscripts. Instead, a less formal version known as 'rustic capitals' was generally used. For even more casual purposes— such as private correspondence—a cursive script was often used, scratched into the surface of the wax-filled tabula with a stylus, thus giving rise to its somewhat disjoined appearance.

By contrast, the increased availability of parchment, with its smooth surface and relatively large writing area, undoubtedly had much to do with the development of the new rounded form of majuscule letter known as the uncial, with its scriptural elegance aligned to the rise and fall of the pen.

7 Early depiction of Greek scrolls as stored in the ancient precursors to the modern library.

8 *The Codex Sinaticus*, written in Greek unicals around 350 AD.

"In the fourth century, it appeared as a perfect book hand beside the square and rustic capital scripts, and from the fifth century onwards, for over five hundred years it was the main book hand of the Christian world...."[4] The fourth century *Codex Sinaticus*, held by the British Library, contains a good example of this hand, written (for the most part) in four columns of majestically executed uncials spread across the broad pages. In the same way John Baskerville would use the hot rolled paper to good effect with the black outline of his letters generations later.

Perhaps unsurprisingly, the fourth century also saw the dramatic shift of the written artefact, moving from the rolled scrolls of antiquity to the 'codex'—a series of bound manuscript sheets. The original intent of this terminology has filtered down to the present day in some of the names for the constituent parts of a book. The word 'codex' is derived from the Latin *caudex* or tree trunk, so it is perfectly in keeping that pages are still referred to as 'leaves' and that the covers are defined as 'boards'—though this later terminology almost certainly relates to the early binding practice of using leather over wooden boards to protect the bound text-block of a book. In the same vein, the word 'book' is itself derived from the Anglo-Saxon word for beech tree.

So the book had finally freed itself from the restraints of the scroll arrangement, becoming taller and narrower, with the text usually written in two columns on the page. To complement this elongated structure, the half uncial letter was developed, with its graceful ascenders and descenders. Paragraphs began to be demarked by large initial letters projecting into the margin, though the remainder of the written text stayed as a continuous block undivided and uniform in appearance well into the ninth century. Variations on the unciar and majuscular hand can be seen developing across Europe. Works such as the seventh century *Book of Durrow* have been rendered in an Irish majuscule, within which initials of vegetative complexity are intertwined.[5]

9 When carving text into stone, the Romans only used capital letters, or majuscules, and rarely used spaces between words.

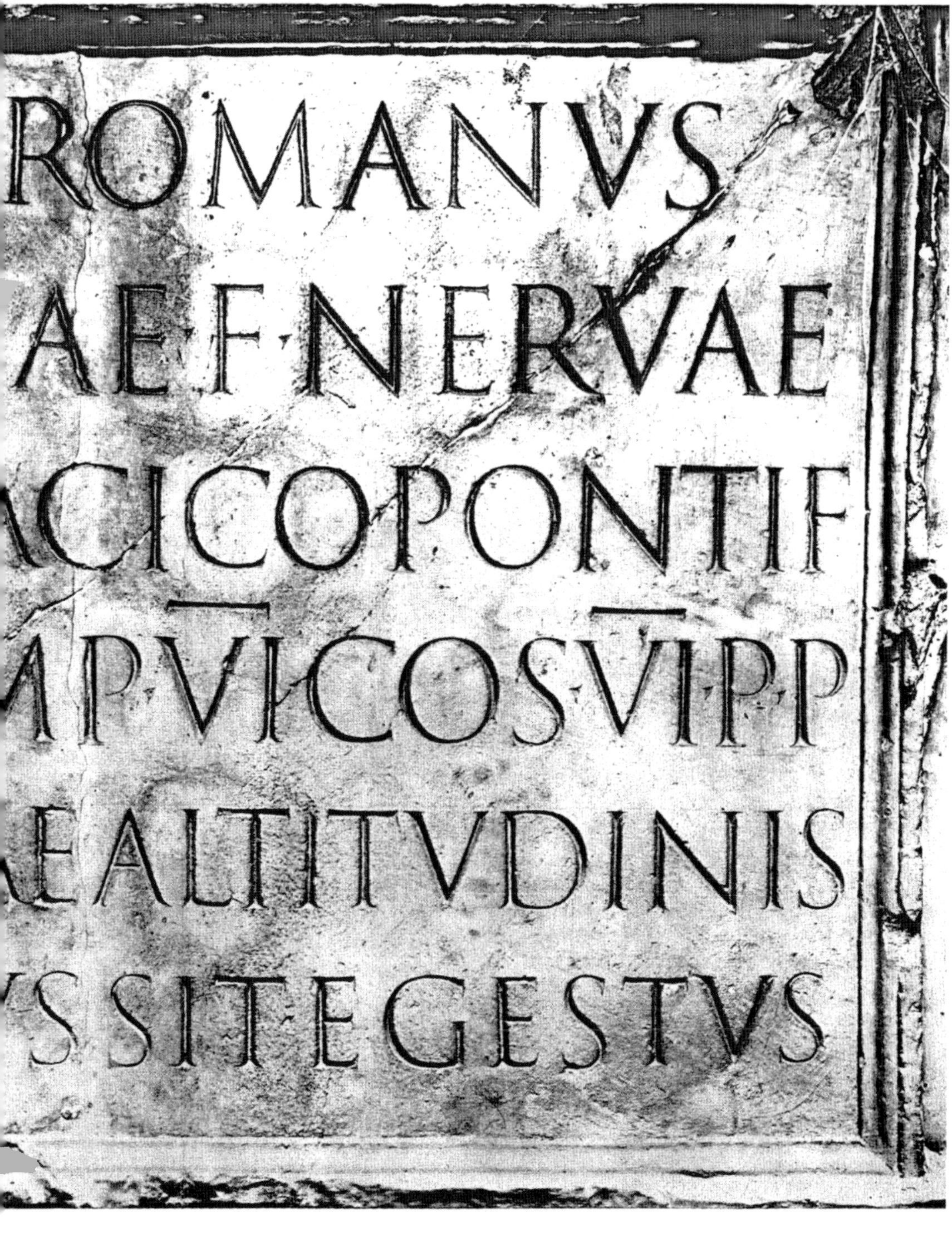

ROMANVS

AEF NERVAE

CICOPONTIF

MPVICOSVIPP

EALTITVDINIS

SSITEGESTVS

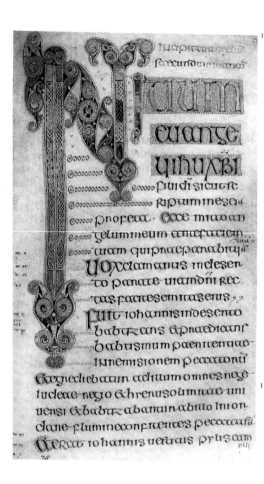
10

11

In France, under the warrior king Charlemagne, and probably influenced by the Anglo-Irish hand, a miniscule script was developed wherein each letter was separately formed and divorced from other characters by the white space on the page. In order to confer gravitas, roman majuscules or uncials were employed for titles and important headings. The Carolingian script spread through the monastic world to become the standard book hand of Western Europe, and can still be seen perfectly rendered in works such as the ninth century copy of Pliny's *Historia Nauralis* held in the Pierpont Morgan Library.[6] The coalescence of majuscules and minuscules into a meaningful written system is mainly due to this script. It was employed almost universally until the twelfth century, when the letters gradually assumed a more angular shape emerging as the blackletter or Gothic script, which was employed in Britain until the sixteenth century and in Germany until well into the twentieth century. Crucially, this was the written letterform that the earliest printers sought to imitate before type

10 Page from the *Book of Durrow*, set in Irish majuscules and produced some time in the seventh century.

11 Carolingian capitals, probably by Alcuin of York, Rome, 796 AD.

12 In Italy, the concentration was on ancient Greek and Roman texts and developed a fine cursive style of writing, circa 1540.

13 Psalter leaf, France, 1210 AD Angular Gothic bookhand on vellum.

designers relegated its inky blackness to the realms of the legal and liturgical tract, preferring instead the light airiness of the humanistic or Renaissance letterforms derived from the Carolingian model and from which they created the family roman type faces.

The fifteenth century in Italy saw the development of a finely rendered cursive hand based on the earlier round miniscule. Being considered to be of classical origin this was called 'antiqua' and was generally employed for the production of literary pieces. With time, the style developed into two forms: the first, a venetian miniscule, nowadays referred to as 'italic' and for many years ascribed in origin to the handwriting of the poet Petrach. It is probably one of the most legible of all character forms ever invented, especially suited to the cramped pages of small-scale productions to which end a printed form was used to great effect by the printer Aldus Manutius in his series of pocket classics. The second form appears as a 'roman' type of letter which was again perfected in northern Italy, chiefly at Venice, where it was developed into the typefaces used in the printing presses during the late fifteenth and early sixteenth centuries. With the spread of printing across Europe it came to be disseminated to the Netherlands, Germany, Spain and France, arriving in Britain around 1520, when it is possible to see Caxton's acolyte, Wynkyn de Worde reject the heavy blackletter forms of his master to embrace the much lighter continental model, setting the stage for the printed book of the next few hundred years.

12

13

1

DAVID PEARSON

Penguin Books—Great Ideas

Penguin Crime   2'6

abcdefghijk
mnopqrstuvwxy

abcdefghijklmnop

abcdefghijkl

abcdefghijklmnopqr

90°

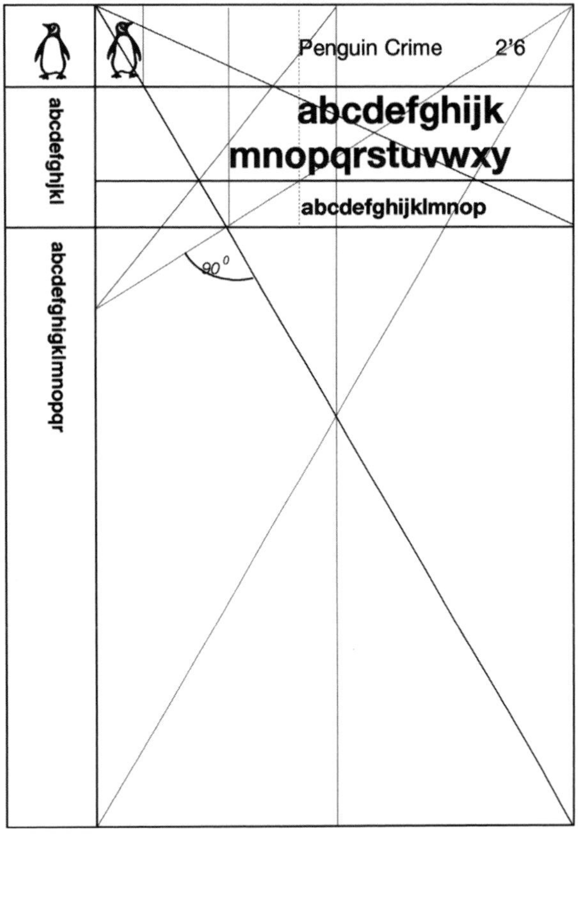

1 The Marber grid, 1961.
Romek was a freelance cover
designer for Penguin from
1961 to 1969.

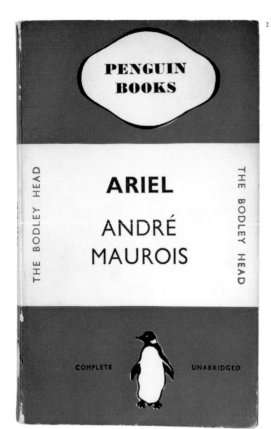

2

2 Penguin no 1:
André Maurois, *Ariel*, 1935.
Cover design by Edward Young.

3 An early proposal for
The Social Contract cover.

4 Jean-Paul Sartre *Words*, 1983.
Cover design by Derek Birdsall.

In Britain today, books fight fiercely for shelf space. Full-bleed pictures and huge type are very much the norm, and the idea that a quietly suggestive cover could be heard through the noise seems to be increasingly overlooked. There is a common notion within publishing that academics will buy a book regardless of its cover whereas your average consumer has to be manipulated all the way to the check-out. This is a belief not found commonly in other European countries, where books are consistently packaged with dignity and a respect for the buying public. Austere-looking covers sit happily next to packets of sweets in Italian railway kiosks, whilst the most commercial French novels need carry no more information than a tiny title and author name on a plain white background.

In Britain, this rather utilitarian approach has never been more neatly executed than by Penguin Books in its early years. The founding of the company in 1935 heralded a new, egalitarian era of publishing. For the first time, the ordinary man or woman in the street was able to buy a pocket-sized paperback for the price of a packet of cigarettes. Book buying was no longer the preserve of the privileged classes, and books could now sell in huge quantities. Significantly, Penguin achieved this early success without the aid of pictures, shiny foil or marketing slogans, just simple, approachable design.

Over the years, the clarity of Penguin's purpose had become somewhat compromised by shifting

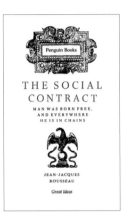

3

THE SOCIAL
CONTRACT

MAN WAS BORN FREE,
AND EVERYWHERE
HE IS IN CHAINS

JEAN-JACQUES
ROUSSEAU

Great Ideas

4

'I loathe my
childhood
and all that
remains of it...'
Words by Jean-
Paul Sartre

production costs and an increasingly competitive marketplace. And in the field of 'classic' literature, in order to maintain their leading position—and to justify their cover price—many of the books had developed into unwieldy tomes loaded with annotation and critical essays which had the effect of narrowing their appeal, resulting in a more academic readership.

In 2004, Simon Winder (a commissioning editor for Penguin Press) began to develop an idea for a mini-series—modest in both pagination and price—that might go some way towards shaking off the stigma that had attached itself to the buying of classic literature. These new books would revert to Penguin's original 'A' format, which would give them back an easy, pamphletty feel and enable a significant price reduction.[1]

The conceit for Great Ideas is to take existing Penguin books and chip pieces off. This is partly to try to encourage buyers to go from the chip back to the classic it came from and partly to remain true to the vision of Allen Lane (the founder of Penguin Books), that the publisher existed to educate and to popularise.

While spanning over 2,000 years of philosophy, the first 20 book selection addresses many very contemporary issues, such as globalisation, the environment, religious intolerance, and so on.

So what is the most appropriate aesthetic for philosophy? How do you sum up a text that tells us everything and, yet nothing at all? Perhaps abstract shapes, patterns or evocative landscapes? At once these solutions feel too contrived, too knowing.

As a junior designer at Penguin, I was given the task of designing the covers. With no existing model to influence proceedings and, therefore no specific sales expectations, my Art Director (Jim Stoddart) deemed it an ideal project for me to cut my teeth on.

Early in the process, illustration was suggested to me as a possible solution, but owing to the subjective nature of the writing it felt like a mistake to dress the covers in imagery that might simply mislead. I imagined that a less literal treatment might better serve the subjects and challenge the reader to project their own meaning onto the covers. If you can activate a reader's interpretive participation you stand a much better chance of making their experience a meaningful one.

On reading the texts, it became apparent that later writers often revered or reviled earlier writers in interesting ways, so there seemed a good reason to make clear visual connections across the series.

I worked up some rough covers to present internally, and although they sported gross historical inaccuracies (blackletter used for Mary Wollstonecraft's passionate

5

MARCUS AU
RELIUS·MED
ITATIONS·A
LITTLE FLES
H, A LITTLE
BREATH, AN
D A REASON
TO RULE AL
L—THAT IS M
YSELF·PENG
UIN BOOKS
GREAT IDEAS

declaration of female independence, for example)
the selection was clear enough in its intention: situating
the writing in its historical and geographical place
through typography.

Type-only covers had become increasingly rare in
publishing, but I remember feeling confident that my
solution was 'on brand', as Penguin have a rich history
of distinctive, type-driven jackets. Also, my feeling was
that the cumulative effect of the covers would give them
sufficient presence when displayed.

An initial concern was sparked by the lack of a publisher's
logo on the covers. To emphasise the period-specific
styling I had decided to represent the company and
series names with words only, arguing that this
treatment—when applied consistently across 20
titles—would then create its own brand identity.

The roughs seemed to have an immediate impact, and
this bought me time to go away and research the project
in full, with the expectation that I would return with
a more complete solution.

During this period I was able to sound out other
designers—namely Phil Baines and Catherine Dixon (my
college tutors), and one of my old classmates, Alistair Hall.
This would ensure two things: that the project would have
an in-built level of quality control (typophiles can be very
unforgiving if you get it wrong) and that collectively the

covers would appear varied and interesting. For example,
when Phil got involved I was struck by how confidently
he used the cover area, and it is this fluctuation in scale
that helped provide pace to the series. Phil's approach
opened my eyes and made me realise that I too could
push the idea further than I had originally imagined. The
series could have quite easily turned into a straight-laced,
visual history of lettering, but we were now finding more
and more abstract ways to represent the subject matter.
This gave the project personality and even a little humour.

Finally, after eight weeks of intense activity, came the
unveiling. I guess I'd begun to feel rather protective of
the work since it was the first project I'd been allowed
to manage, so I wanted to give it the strongest chance of
success. To do this, I held back until I was ready to show
all 20 covers at the same time, thus making the strongest
possible statement.

The temptation of all clients is to make small changes—
partly to acquire some ownership of the idea themselves
and partly out of well intentioned attempts to second-
guess the market. Happily, in this instance, the Penguin
press managing director—Stefan McGrath—stuck his
neck out and insisted that every cover be preserved in an
unadulterated state. This was a very bold decision, and I
noticed more than a few worried looks, but he simply
felt that the process of making changes—once begun—
would never end and that the integrity of the project
would be compromised.[2]

6

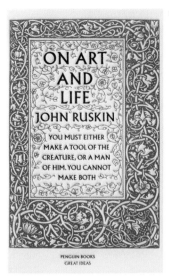

7

Thomas à Kempis
The Inner Life

A true understanding and humble estimate of oneself is the highest and most valuable of all lessons. To take no account of oneself, but always to think well and highly of others is the highest wisdom and perfection. Should you see another person openly doing evil, or carrying out a wicked purpose, do not on that account consider yourself better than him, for you cannot tell how long you will remain in a state of grace. We are all frail; consider none more frail than yourself.

Penguin Books
Great Ideas

8

FRIEDRICH
NIET3SCHE
WHY I AM
SO WISE

I know my fate. One day there will be associated with my name the recollection of something frightful—of a crisis like no other before on earth, of the profoundest collision of conscience.

Penguin Books   **Great Ideas**

9

5 Marcus Aurelius,
Meditations, 2004.
Cover design by Phil Baines.

6 John Ruskin,
On Art and Life, 2004.
Cover design by David Pearson.

7 Thomas Kempis,
The Inner Life, 2004.
Cover design by David Pearson.

8 Friedrich Nietzsche,
Why I am So Wise, 2004.
Cover design by Phil Baines.

9 Jonathan Swift,
A Tale of a Tub, 2004.
Cover design by David Pearson.

10

10

With approval won, the next step was to proof the covers.[3] Of course, we did not have an unlimited budget, and we had to monitor quite closely what was spent. Once the economical decision was made to use only two colours (black and red, which is the traditional second printing colour), it meant that more elaborate finishes could be afforded. The debossing of type tips a nod to letterpress printing (albeit in a rather amplified way) while the choice of an uncoated, off-white stock reinforces the link with traditional printing.[4]

In book publishing, it can be a contentious decision to leave a cover uncoated, as it tends to get rather dirty, but I never saw this as a problem since the books would only acquire a stronger sense of erudition the more beaten up they became.

These days, the sales team normally show what is new at Penguin on their laptops. The trouble is, in PowerPoint you gain no sense of a cover's tactile qualities.

In one instance, a Penguin salesman (Andy Taylor) pretended that his computer was broken in order to get the proofs into the hands of his customers, and he insists that this made all the difference.

Great Ideas was launched on 2 September 2004, and sales currently stand at three million copies worldwide. Second and third series have since been commissioned—in blue and green respectively—and things may not end there.

10 George Orwell,
Why I Write (detail), 2004.
Cover design by Alistair Hall.

11 St Augustine
Confessions of a Sinner, 2004.
Cover design by Catherine Dixon.

12 Linotype Vere Dignum:
Regular (top) and Decorative.
Designed by Phil Baines.

OHAMBURGEFONTIV [12]

OHAMBURGEFONS

JT AUGUJTINE

CONFEJJIONG

OF A JINNER

AJ A YOUTH
I HAD PRAYED To YOU
FOR CHAJTITY AND JAID, GIVE ME
CHAJTITY &
CONTINENCE
BUT
NOT
YET

PENGUIN BOOKJ · GREAT IDEAJ

The series' success should be attributed to many different factors: Simon's original idea was a great one, implying that world-changing thought and writing equates to Penguin, while the finished books reflected Allen Lane's philosophy that good design should cost no more than bad; but above all the publisher displayed an unfaltering level of confidence in the project, ensuring that its message remained clear and its purpose true.

The Covers: Confessions of a Sinner (series I)

There is no early Christian font revival contemporary with St Augustine, so designer Catherine Dixon decided on a more lateral approach for Confessions of a Sinner (Great Idea no 3):

…My work focused instead on ideas about how lettering could be used in a certain celebratory and decorative sense. I also wanted to retain a crudeness in the letterforms used. The Vere Dignum font offered both these things. It also reflected ideas about visual excess and restraint as it has an over indulgent, curly variant of the plain base font. I have to say, though, that it bothered me quite a lot at first that the letterforms were not historically legitimate. But that is to miss the point of the series idea, I think. That has far more to do with a way of looking at aspects of past practice and extracting the ideas informing that practice, as much as it is about copying the visual manifestations of different styles.

13

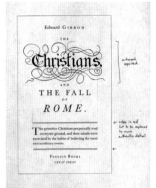

14

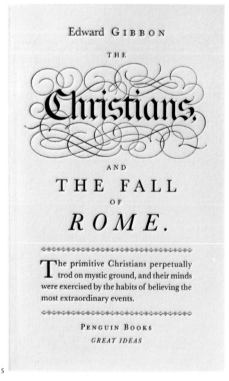

15

The Covers: *Christians and the Fall of Rome* (series I)

The *Christians and the Fall of Rome* (Great Idea no 9) mirrors the title page design of Baskerville's Bible for Cambridge University Press, 1776.

As he developed the cover, Phil decided that his favourite band—The Fall—should be entitled to a special mention.

The Covers: *Books v Cigarettes* (series III)

Far be it from me to imply that laziness has ever gripped a Penguin design department, but even the briefest look through the company's archive presents a very clear pattern: Penguin have often turned to the humble circle in order to solve a design brief. So obvious is this trend (there are literally hundreds of examples) that when it came to designing George Orwell's *Books v Cigarettes* (Great Idea no 57), the revival of the big circle felt like a fitting tribute to this quintessentially Penguin author.

Adopting Romek Marber's Penguin crime grid, the cover suggests that a cigarette stub (or is that a bullet hole?) has actually punctured the book's cover, fatally wounding it.

With Penguin's 'crime green' already in place as our series colour, all that remained was to persuade Penguin that an extra colour was required.[5] Red had made fleeting appearances in Romek's own crime covers

—usually to denote blood—and such sparing use of embellishment was symptomatic of Penguin's early rigour. Although it didn't make me very popular with the other designers, its addition to our palette felt like a fitting indulgence for one of the list's biggest-selling authors.

The typeface used is Intertype Standard (a version of Berthold's Akzidenz Grotesk) and this was directly lifted from a selection of previous Penguin covers

Early titles in Romek's crime series featured minimal use of capitalisation, so this model was retained for our own version, for example using 'cigarettes' instead of 'Cigarettes'. Overprinting also makes an appearance here, in what is one of our looser interpretations of a typographic cover.[6]

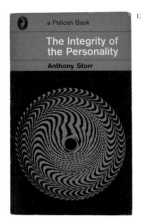

16

17

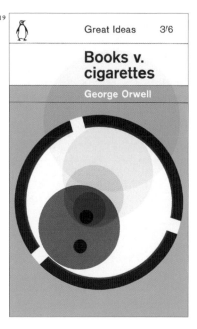

18

19

13 John Baskerville's title
page, for his 1776 Bible.

14 Rough layout by Phil Baines
for *The Christians and the Fall of Rome*.

15 Edward Gibbon,
*The Christians and the Fall
of Rome*, 2004.
Cover design by Phil Baines.

16, 17 'Big circles': Anthony
Storr, *The Integrity of the Personality*,
1970. Cover photograph: Snark
International; *Radical School Reform*,
1972 (uncredited).

18 Josephine Tey,
The Daughter of Time, 1961.
Cover design by Romek Marber.

19 George Orwell,
Books v Cigarettes, 2008.
Cover design by David Pearson.

20

MM AA RR CC OO
MM AA RR CC OO

PP OO LL OO
PP OO LL OO

TRAVELS IN THE LAND OF

KK UU BB II LL AA II
KK UU BB II LL AA II

KK HH AA NN
KK HH AA NN

EVERY
ONE SHOU
LD KNOW TH   AT T
HIS GREAT KHA   N IS TH
E MIGHTIEST MA   N, WHETH
ER IN RESPECT OF S   UBJECTS OR
OF TERRITORY OR OF   TREASURE, WH
O IS IN THE WORLD TODAY OR WHO HAS EVER
BEEN ... EVERYONE WILL BE CONVINCED THAT
HE IS INDEED THE GREATEST LORD THE WORL
D HAS EVER KNOWN ¶ EVERYONE SHOULD KN
OW THAT THIS GREAT KHAN IS THE MIGHTIEST
MAN, WHETHER IN RESPECT OF SUBJECTS OR O
F TERRITORY OR OF TREASURE, WHO IS IN THE
WORLD TODAY OR WHO HAS EVER BEEN ... EVER
YONE WILL BE CONVINCED THAT HE IS INDEED
THE GREATEST LORD THE WORLD HAS EVER KN
OWN ¶ EVERYONE SHOULD KNOW THAT THIS G
REAT KHAN IS THE MIGHTIEST MAN, WHETHER
IN RESPECT OF SUBJECTS OR OF TERRITORY ...
PENGUIN BOOKS ¶ GREAT IDEAS

21

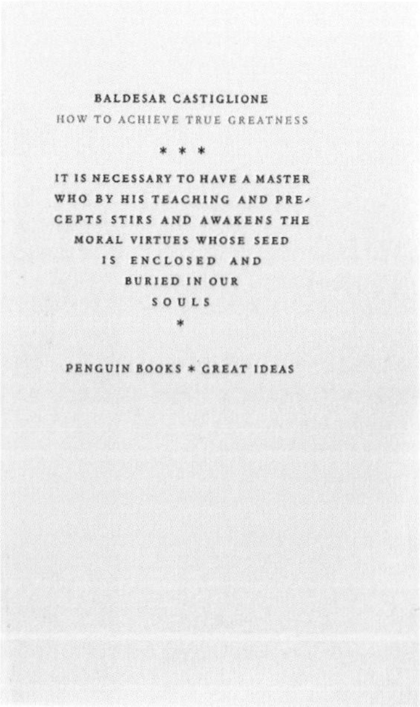

BALDESAR CASTIGLIONE
HOW TO ACHIEVE TRUE GREATNESS

* * *

IT IS NECESSARY TO HAVE A MASTER
WHO BY HIS TEACHING AND PRE-
CEPTS STIRS AND AWAKENS THE
MORAL VIRTUES WHOSE SEED
IS ENCLOSED AND
BURIED IN OUR
SOULS

*

PENGUIN BOOKS * GREAT IDEAS

22 23

Of
EMPIRE
FRANCIS BACON

Read not to contradict and
confute; nor to believe and
take for granted; nor to find
talk and discourse;
but to weigh and consider.

Penguin Books, Great Ideas

24

NO ONE CAN BE SAID TO HAVE A HAPPY LIFE WHEN ITS
VIOLENT TERMINATION BRINGS HIS SLAYERS NOT MERELY IMPUNITY BUT THE HEIGHT OF GLORY

C
AN ATTACK
I
ON AN ENEMY
C
OF FREEDOM
E
PENGUIN BOOKS
R
GREAT IDEAS
O

20 Marco Polo, *Travels in the Land of Kubilai Khan*, 2005.
Cover design by Phil Baines.

21 Baldesar Castiglione, *How to Achieve True Greatness*, 2005.
Cover design by Phil Baines.

22 Albert Camus, *Myth of Sisyphus*, 2005.
Cover design by David Pearson.

23 Francis Bacon, *Of Empire*, 2005.
Cover design by David Pearson.

24 Cicero, *An Attack on an Enemy of Freedom*, 2005.
Cover design by Phil Baines.

25

26

27

25 Letter sampling using
Adobe Photoshop.

26 Robert Burton,
Some Anatomies of Melancholy, 2008.
Cover design by Catherine Dixon.

27 Sigmund Freud,
The Future of an Illusion, 2008.
Cover design by David Pearson.

28 Leo Tolstoy, *Confession*, 2008.
Cover design by David Pearson.

29 Frantz Fanon,
Concerning Violence, 2008.
Cover design by Phil Baines.

FRIEDRICH·
NIETZSCHE·
MAN·ALONE·
WITH·HIM·
SELF

Every superior human being will instinctively aspire after a secret citadel where he is set free from the crowd, the many, the majority.

Penguin Books Great Ideas

30

PLUTARCH
IN CONSOLATION
TO HIS WIFE
WE MUST NOT
SLUMP IN
DEJECTION
OR SHUT
OURSELVES
AWAY
PENGUIN BOOKS
GREAT IDEAS

31

AN APPEAL TO THE
TOILING, OPPRESSED
AND EXHAUSTED
PEOPLES OF
EUROPE

THEY TURN THEIR PEOPLE'S BLOOD INTO THEIR MASTER'S GOLD

LEON TROTSKY
PENGUIN BOOKS GREAT IDEAS

32

30 Friedrich Nietzcshe,
Man Alone with Himself, 2008.
Cover design by Phil Baines.

31 Plutarch,
In Consolation to his Wife, 2008.
Cover design by Catherine Dixon
and David Pearson.

32 Leon Trotsky, *An Appeal to the
Toiling Oppressed and Exhausted Peoples
of Europe*, 2008.
Cover design by David Pearson.

33 Albert Camus, *Fastidious
Assassins*, 2008.
Cover design by David Pearson.

34 Ralph Waldo Emerson,
Nature, 2008.
Cover design by David Pearson.

33

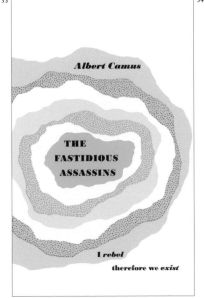

Albert Camus

THE
FASTIDIOUS
ASSASSINS

I *rebel*

therefore we *exist*

34

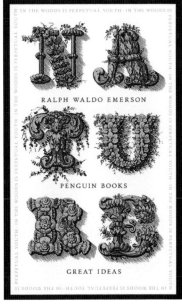

RALPH WALDO EMERSON

PENGUIN BOOKS

GREAT IDEAS

2 PRINTING AND PROCESS

PRINTING AND PROCESS

The copying of manuscripts was a laborious process and the majority of books in the fourteenth century were to be found only in the great libraries, or the households of the moneyed few.[1] Even the moderately well-off were devoid of even the most basic reading matter. The Peasant's Revolt in 1381 might have questioned temporal authority but it was the challenge to the theological status quo led by the exponents of the Reformation, and a new-found thirst for the foundation texts of classical knowledge, that gestated a new demand for books in ever greater numbers. The essential elements for the production of printed matter in quantity were already latent in the world and needed only a catalyst to be brought together. Both the Chinese and the Koreans had been producing printed images and texts for hundreds of years. Initially, these were cut entirely onto wooden blocks, then with the texts executed from crude moveable types cast from either bronze or clay. The craft of printing had travelled down the trade routes but as yet its potential as a reproductive process had not, in Europe, been realised. Paper also originated in the Far East, first recorded

1 Image of a scribe copying the Bible in a medieval scriptorium, 1893.

2 Paper had been first invented in the Far East, and gradutally migrated to Europe through trade routes.

in China in 105 AD. It first arrived on European shores in Spain during 1276, and before long the mills at Fabiano in Italy were in operation, soon becoming one of the primary paper producers in Europe. By the fifteenth century, paper was freely available and woodcut prints encompassing small lettered inscriptions were being produced for the popular market. One of the earliest examples of this that can be directly dated in that of St Christopher and depicts the saint as the bearer of the infant Jesus who is held aloft from the waves crashing onto distant rocky shores. Underneath is a Latin verse followed by the date 1423.[2] The fundamental problem though, still lay in the ability to reproduce large amounts of lettering to a consistently high standard, thus obviating the need for laborious copying or carving of individual letters into wood. Drawing on the inspiration of the Chinese, it would take a German goldsmith of dubious reputation to solve the riddle.

How then should the first book printed from moveable type appear meteor-like and fully formed from these humble beginnings? The genesis of the great 42-line Bible created by Johann Gutenberg at Mainz sometime around 1455 is still, partly, shrouded in mystery. Indeed, until quite recently there was some doubt as to the identity of the first printer, with claim and counter claim rebounding around Europe. Other contestants to the title include (to name a few) Gutenberg's accomplice Johann Fust and, the redoubtable Dutchman, Laurens Coster.[3] Gutenberg's breakthrough apparently stems from his background as a goldsmith and fine metalworker. Type relies on the relief printing process in that it is the raised portion of the inked letter that comes into contact with the paper. Manufacturing that type accurately required considerable skill, first in making the master punches from which moulds can be formed, and then in casting the individual type pieces from a suitable alloy.

Manufacture of Type

Though none of his equipment survives and neither he nor any of his contemporaries left any indication of his

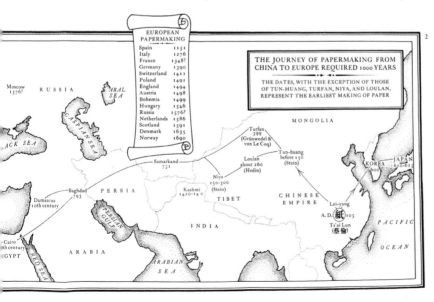

3

AD EBREOS

fuit:nūc aūt et michi ꝯ tibi vtilis:quē
remisi tibi . Tu aūt illū vt mea viscera
suscipe.Quē ego volueꝛā mecū detine
re:vt pro te michi ministraret ī vincu
lis euangelij. Hinc cōsilio aūt tuo ni
chil volui facere:vti ne velut ex necessi
tate bonū tuū esset:sed volūtariū . For
sitan eni ideo discessit ad horā a te:vt
eternū illū reciperes:iam nō vt seruum
sed pro seruo carissimū fratrem :maxime
michi.Quāto aūt magis tibi:et ī car
ne et ī dūo: Si ego habes me sociū:
suscipe illū sicut me. Si aūt aliqd no
cuit tibi aut debet:hoc michi imputa.
Ego paulus scripsi mea manu . Ego
reddam:vt non dicā tibi ꝙ ꝯ teipm mi
chi debes. Ita frater ego te fruar in do
mino:reficere viscera mea ī cristo . Con
fidens in obediētia tua scripsi tibi:scies
qñ et sup id qd dico facies. Simul et
para michi hospiciū:nā spero ꝑ oratio
nes vras donari me vobis. Salutat
te epafras concaptiuus me9 in cristo ihe
su:marc9 aristarchus demas ꝯ lucas
adiutores mei. Gratia dūi nri ihesu
cristi cū spiritu vestro amen . Explicit
epls ad phylemonem incipit argu
mentū in eplam ad hebreos :

IN primis dicendū est cur aptus pau
lus ī hac epla scribendo nō seruauerit
morem suū:vt vel vocabulū nominis
sui vel ordinis describeret dignitatem.
Hec causa est ꝙ ad eos scribens ꝙ ex cir
cuncisione crediderant ꝗ̄i gentiū apo
stolus ꝯ nō hebreos:sciens quoꝯ eor
superbiam:suāꝯ humilitate ipse demo
strans meritū officij sui noluit anteferre.
Nā simili modo etiā iohānes apus
propter humilitate in epla sua nome
suū eade ratioe nō pnuit. Hanc ergo
eplam fertur apostol9 ad hebreos con
scriptā hebraica lingua misisse:cuius

sensum ꝯ ordinē retinens lucas euan
gelista post excessum apostoli pauli
greco sermone cōposuit. Explicit argu
mentū Incipit epla ad hebreos:

MUltipharie mltisꝯ
modis olim deus
loquēs patribus in
prophetis :nouissi
me diebz istis locu
tus e nobis in filio
quē ostituit heredem vniuersoꝛ:ꝑ quē
fecit et secla.Qui cū sit splendoꝛ glorie:
et figura substātie eius ·portansꝯ oia
verbo virtutis sue purgatione pecca
torū faciens : sedet ad dexterā maiesta
tis in excelsis tanto melioꝛ angelis ef
fectus:quanto differentius pre illis no
men hereditauit.Cui eni dixit aliquā
do angeloꝛ filius meus es tu ego ho
die genui te? Et rursum.Ego ero illi i
patrem:ꝯ ipe erit michi in filiū . Et cū
iterum introducit pmogenitū in oꝛbe
terre dicit.Et adorent eum omnes an
geli dei. Et ad angelos quidem dicit.
Qui facit angelos suos spiritus:et mi
nistros suos flammā ignis. Ad filiū
autem.Thronus tuus de9 in seculum
seculi:virga equitatis virga regni tui.
Dilexisti iusticiā et odisti iniquatem:
propterea vnxit te deus deus tuus o
leo exultationis pre participibz tuis.
Et tu in principio dūe terrā fundasti:
et opera manuū tuarum sunt celi. Ipi
peribunt tu autem pmanebis:ꝯ omnes
ut vestimentū veterascent . Et velut a
mictum mutabis eos ꝯ mutabūtur:
tu autem idem ipse es:ꝯ anni tui non
deficient. Ad quē aūt angelorum di
xit aliquādo sede a dextris meis: quo
adusqꝯ ponā inimicos tuos scabellū
pedū tuoꝯ? Nōne oūes? sunt aministra
torij spirit9:ī ministeriū missi propter

3, 4 Pages from Johann
Gutenberg's famed 42-line
Bible, the first document to be
printed with moveable type in
the Western world.

Photography by Matthew Pull.

processes, Gutenberg must have produced matrices formed by striking a punch or punches into some small slab of soft metal such as copper. An adjustable mould would then have accommodated one matrix at a time and permitted molten lead to be poured into the cavity. The result is a piece of type each consisting of a single letter (aside from ligatures) on a column of lead (the body) of a standard height with a letterform on one end replicating that of the punch.

In the seventeenth century, Joseph Moxon gave the first comprehensive account of this process in English:

> If the letter-cutter be to cut a whole set of punches of the same body of roman and italica, he provides about 240 or 260 of these punches, because so many will be used in the roman and italica capitals and lower case, double letters, swash letters, accented letters, figures, points, etc. But this number of punches are to have several heights and thicknesses, though the letters to be cut on them are all of the same body.... The steel punches being thus finish'd,

as afore was shewed, they are to be sunk or struck into pieces of copper, about an inch and an half long, and one quarter of an inch deep; but the thickness not assignable, because of the different thickness of the letters.... But before these punches are sunk into the copper, the letter founder must provide a mold to justify the matrices by.... Every mold is made of two parts, and under and an upper.... And the sliding of these two parts of the mold backwards, makes the shank of the letter thicker, because the bodies in each part stand wider asunder; and the sliding them forwards makes the shank of the letter thinner, because the bodies on each part of the mold stand closer together.[4]

Gutenberg's skill was in the formulation of the alloy from which to cast the type and in the method of adjusting the mould to accept the differing widths of letters in the Latin alphabet.

The strong allegiance of Gutenberg's, and indeed the majority of the early printers', typefaces to the letterforms used in contemporary manuscripts can be traced

4

back to the conventions of the written text laid down nearly a millennium before. No doubt conscious to introduce new technology whilst remaining within the careful tradition of book making, the 42-line Bible and succeeding works (with their columns of closely packed and heavily blackened lettering interspersed and enlivened only by decorative initials) could be taken to be the product of the medieval scriptorium from a distance. There is another good reason for the look of Gutenberg's Bible, Peter Schöffer, who in 1457 would collaborate with Johann Fust on an elaborate Psalter, was almost certainly involved in the production of the 42-line Bible.[5] "He has traditionally been identified as a scribe or calligrapher on the basis of the colophon of a manuscript destroyed at Strasburg in the Prussian siege of 1870, which stated that he had copied the book at Paris in 1449. It is therefore assumed that Schöffer may have been particularly concerned with the type design or layout for the 42-line Bible, the 1457 Psalter, and the later books that he printed in partnership with Fust or alone."[6] Just 48 copies of the 42-line Bible—36 on paper and 12

printed on vellum—are known to have survived into the twentieth century in either complete or partial form. This is from a probable edition of between 160 and 180 copies in total.

Very little is known of Gutenberg's working practices. In 1900, the scholar Paul Schwenke concluded that six compositors and six presses could have been in use at any one time, though little recent research has been done to back this up.[7] It is impossible to say exactly what these presses would have looked like, but an idea can possibly be gained from some of the illustrations nearly contemporary with Gutenberg's 42-line Bible. The earliest picture of a printing press dates from 1499, and appears in an edition of the *Danse Macabre* published in Lyone by Mathias Huss. This is a two-pull wooden screw press in which the two pages of a folio sheet could be set up together in a single forme. After an impression had been taken from the first page, the forme could be cranked forward by means of the windlass handle attached to the bed and the other page printed off. However, it is generally acknowledged

5, 6 Johann Gutenberg's typeface as used in his famed 42-line Bible.

7 Illustration of the wooden or 'common' press, used in printing rooms until the advent of the cast-iron Stanhope press in the early nineteenth century.
Illustration by Emma Gibson.
Image courtesy of the artist.

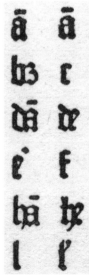

that until the 1470s at least, the majority of books were printed on single pull presses with one page being produced at a time.

In the 1499 illustration, the essential elements of the press workshop that would endure for nearly five centuries are already visible. One pressman—the 'puller'—stands by the press ready to wind the forme in under the platen before taking the impression by pulling on the bar and thus lowering the platen, forcing inky type against the paper. The other pressman—known as the 'beater'—stands holding an inking ball. Two inking balls were usually used to pound ink into the forme, each comprising a shaped wooden handle or stock to one end of which was nailed a ball of untanned leather stuffed with wool or hair. Ink, generally carbon and linseed oil based, was picked up from a slab which can often be seen attached to the side of the press, the two inking balls being rolled together before being beaten onto the type. This method of applying ink would remain virtually unchanged until the advent of the inking roller some three

and a half centuries later. Even by 1824, John Johnson, author of the printer's manual *Typographia* maintained that "with respect to rollers... having pronounced that they would not execute the work equal to the balls: this opinion time has fully verified... as to the last, they are totally unfit to produce any impressions worthy of notice".[8] James Moran has described the working of the press team as follows:

Two men usually worked at the press, taking turns as 'puller' and 'beater' (the one who applied the ink to the forme). The forme having been inked and the paper brought down onto the type, the puller turned the rounce with his left hand, giving about one turn to bring half the carriage under the platen. Placing his right foot on the foot step he grasped the bar with his right hand, sliding it down and giving a straight pull. The spindle turned and forced the platen on to the back of the typan, pressing the paper on to the inked type. The bar was gently returned, the platen rising clear of the typan, and the rounce was given a further turn

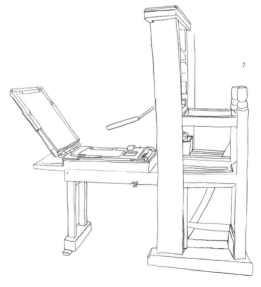

7

bringing the front half of the carriage beneath the platen. A further pull printed the rest of the sheet. The bar was returned, and the carriage run right out so that the paper could be changed and the forme re-inked.[9]

Both the two-pull wooden press and the associated equipment would survive virtually unchanged until the advent of Stanhope's cast iron press in the early years of the nineteenth century. Even then, the essential elements of hand press work remained in use in small workshops well into the twentieth century.

The setting of the type was carried out by the compositor. In the earliest illustrations he sat at a low table taking the type from the case in front of him. Later, the cases of type would be supported at an angle on a high desk. Writing in 1838, Charles Timperley—in *The Printers' Manual*—was adamant that the compositor should "work with his case level at his breast, (though it) may at first tire his arms, yet use will so inure him to it, that it becomes afterwards equally unpleasant to work at a low

frame".[10] Type was laid out in cases with the most commonly used letters, spacing materials and punctuation most readily to hand. However there was no standardisation to this method, and as late as 1771, Philip Luckombe complained that "the disposition of (type) sorts differs almost in every printing house, more or less, it follows that such irregularities must have their effects accordingly; of which we do not want for instances".[11] These "instances" to which he refers would include the speed and accuracy of the compositor, which would not only be of concern to the printing house managers, but to the man himself whose daily wage would be affected. Another disadvantage noted by Luckombe is that when purchasing cases of type second hand "all such sorts must be transposed whose situation does not agree with the plan by which the buyer's letter is laid".[12] However, by the early years of the nineteenth century, Timperley was able to observe that whilst case layout differed in most offices, there was at least some consensus. Increasingly, standardisation had crept in and for the last hundred

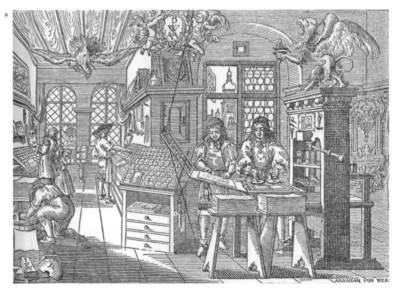

8 An early illustration of inking balls, in Joseph Moxon, *Mechanik Exercises on the Whole Art of Printing,* 1683.

9 *L'Atelier Au XVIIe Siècle,* wood block print from Abraham von Werdt, displaying the workings of the press room, complete with 'puller' and 'beater'.

10 The sheet of paper fed into the press can be printed with either two, four, eight or 12 pages. This layout is called the imposition, in Philip Luckcombe's *The History and Art of Printing,* 1771.

years or so the layout of upper and lower cases and of a combined case has not meaningfully changed.

Compositors in the fifteenth century must have, like their later counterparts, brought the type together in lines, inserting spacing material between the words and setting the lines to an even length. They are likely to have used wooden composing sticks to hold the individual sorts as they were picked from the cases. When a line or more was accommodated in the stick, it could then be transferred to a wooden tray, or galley, for temporary storage. From the galley, a quick proof could have been taken if so required, which in later years was given the term 'galley proof'. If deemed correct, the lines of type would then have been formed into pages and locked into a metal frame (the 'chase'), which would be held securely on the bed of the press. In subsequent centuries, the layout of the pages within the chase followed well-established practice and depended upon whether the book was to be printed with two (folio), four (quarto) or eight (octavo) pages to the sheet.

This was known as 'imposition', and by the length of text and illustration devoted to its explanation in printer's books of instruction, it must have exercised considerable confusion for compositors across history, especially when combinations of 32 or 64 pages were required to be laid out on a single sheet.

Unlike later printers, Gutenberg did not have the luxury of purchasing his type on the second-hand market. Instead, he had to commission the punches and cast the type himself. The fount used in the 42-line Bible comprises some 270 different characters, so as to provide a printed approximation of the Gothic Textura hand used in the writing of liturgical books commonly found in the Mainz region. This is approximately three times the number of sorts found in a modern roman fount. As well as the normal upper and lower case letters, Gutenberg's fount contained numerous abbreviations, ligatures and special abutting sorts. As Janet Ing has observed "both the ligatures and abutting types served to improve the close, even spacing between verticals that was a feature of the textura hand…. Tight letter-fitting was also achieved by the use of ligatures, which typically brought together, onto one piece of metal, two letters such as b and o so that, as in a manuscript hand, they shared a single vertical stroke."[13]

Until recently, it was assumed that Gutenberg followed the accepted practice of cutting a single punch for each sort as described by Moxon. Some of the early sorts were cast on a body slightly larger than that necessary to accommodate the face, but were later filed down to the size used throughout the rest of the Bible. However, recent research by Paul Needham, librarian of the Scheide Library, and Blaise Agüera y Arcas, have concluded that Gutenberg may have used an earlier technology that involves casting letters in moulds of sand—moulds that could not be reused because they had to be broken apart to get the letters out.[14]

The manufacture of type required a considerable investment, not only in time and skill, but also in financial terms, an investment that not all printers were

11

12

willing to make. At the same time as the Mainz printers were perfecting the Bibles, and later the great Psalter, other printers were working in the less refined medium of wood. Blockbooks were a natural development of such prints as the 1423 St Christopher, providing a simple and accessible way of communicating popular Bible stories and didactic tales. They are mostly undated, with comparatively crudely executed texts and woodcuts leading many to assume that they predate more refined typeset volumes. Now they are generally considered to run contiguously with the works of the early exponents of type. Their texts are those already made popular by manuscript distribution; the *Ars moriendi*—mediations of a Christian life and death, the *Apocalypsis sancti Johannis* and the *Biblia Pauperum*, all of which saw editions published in the 1460s and 70s.

With the Mainz revolution in moveable type, wood would not be used again as a medium for the printing of large amounts of lettering until the nineteenth century, when large decorative faces were used for some of the more exuberant posters and advertising broadsides. Curiously, the idea of a single unified substrate—the wooden plank of the blockbook—would also make a comeback during that same period with the advent of the stereotype. This produced a printing plate made by taking an impression from pre-set type, or indeed even a cut wooden block. A mould was made using Plaster of Paris or papier mache, into which stereotype metal, similar to typemetal, is poured in to produce a 'matrix'. The process was originally outlined in 1690, and the first book printed from stereotype plates is a Syriac-Latin Testament of 1708.[15] The idea of a single unified substrate for typesetting also recurred with the Linotype machine, which produced slugs of type cast as one unit rather than separate sorts or pieces of type. This system endured until the very end of relief printing in Europe, and in some parts of the world is still in use today. In some small way, then, the ideology of the blockbook maker has endured longer than that of Gutenberg, though in a very different medium and with many fundamental modifications.

11 An early example of a blockbook. Illustration from *Ars Moriendi*, circa 1460s.

12 Galley proof with corrections, 1861.

13 The Stanhope press was the first press made entirely out of cast iron and had many levers to magnify the pressure onto the page. It became very popular with newspaper printers in the early 1800s.

Illustration by Emma Gibson.

Image courtesy of the artist.

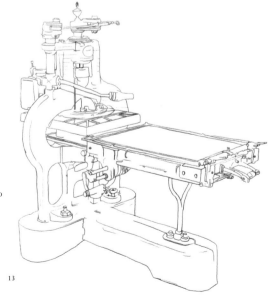

13

2
ALEXANDER W WHITE

Type through a Colander

1 Pieces of metal type at work,
St Bride Library.

Photography Jarek Kotomski.

I recently gave a talk to the student body at a certain large, southern design school, wearing, at least for the first several minutes, a large stainless steel colander on my head. The point I wanted to make was that readers have come to wear a similar, if less visible, barrier to uninvited incoming messages. They have—we have—been conditioned by increasingly relentless exposure to resist both sales and editorial design. The only way to get your message through is by fashioning it into a point finer than the holes in the colander.

It is easy to make a typographic thing, an ordinary piece of typesetting determined more by computer defaults than artistic vision and craft. It is much more difficult to develop a type treatment that conducts information and personality like electricity through a wire.

While it is true that visuals get a reader to look, type delivers the message and the meaning, the tone of voice and feeling. Pacing and visual tone of voice are essential considerations to type's effectiveness. Spacing is the critical aspect of type that divides plain typesetting from fine typography.

What makes type good? The most popular way to improve one's use of type has been to buy design annuals and copy or 'be inspired' by the samples that happen to strike us as looking good. This is based on opinion and whim, not understanding what would most effectively get a particular idea across. Rarely does a typographic message break through my defences and get noticed. When I finish skimming a magazine, for example, I often try to recall the single outstanding ad or feature opener I have seen. With rare exceptions, I cannot. How can it be that not one of a very finite group, maybe 50 opportunities, has broken through with a message and presentation that made even a minimally lasting impact? And I'm looking for impact, whereas most readers are training themselves to avoid the increasing noisiness of editorial and advertising design.

Unlike mathematics, where there can only be a single 'right' answer, design in general and typography in particular have many alternate solutions. It is up to the designer to find the best among these. Design is neither an opportunity to show off one's latest visual notions for one's colleagues nor a mere task of creating legible monotony. Why? Because flashiness for its own sake disguises the true value of the message while sameness puts uncommitted readers, i.e., browsers, to sleep.

Typography and design are much simpler when you remember it is a process, not a result:

- Know the material. Digest it fully. At the very least, read it.

- Take apart the problem you have been given. Redefinition is essential because you have been given only the apparent problem. A redefinition is complete when the solution presents itself, when the solution is not a random stab in the dark.

- Distill the essential from the plentiful. This step is complete when nothing is missing and nothing is extraneous. This is the definition of elegance.

- Abstract the main point typographically so its importance to the reader is clear and it is visually arresting. A message that doesn't stop readers won't be read. Abstraction makes an idea clearer by removing unnecessary details. Abstraction can be harmful, though, when it obscures the message by removing identifiable markers.

- Unify all elements by balancing them in a three-level hierarchy—most important, least important, and everything else similarly in the middle—so readers see organisation and clarity. More than three levels is counterproductive because it unnecessarily complicates the mid-level elements. Design—whether graphic or typographic—is the process of taking unrelated parts and putting them together in an organised single arrangement.

- Typographers are in service to their readers by accelerating learning and making content stick. We have seen type evolve from being prepared and proofread by craftsmen to just another responsibility among many of the design professional.

From Gutenberg's invention in about 1450 through the early 1800s, the printer was the typesetter and, quite often, the type designer as well. For the next hundred years, the printer bought type from a foundry, a specialist who frequently developed his own technology for setting the characters. The typefounder thereby cornered the market on his particular typefaces, so if a printer eventually wanted an additional size of type in a family, there was only one source from whom to get it. As the twentieth century progressed, offset lithography was introduced, allowing a printing plate to be made from a photographic negative. Some printers found they particularly enjoyed organising visual materials in readiness for reproduction. They evolved into 'graphic designers', a term that was invented in 1922—indicating the timely need—by William Addison Dwiggins. These new designers began expanding the possibilities of printing and technology: letterforms and their spacing became much more flexible and permutable.

Though great strides are being made in computer typography, we are still seeing a lot of type set with default attributes—both at text and display sizes. Typography can only be mastered one hard lesson at a time. It is not for every designer because it requires a particular attitude and a gift for details. That is perhaps why we see so much bad typesetting. Here are a few tips to keep you moving in the right direction:

➤ Typography must be clean of accidental variations. The spacing must be perfectly adjusted to make it either invisible (the Holy Grail) or clearly, intentionally manipulated. Those who know, look at text type for signs of a designer's real understanding and sensitivity to letterforms. Everyone has decent display type, so less about the designer can be gleaned from it.

➤ Restrict typeface use. Develop a type palette that uses the least possible number of typefaces, sizes, and weights, while still allowing for flexibility as deserving circumstances warrant. When in doubt, do not make a special change. Your readers are well served if you err on the side of typographic consistency. If your system is well conceived, the variations in your regular typographic arsenal will cover any situation.

➤ Standardise type placement and type specifications. Column structure and text treatment are pervasive in a publication or a campaign or web site. In combination, structure and treatment create the product's personality. After deciding on type specifications, determine where every element will be placed, how far from the trim, how far from other type elements. Space management is what will elevate your product above your competitors' and it will make readers trust the content.

➤ Flush-left/ragged-right type is an all-purpose setting. Word spacing in flush-left/ragged-right type is always consistent, regardless of the column width. Justified type, on the other hand, achieves two smooth edges at the expense of even word spacing: each line of type is sucked out to or shoved into the full measure, and word spacing is expanded or squeezed as needed. This is a minor distraction in lines of type that contain about 50 characters, but shorter justified lines create horribly uneven word spaces. Avoid the problem by setting all type flush left/ragged right—and allow hyphenation. The idea that such a setting looks more casual, or that justified type looks more dignified, is nonsense. What is far more important is how the display type is handled and how it relates to the text.

Typography cannot be faked. It is either clear, interpretive of the content, and appropriate to its message, or it is a random treatment that only superficially looks daring and current.

3 LETTERS

LETTERS

Letters come in many forms. These differing forms have developed for a variety of reasons, some as a result of the historical precedent of handwritten forms, some from typographic innovations and others still as a response to some new demand of the printed word, as in greater clarity of form required for advertising or public notices. As more typefaces became available, there was a need to classify them and to find a method of denoting the size of a face as it was printed on the page.

When Gutenberg founded the type for the 42-line Bible, he had only to worry about a single face—there was one choice—the textura or Gothic blackletter form based on the conventions of the written script in use within Germany during the fifteenth century. Soon the ascendancy of the blackletter was challenged by the humanistic scripts of northern Italy and perhaps most crucially by those forms designed by Nicolas Jensen. As master of the Royal Mint at Tours, Jensen had been sent to Germany to learn the new art of printing. After moving around Europe for a while he ended up in Venice where,

Quidā eius libros nō ipſius eſſe ſed Dionyſii & Zophiri co
lophonioru tradunt:qui iocādi cauſa cōſcribentes ei ut diſ
ponere idoneo dederunt. Fuerunt autē Menippi ſex. Prius
qui de lydis ſcripſit: Xanthūq; breuiauit. Secūdus hic ipſe.
Tertius ſtratonicus ſophiſta. Quartus ſculptor . Quintus
& ſextus pictores: utroſq; memorat apollodorus. Cynici au
tem uolumina tredecī ſunt. Neniæ: teſtamenta: epiſtolæ cō
poſitæ ex deorum pſona ad phyſicos & mathematicos grā
maticoſq;: & epicuri fœtus: & eas quæ ab ipſis religioſe co
luntur imagines: & alia.

1

in 1470, he cut the first roman typeface based on the humanist minuscule scripts used in Venice during the fifteenth century. They were written obliquely with a broad flat pen producing letters of varying stroke thicknesses. The resulting typeface was open and round with bracketed serifs and an oblique vertical stress making it eminently readable in large bodies of text. Whereas Gutenberg's face had been based wholeheartedly upon the style of lettering employed in handwritten manuscripts, Jensen's letterforms only nodded to humanist handwriting. Instead, these were the first characters to be developed on sound typographic principles, with a defined width and height for each letter designed, so that each individual piece of type could be combined with any other piece of type to produce an even and universally pleasing result.

Venice was also the birthplace of the first italic face. Sometimes known as cursive type, the prototype italic was cut for the printer and publisher Aldus Manutius at Venice by Francesco Griffo sometime around 1499. Derived from the informal sloped humanist scripts

of the period, italic is defined by its pronounced right slope and its somewhat cramped appearance. Manutius was the first to recognise the potential market for small pocket editions of the classics and in order to produce these small format books, he would need a face that would make the most economical use of the page. He had, though, only commissioned lower case italic letters with small roman capitals being used when required. The first italic capitals were used in Vienna by the printer Singrenius around 1524 and Caxton's acolyte, Wynkyn de Worde, was the first to use italic in England in 1528.

Although Manutius and his contemporaries had originally used italic to set complete texts, by the end of the eighteenth century the practice had been dismissed. Even the setting of prefaces and introductory matter in italic, as was common in the seventeenth century, was increasingly being frowned upon. As Philip Luckombe noted in 1771, in his instructional manual *The History and Art of Printing*, "italic was originally designed… to distinguish such parts of a book as said not to belong to

1 An example of Nicolas Jenson's roman typeface in *Laertius*, 1475.

2, 3 Constantinus Lascaris, *Erotemata*, printed by Aldus Manutius, 1494–95.

the body thereof, as prefaces, summaries, and contents… at present the letter is used more sparingly, since all the different parts of a work may now be very properly varied by the different sizes of roman".[1] Today, italics are cut to accompany most roman faces where they are used for textual emphasis and for display purposes. Italic should not, however, be confused with sloped type which, although similarly inclined to the right does not demonstrate the calligraphic features of italic faces up to the start of the twentieth century. A comparison between vertical roman and a sloped roman of the same type family will show that certain modifications have been made to the curved strokes of the c, g, o and so on, together with a relative extension of the base strokes of the b, d, e, etc. Good examples of sloped faces include the version of Eric Gill's roman face, Perpetua, cut in 1929 by the Monotype Corporation to accompany his original 1925 design.

Size

In a 1766 type specimen sheet, the Bristol letter founders of Isaac Moore and Co lists roman and italic faces in 11 different sizes, ranging from the smallest 'Long Primer Roman No 2' to a huge 'Four Line Pica', together with sundry fleurons, borders and other typographic ornaments.[2] By 1838, Timperley was able to describe some 19 different sizes of letter used in British workshops to which he added the comparative sizes and names of currently in employed by his French, German and Dutch counterparts.[3] It should be noted that even within Britain, there was no standardisation of the body size of these letters. Thus a Brevier supplied from one foundry could be of a different size to that available from another. If founts from two different foundries were to be employed together, a good deal of making up might be necessary with consequent implications for speed and cost.

The same lack of standardisation operated on the Continent where, as can be seen from Timperley's table, where the French German and Dutch were equally inventive in their designation. A system for defining type by point size, though, had been proposed as early as 1737,

4

ABCDEFGHIJKLMNOPQRST
UVWXYZ&fiflffffifflæœÆŒ
abcdefghijklmnopqrstuvwxyz
£1234567890.,:;!?''-([—

ABCDEFGHIJKLMNOPQRSTUV
WXYZ& fiflffffifflæœÆŒ
abcdefghijklmnopqrstuvwxyz
£1234567890.,:;!?''-([

4 Eric Gill's roman face, Perpetua, as cut by Monotype in 1929.

5 Isaac Moore, Specimen Sheet, 1766.

6 Charles T. Timperley, Comparative table of English, French, German and Dutch type sizes, from *The Printers' Manual*, 1838.

when the Parisian type founder Pierre Fournier le Jeune pegged a single unit at 0.349 mm. Some four decades later and another Parisian, François Ambroise Didot, resurrected the idea this time devising a system based on a single point of 0.3759 mm. It would take a disastrous fire in 1871 at the Chicago foundry of Marder, Luse & Company to change things for good. Re-equipping after the fire, the foundry commissioned Nelson Hawks to re-cut all of its punches and matrices to a new size. Hawks decided to fix the point at 0.3515 mm (0.01387 inches, or approximately 72 points to the inch) basing his measurement on a popular pica type of the day, giving rise to a degree of standardisation. This new system was adopted by the American Type Founders' Association (ATF) in 1886 and by British printers in 1898 and became the standard system used throughout Britain and America, though the Didot standard prevailed on the Continent for many years. However, with the rise of computerised graphics, a new problem presented itself. If one Hawks point equals 0.352298 mm, then 72 points on the Hawks system would

equal 2.5365456 cm, which was hardly a useful sum for computerised graphics. When PostScript was created by Warnock and Geschke in the 1980s, a point was defined as exactly 1/72nd of an inch (0.3527552 mm), which offers a much more stable mathematical base for sizing faces. The PostScript point has since become the standard point size for all computer graphics applications

Type can still be divided into two categories dependant upon size: text type and display type. In general, the former includes anything up to 14 point, whilst display types would comprise anything over 14 point, the larger sizes traditionally being cut in wood rather than cast in type metal.

It should be noted, though, that stating that type is 10, 12 or even 72 point does not necessarily provide an indication of the size of the face as it is printed on the page. Point size refers specifically to the body size, in metal type this is the metal body upon which the face is cast. It is what is known as the 'x height'—the size from head to foot of a lower case x—that conveys the visual impression of the size of a letter. Typefaces of the same point size are rendered larger or smaller on the page where their x height varies. This may be because the face has been designed as large on the body with short ascenders and descenders, or conversely it may be cast small on the body with correspondingly long ascenders and descenders.

Classifying Typefaces

Instructing the young printer in 1838, Timperely observes that "printers divide a fount of letter into two classes—the upper case, and the lower case. The upper case sorts are capitals, small letters, accented letters, fractions, and references. The lower case consists of small letters, double letters, points, figures, spaces, quadrats, etc."[4] The terms 'upper case' and 'lower case' are derived from the practice of locating two cases at the composing desk, one above the other. The upper case would contain the capital or 'upper case' letters together with reference marks and accents, whilst the lower case would accommodate 'lower

case' or small letters. Timpereley, like his contemporary Johnson, only had a limited repertoire of typefaces available for use. Aside from the ubiquitous roman in its various guises, there were:

Gothic or blackletter which, he notes "was seldom used except in law works, particularly statute law; it was at length expelled from these, and only made its appearance in the heads of statutes, etc".[5] "Script type which, according to the observation of Rowe Mores "is a flimsy type, imitating a pseudo-Italian hand-writing, and fitted for ladies and beaux-candidates for fair palace donative, who court a plattin to save unnecessary trouble, and to conceal their management of a pen".[6] "Ronde type, in imitation of secretary, has been very lately introduced to the notice of the profession, and, may, in some particular circulars, be of service....A type called German Text has also been lately introduced."[7]

Along with various fleurons, decorative borders and other similar accoutrements, these letterforms represented the entire typographic vocabulary of an early

7
PERPETUA REGULAR 55 PT

BASKERVILLE REGULAR 55 PT

FUTURA BOOK 55 PT

AVANT GARDE BOOK 55 PT

8

7 Even though these four typefaces are all set in the same point size, they differ in actual size on the page.

8 W De Worde, *Thordynary of Crysten Men,* 1506.

9 First Latin script to be used in England, 1672.

nineteenth century printer. This accounts for the almost universal sameness of most printing up to this date. But there was a revolution underway, being led by display faces that would soon percolate down to the pages of every book, offering printers—and later typographers— endless possibilities. With diversity, though, there comes the problem of classification, of offering a cogent taxonomy. This is an issue that vexed the French social anthropologist and philosopher Michel Foucault, who in his preface to *The Order of Things* posits a similar problem in the form of "a breaking up (of) all the ordered surfaces and all the planes with which we are accustomed to tame the wild profusion of existing things, and continuing long afterwards to disturb and threaten with collapse our age-old distinction between the Same and the Other".[8] Quoting himself from a passage in Borges that refers to the divisions of Chinese encyclopaedia, he concludes that "each of these strange categories can be assigned a precise meaning and a demonstrable content".[9] This acknowledges both the need for order and the recognition that whilst type forms are the same in conforming to standard alphabets they are 'other' in the form of the letters themselves, which often embody "a cultural significance, a meaning beyond that of the actual words".[10]

Just as Linnaeus attempted to tie down a system for classifying the natural world, so too have there been various attempts to bring the huge variety of typefaces into some kind of meaningful taxonomic system, whereby any typeface can be classified according to its visual characteristics. One of the most effective of these is that initiated by the French designer Maximilien Vox in which he invented a new naming convention to avoid some of the old associations and confusions which had arisen from various old naming conventions. This was the system of classification adopted by the British Standards Committee (BS) in 1967. Over the years it has been revised several times and in its present guise it is divided into 11 different basic groups of letterforms.

9

GROUP 1
HUMANIST

The earliest roman type faces having their origins in the humanist minuscule scripts first used in Venice in the fifteenth century and written obliquely with a broad flat pen producing letters of varying stroke thicknesses.

They are characterised by having very little contrast between the thicks and the thins, heavily bracketed serifs and an oblique vertical stress. (The upper case letters are shorter than the ascenders of the lower case letters). Formerly known as "venetian", the letterforms are open and round, making the faces in this class eminently readable in large bodies of text.

GROUP 2
GARALD

This group of roman types is derived from those cut by Francesco Griffo for Aldus Manutius at Venice and those inspired by the Aldine tradition as principally exemplified by Claude Garamond's faces used from 1530 in France. The term "garald" was developed by merging <u>Gar</u>amond and <u>Ald</u>us.

These faces generally exhibit greater contrast in the relative thickness of the strokes than in humanist designs (see above). The serifs are scooped, sturdy, without being heavy and the axis of the curves is inclined to the left. Lower case letters have a horizontal bar and the serifs of the ascenders in these letters are oblique.

Traditionally, both Group 1 and Group 2 letters have been referred to as 'old face'—hence Caslon Old Face—with no distinction made between letterforms.

GROUP 3
TRANSITIONAL

So-called because they are considered to be transitional between Garald 'old face' and Didone or 'modern'.

The father of all transitional faces is generally considered to be the Romains

de Roi cut by the Frenchman Phillipe Grandjean in 1694 exclusively for the French king Louis XIV's printing. This face is distinguished by flat unbracketed serifs. The use of the type outside of the royal printing house was forbidden by law, but subtly modified versions were produced by other type founders, most notably Pierre Simon Fournier and Pierre-François Didot.

In Britain, John Baskerville re-appraised Grandjean's work with the finely chiseled type first used in his 1757 *Virgil*.

Letters demonstrate an axis that is vertical or slightly inclined to the left. Serifs are less heavily bracketed and are more refined than in old face, and there is a greater contrast between the thicks and the thins. The ascenders in the lower case are oblique. Many of these characteristics are seen in the letterforms used by copper-plate engravers of the period.

Letters tend to be exceptionally wide for their x height, closely fitted and of well-defined proportion.

GROUP 4
DIDONE

So-called because they are considered to embody the features of both <u>Did</u>ot and Bod<u>oni</u>, members of the didone group were once referred to as 'modern faces'. Drawing on the designs of both Fournier and Didot, and inspired by Baskerville's productions, the Italian type-founder Giambattista Bodoni "carried the exaggeration of the thin and thick strokes of the letters still further, until Baskerville's type by the side of the Italian looks serious and dignified".[11]

This exaggeration of the hairline serif was made possible by improvements in press and paper technology making it possible to print such fine-lined details.

Faces in this group exhibit typically strong contrast between the thick and

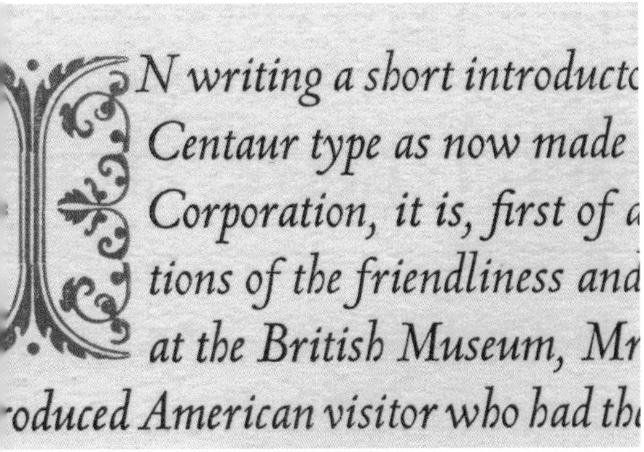

N writing a short introduct[o]
Centaur type as now made
Corporation, it is, first of [a]
tions of the friendliness and
at the British Museum, Mr
[pr]oduced American visitor who had th[e]

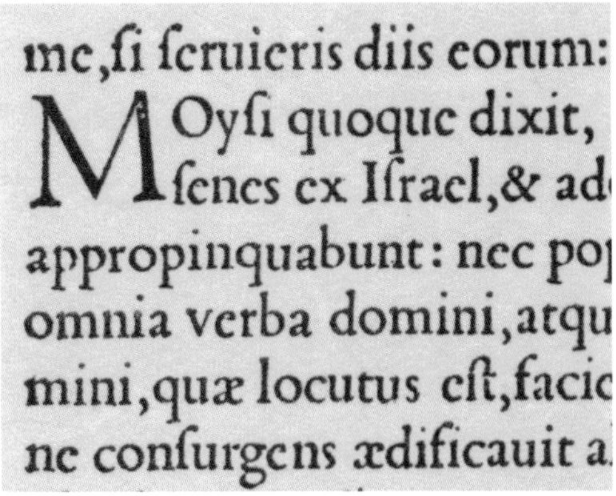

11

12

me, fi feruieris diis eorum:
Oyfi quoque dixit,
fenes ex Ifrael, & ad
appropinquabunt: nec po[p]
omnia verba domini, atqu[e]
mini, quæ locutus eft, facio
ne confurgens ædificauit a[d]

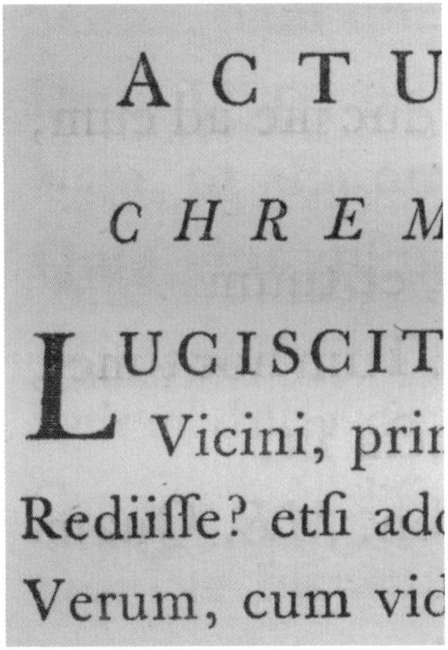

ACTU
CHREM
LUCISCIT
Vicini, pri[n]
Rediiffe? etfi ad[d]
Verum, cum vi[d]

13

14

ABCDEFGHIJKLMN
abcdefghijklm
12345

ABCDEFGHIJKLM
abcdefghijklm
ABCDEFGHIJKLM
abcdefghijklm

ABCDEFGHIJKLM
abcdefghijklm
ABCDEFGHIJKLM

11 Humanist example: Centaur Monotype, in Alfred W Pollard's *The Trained Printer and the Amateur, and the Pleasure of Small Books*, 1929.

12 Garald Example: Robert Estienne's *Biblia Latina*, 1953.

13 Transitional example: Baskerville typeface in *Publii terentii afri Comoediae*, Birminghamiae, 1772.

14 Didone example: Bodoni Monotype Specimen.

abcdef
ghijk
lmnop
qrst u
vwxyz

15

ABCDEFGHIJKLMNP
abcdefghijklmnopqrs
£1234567890*abcde*
NPQRSTUWXYZ&123

ABCDEFGHJKLMNC
&abcdefghjklmnopq
123456789!? *abcdef*
NOPQRSTUWXYZ£

16

17

ABCDE

18

15 Slab serif example:
Halbfette Egyptian.

16 Linear example: Monotype
Frutiger Univers, 1964.

17 Glyphic example: detail of
Perpetua Monotype, 1929.

18 Script example: Specimen
from the early 1700s.

the thin strokes. Serifs are reduced to fine lines with no noticeable bracketing and three is an overall pronounced vertical stress. The ascenders of the lower case are horizontal.

GROUP 5
SLAB-SERIF

Sometimes also known as 'Egyptian', slab serif is defined by its monoline form terminated with thick square-faced serifs and probably has its origins in the letterforms developed by sign painters around the beginning of the nineteenth century.

The characteristics are thick slab serifs and thick main strokes with little contrast between the thicks and thins.

Types in this class are well-suited to situations where a bold legible statement is required and are especially popular for children's books and display work.

GROUP 6
LINEAL

A wide-ranging group of type faces without serifs generally known as 'sans-serif' or just 'sans'. Less commonly they are referred to as 'grotesque' or 'grot' in Britain and 'Gothic' in America.

BS 2961 breaks sans-serif faces down into four further divisions:

i. Grotesque type faces of nineteenth century origins. There is some variation in thickness of strokes which often end in an oblique termination.

ii. Neo-grotesque. Good examples are Helvetica, introduced by the Swiss type foundry, Haas, in 1957, and Adrian Frutiger's Univers which was commissioned by Deberny and Peignot and coincidentally appeared in the same year. These have greater evenness in the strokes than with grot faces with no noticeable stress. The ends of the curved strokes are usually horizontal.

iii. 'Geometric' faces for which the basis is geometric shapes—triangles, circles, etc. They are executed in monocline leading to very little differentiation between letters.

iv. Humanist sans typefaces are based on the proportions of inscriptional Roman capitals and humanist or garald lower case, rather than early grotesques. There is some contrast to the strokes.

The clean even, or almost even, design of the lineal types make them very readable. But because there are no serifs to aid in the horizontal flow of the lines, sans serif types should always be leaded.

GROUP 7
GLYPHIC

Based on letters which have their origins in the stonecutter's workshop rather than those of calligraphic form. Members of the glyphic group are characterised by the elegant incised capitals used on monuments and important buildings. Eric Gill's Perpetua has been used both for inscriptional work on buildings and as a typeface in books as has Bethold Wolpe's *Albertus*.

GROUP 8
SCRIPT

Script typefaces imitate cursive writing as opposed to those which are drawn. Script can be further divided into 'copperplate' and 'cursive'.

i. Copperplate is imitative of that form of lettering traditionally associated with the fine engraved script employed by copperplate engravers. The style is to be found exemplified in writing tuition books such as those by George Bickham. Timperely notes in 1838, that "M Firmin Didot has the merit of inventing or introducing a script of a peculiar form; but a great obstacle in bringing it into general use, was the difficulty in composition, in learning the necessary variations and combinations of character; as some characters, the r for instance, have eight variations; but when properly combined, gives and appearance which scarcely admits of improvement."[12]

ii. Cursive is used to describe types which resemble a less formal style of writing.

GROUP 9
GRAPHIC

The graphic group is made up of typefaces derived from hand-drawn originals, executed with a brush, pen or pencil but not forming a coherent script. As such they are unsuitable for text setting but lend themselves to display work. It is in this category that type designers can give full rein to their wilder fantasies.

GROUP 10
BLACKLETTER

Blackletter represents the earliest form of type as exemplified in Gutenberg's 42-line Bible. These in turn were based on the conventions of the written script in use in Germany during the fifteenth century. It is sometime referred to as Textura or 'Gothic', of which Timperley notes that "it is called Gothic by some; and Old English by others; but printers call it blackletter, on account of its taking a larger compass than either roman or italic, the full and spreading strokes thereof appearing more black upon the paper. On the introduction of the roman character, its use began to decline, and it was seldom used except in law works, in the heads of statutes, etc."[13]

Blackletter has been further classified into four main groups:[14]

i. Gotisch (English 'textura'). Compressed and angular types, without curves in the lower case letters. The lower case letters terminate at both the head and the foot in oblique rectangles.

ii. Rundgotisch (English 'rotunda'). An Italiante version of textura, transitional between it and Schwahacher. The letters are more rounded and do not end in oblique rectangles.

iii. Schwahacher. A popular vernacular type exemplified in Caxton's early printed works. McLean quotes Alexander Nesbitt who says it "has 'mandorla' rounds in lower case, and can be used where a religious feeling is to be avoided".[15] It has its origins in a cursive writing of which the French version was called *lettre bâtarde*.

iv. Fraktur. The most commonly encountered blackletter used in Germany in recent years. McLean quotes Nesbitt saying that "it is the result of Renaissance influence upon Gothic letters—to be more definite, the influence of the baroque element of the Renaissance... one need but examine some of Albrecht Dürer's title pages to see the introduction of the Baroque flourishes and movement".[16] Characteristically, the lower case letters sometimes have forked tops, the a is not looped and the g has an open curved tail.

GROUP 11
NON-LATIN TYPE FORMS

Traditionally known by British printers as 'exotics', these include Cyrillic, Arabic and oriental typefaces.

19 Graphic example: 24-line Gothic for Two Colours no 972–4 from the Bonnewell & Co, Caxton letter works. Photography by Matthew Pull.

20 Blackletter example: Catholic Litany and Ritual hours, written in old gothic characters on vellum, mid-fifteenth century.

21 Non-latin type form example: Contemporary example of Japanese typeforms.

Panose

In more recent times, the Panose
System has been increasingly popular
in typographical classification. Unlike
the BS classification which relies on a
taxoniomatic approach, Panose is based
soley on the visual characteristics of
individual letterforms. Thus it can be
a more effective tool in identifying an
unknown font from a sample image,
or in matching a known font to other
members of its visual family from
a body of candidates.

Panose definitions exist for Latin Text,
Latin Script, Latin Decorative, Iconographic,
Japanese Text, Cyrillic Text and Hebrew.
The original Panose System was developed
in 1985 by Benjamin Bauermeister and
produced a seven hexadecimal digit
number (later expanded to ten digits) for
each font. Each digit was computed from
a specific visual metric, such as the weight
of the font and the presence or absence
of serifs.

22 *A Manual of Comparative Typography*,
Benjamin Bauermeister, Van
Nostrand Reinhold Company
Inc, 1988.

Times Roman

ABCDEFG
HIJKLMN
OPQRSTU
VWXYZ
abcdefghijk
lmnopqrstu
vwxyz
123456789
0.,:;''&!?$

Times Roman 46 point

ABCDEFGHIJKLMN
OPQRSTUVWXYZ
abcdefghijklmnopqrstu
vwxyz
1234567890.,:;''&!?$

Times Italic 24 point

PANOSE abegmoqst

Times Semi Bold 24 point

PANOSE abegmoqst

Times Semi Bold Italic 24 point

PANOSE abegmoqst

Times Bold 24 point

PANOSE abegmoqst

Times Bold Italic 24 point

PANOSE abegmoqst

Times Extra Bold 24 point

Supplier	Linotronic 202 Digital Typesetter
Usage	Text, Display
Similar Fonts	Times Europa
Available Media	
Digital, DT, Photo, Hot, Bit, PS	
Alternate Names	
Dutch 801(BS), English(Alpha), English Times(CG), London Roman(Wang), Pegasus Press Roman(IBM), TR(Itek), Times New Roman(BH)	

	1	2	3	4	5	6	7	8	9	0
serif	●	68	93	X	X	X	(168)	X	(219)	X
proportion	●	(39)	X	X	X	X				
contrast	2	●	(31)	35	X	X				
arm style	(13)	22	●	X	X	X	X	X	X	
form	●	X	X	X	X	X				
midline	X	●	X	(27)	X	(28)	X	X		
x height	X	●	X	X						

22

3
WILL HILL

Old Forms; New Ideas: Typographic Revival and the Uses of History

1 The Civilite type family
designed by Robert Granjon
in 1557.

Through the course of the twentieth century, successive phases of type production technology have prompted the review and redesign of existing typefaces and the demand for new ones. Mechanised typecasting using Linotype and Monotype systems, the development of increasingly sophisticated phototypesetting technology, and finally the advent of digital type, have created the need to adapt existing faces to new media and the opportunity to review, adapt and modify classic forms to meet changing user needs.

As the technology of type production has developed from device-dependent industrial processes to the increasingly democratised world of digital typography, so critical and creative perspectives upon type design have developed in diversity and sophistication. The revival of historic type forms has evolved from a practical imperative into a complex medium of enquiry, through which type design examines its relationship to its history.

The digital revolution has had a threefold impact upon type design, prompting change in the methods of type production, the media of type storage and distribution, and the patterns of type consumption. Peter Bil'ak has observed that: "Within a few years, designers had created the same number of new typefaces as they had done in the whole 500 year history of typography."

Relationships between reader, type user, publisher and designer have been reconfigured, repositioning the typeface as a mass cultural product. Like other aspects of popular culture, such as fashion or music, type evokes the *zeitgeist* through a continuous cycle of change and redundancy, and requires multiplicity of form and style in order to fulfill public appetites.

As type design technology has become more personalised, and the technology of storage and distribution has become more accessible, these conditions have made possible the emerging idea of type design as a medium of enquiry and discourse. This process is at times irreverent, playful or ironic, reflecting a pluralistic view of historical authenticity.

Typographic revivals in the first half of the twentieth century were generally driven by defined values and measurable goals. These included the preservation of established forms through their adaptation to new technologies, the restoration of types overlooked by recent history, and the use of historical example to inform the design of new types. These initiatives share a Modernist ideal of progressive improvement. By contrast, type revivals in the postmodern era have been divergent and speculative, expressing pluralistic approaches through mutable form. Type design and typographic revival have emerged as a medium of critical debate, argument and subversion.

The concept of typographic revival can be traced to the types designed by William Morris for the Kelmscott Press. These mark a significant cultural development in that for the first time we see developments in type design, proposed as the deliberate expression of an ideology, related not only to a distinct design aesthetic but to a coherent and integrated social and political outlook. Based upon the types cast by Nicholas Jenson in the fifteenth century, Morris' Golden Type is not simply the expression of his aesthetic or functional preference. Like the term 'Pre-Raphaelite', it identifies a historical ideal in opposition to the conditions of Morris' own times.

In nomine Patris, & Filij, & Spiritus Sancti Dei unius

Euangelium Patris excellentis Lucę Euangeliftę. Aperitio Euangelij gloriofi.

Quoniam quidem multi noluerunt ordinare narrationem eorum quæ

completa funt in nobis, ficut tradiderunt nobis illi, quí ab

initio uiderant, & fuerant miniftri fermonis: uifum eft & mihi,

cum effem affecutus omnia, fecundum ueritatem fcribere tibi

2 Robert Granjon designed
the types for this sacred Arabic
book, circa 1590.

Some revivals are driven by market demand, some are undertaken as a medium of typographic research, while others explore hypotheses or personal perspectives upon type history.

In the broadest sense, all typefaces have a dimension of revival. All types are related to a continuity of recognisable letterforms, and the design of a new typeface unavoidably references past designs. The process involves complex decisions on the way in which the new design reflects its historic models. Any attempt to 'reconstruct' a historic typeface quickly encounters questions of individual selection and the need for synthesis. It is best understood as an act of interpretation rather than a wholly unique creative activity.

In considering the wide range of faces described as 'revivals' it becomes clear that they reflect variations of design philosophy.

A number of analogies have been used to describe the relationship between revival typefaces and their source material. Matthew Carter has described his Galliard as an 'anthology' of key characteristics of Robert Granjon's types, a personal synthesis rather than a specific revival of one face. Frederic Warde described Bruce Rogers' Centaur as a 'paraphrase' of Jenson, while John Downer compares type revival to the process of portraiture.

Robert Bringhurst comments upon synthesis and interpretation in Giovanni Mardersteig's Dante: "Mardersteig was the greatest modern scholar of Francesco Griffo's work, and his Dante, though not in fact a copy of any of Griffo's types—has more of Griffo's spirit than any other face now commercially available."

Approaches to typographic revival range from literal reconstruction at one extreme to increasingly interpretative or synthetic approaches at the other. The British Monotype offices in the 1920s and 1930s made a distinction between 'rough' and 'smooth' revivals, and these distinctions remain applicable to current digital design.

The late Justin Howes described his founder's Caslon typeface family as "no-holds barred" revivals. A highly accurate and un-moderated set of types transcribed from the original punches, they represent an extreme of literal reconstruction. Each size of Caslon's types is recreated as a distinct font, reinstating those variations which characterised the art of the hand punchcutter.

Jonathan Hoefler's HTF Historicals series was the outcome of direct digital transcription of key historic faces (including Granjon's Civilite, and the Fell types) scanned from original printed specimens. Originating as an experiment demonstrating the limitations of such a literal method, this project critiques the idea of the revival face as a simple replica of the original, examining the ambiguities of 'authenticity' and fidelity to historic sources.

Even the literal and accurate reconstruction of a historic model will nevertheless present the designer with a large number of interpretative decisions. If a text type is to meet present day user expectations, it will be necessary to include features which have no equivalent in the original source of the revival. For example, a revival based upon a fifteenth or early sixteenth century source or model, the original will not have a 'companion' italic form, since the earliest italic types were conceived as free-standing

text faces. A suitable companion italic may be sourced on the basis of chronology and origin, based upon an italic typeface designed by the same hand or in the same period and region. Alternatively, designing a new italic may provide opportunities for the creative interpretation of a historic form.

Similar questions occur over the design of bold and bold italic fonts. A type dating from before the nineteenth century will not have a definitive bold companion, and the manner in which a designer extrapolates a bold version from the roman presents a range of defining decisions, including the increase in contrast, and the interval of weight between the bold and the regular weight.

If the face has already been the subject of revival in the twentieth century (either for metal or photosetting), earlier revivals may provide possible solutions to these dilemmas. The extent and manner with which these intermediate sources are absorbed into a new revival will vary widely according to the designers methodology and the philosophy which informs the face. The designer may opt to incorporate aspects of earlier revivals alongside original sources, as the most recent stage in a cumulative process. In other instances (such as recent Adobe revivals of Caslon or Garamond) a new design may return to original sources in order to reform faces that have been compromised by successive re-cuts for different technologies.

The literal reconstruction of any typeface originated through hand-cut punches, presents the designer with critical choices over the size of punch from which the revival face is made. (The punches cut for different sizes of a typeface will show noticeable differences of stroke weight and contrast). The designer may refer to a range of punch sizes, and produce from this a synthesis of common features. The resulting face will be less accurate as a transcription, but may serve better to evoke the spirit of the original.

Romantic notions of the 'antique' recur through typographic history; in the use of stylistic categories such as 'antiqua' (antika) or 'old style', or attaching the terminology of antiquity to new designs through the terms 'Egyptian' or 'Gothic'.

Postmodern perspectives on history are typically enquiring or subversive, and postmodern type designs have reflected critical examination of the ideas we bring to history itself. This tendency is reflected in Jonathan Hoefler's Fetish 338, a deliberately eclectic display face which parodies historical style. Hoefler comments:

HTF Fetish No 338 comments on the mythopoetic notion of 'classicism' which figures so prominently in all levels of graphic design in America. It parodies the notions of 'fanciness' in which not only designers but the lay public participate; its forms are as welcome in the pages of Rolling Stone as in the menu of Ye Olde Coffee Shoppe. While it quotes freely from a formal vocabulary of disparate historical styles (such as the Gothic, Victorian, Byzantine, Celtic and Moorish), it is ultimately an invention, one which is endemic only to a vague, romantic heritage to which no American truly belongs, but to which many aspire.

The architectural critic Charles Jencks described the postmodern buildings of Ralph Erskine and

Robert Venturi as being "double-coded", combining contemporary building materials with elements from earlier traditional and vernacular architectures.

'Parodic dialogue' can be seen in Hoefler's Fetish, and recent type design reveals a shift of focus away from the paradox of 'authenticity' and towards diversity in the contradictory use of historical models. These approaches explore the possibility that type design can propose alternative readings of history, revisiting historic sources and developing them in different directions, questioning the basis of many orthodox narratives.

Zuzana Licko's Mrs Eaves is a Baskerville revival, notable for the introduction of a colourful family of unique ligatures that have no historical precedent. The revival is a distinctively postmodern one. In creating a new set of forms without a basis in Baskerville's era, Licko's design queries the notion of historical 'authenticity', and proposes instead a typographic bricolage designed over the structure of a historical model.

These examples reveal typographic revival as a relative concept involving multiple levels of interpretation, selectivity and intervention. These are determined both by commercial circumstance and individual sensibility, and reflect differing theoretical perspectives and cultural conditions. The diversity of approach and philosophy expressed through typeface design, serves to demonstrate the complexity and depth of type as a cultural artefact.

4 PUBLIC TYPE

PUBLIC TYPE

By the 1780s, in spite of the advances of Fell, Caslon, Baskerville and their like, very little had changed since the printers of fifteenth century Italy set the typographic style that would endure for three centuries. The familiar roman face still endured as a serve-all for books, pamphlets, squibs and advertising sheets with virtually no variety. In a modern world where a huge range of letterforms are taken for granted, it might seem strange that early printers could still be creative with so minimal a typographic palette. A printer in the 1750s using Caslon's faces would have only had the choice of roman, italic and blackfaces (as well as several ancient faces such as Greek, Coptick and Hebrew) in sizes from Brevier upwards to French Cannon. Yet all was soon set to change.

Developments in ground breaking typographies from the presses in Parma and elsewhere would have been noticed by the upper and middle class cognoscenti—who could afford these luxury books—but for the majority of the populace these items were far from reach. As Philip Ward has pointed out:

IMBECILE
WARD KEEPERS
WANTED.

The Guardians of Mile End Old Town require the services of a MALE and FEMALE, to take charge of the HARMLESS LUNATICS in the Workhouse Infirmary. Candidates must be active, healthy, patient, without encumbrance, and between twenty-five and fifty years of age.

SALARY } MALE - - £25.
FEMALE - £20.

With Board, Lodging, and Washing,
A MAN AND WIFE PREFERRED.

Applications in the Candidate's own hand-writing, marked on the outside "M" or "F," as the case may be, stating age, and where previously employed, accompanied by THREE TESTIMONIALS, of recent date, must reach me before Twelve o'Clock on THURSDAY, 19th instant, on which day at Three, applicants must attend at their own expense. A selection will then be made, and the appointment take place at Six in the Evening, of the said 19th. No one need apply whose character for honesty, sobriety, and competency, will not bear the strictest investigation. Canvassing the Guardians is prohibited.

(By Order,)

E. J. SOUTHWELL,
Clerk.

Workhouse, Bancroft Road, Stepney, N.E.
7th December, 1861

1

SALARY }

With Boar

A MAN AN

The mass of ordinary people in England have never had enough education for the appreciation of full-length books, or sufficient leisure to read them if they had the learning. In the middle of the eighteenth century, the cheapest book cost 2s6d for an octavo, while a quarto might well cost 10s and a folio as much as 13s and more…. Until the spread of newspapers in the 1850s and the gradual implementation of compulsory education from the 1970s, almanacks, penny broadsheets and chapbooks formed the sole reading matter to be found in many poorer homes, and no study of the literature in England is complete without a respectful reference to the broadside ballad or chapbook, those ambassadors of literacy.[1]

The comic penny ballad sheets may have been sold for a penny but posters and advertising scamps were free to all and represented a further engagement between the printer and the public. Improvements in press technology, principally with the introduction of the cast iron Stanhope press and then the improved Cope and Sherwin machines, coupled with the increased availability of cheap wood pulp papers in larger sheet sizes meant that throughout the early years of the nineteenth century it became possible to print ever larger posters.

Later on, the steam presses would roll these boundaries back even further. Even to the least discerning eye it was obvious that the staid stable to roman faces would no longer suffice with the result that the sturdily aesthetic designs of Bodoni and the like were pulled through into the popular sphere. The London of the 1830s was at the epicentre of a growing empire. Indeed the whole country, increasingly industrialised and self-aware, was starting to demand more in the way of products, entertainments and information. With this demand came advertising and a whole new outlet for print culture. The poster-mongers required maximum impact with little concern for the refinements of the book. Modern faces proved to satisfy the need for the kind of bold statement that the early nineteenth century advertisers demanded of their posters.

1, 2, 3 Posters featuring
the new display faces,
circa early 1800s.

But it was not the modern faces that had been known in Parma—instead the posters and broadsides of the early 1800s are emblazoned with weighty Clarendons, their heavy blackened serifs adding a grim fortitude to announcements they depicted. Printers sometimes added the equally mordant Egyptian-style letters, a style to be perfectly described by its later popular reference—the slab serif.

The slab serif exemplifies the *modus operandi* of street publishing right up until the twentieth century, eschewing typographic finesse in favour of bold visual statements. Like Bodoni, and to a certain extent Baskerville, upper case predominates for impact with the main words often centred and set in the larger sizes. Slab serif, defined by its monoline form terminated with thick square-faced serifs, probably had its origins in the letterforms developed by sign painters around the beginning of the nineteenth century. It was still being used more than a hundred years later and continued, in a somewhat debased format, to live on in box-makers stencils well into the twentieth century.

4 1817, Figgins Antique, first showing of the slab serifed antique, also known as 'the Egyptian', 1815.

4

NES PICA IN SHADE.

ITURE,

NES PICA ANTIQUE.

KIND

INES PICA OPEN.

STONE,

NONPAREIL ANTIQUE.

MNOPQRSTUVWXYZ,;:.-'

V. FIGGINS.

Whereas the finely chiselled lines of Baskerville and Bodoni reek of sophisticated refinement, the Clarendons and Egyptians go for face-on impact, a differentiation which must have been obvious to the early sign writers whose primary objective would have been to communicate their message as effectively and immediately as possible. Today, these faces are still used for that very purpose, communicating short statements and names with maximum exposure, and as such are perfect for headlines, titles and slogans.

The first three decades of the nineteenth century saw an increasing demand for display faces. The kind of expanding type mould used by Gutenberg would not have been suitable for casting these very large letters. Casting such letters in type metal—by then a mixture of lead, tin and antimony—would have been both very expensive and weighty, especially when locked up into a large forme. Instead, in what might seem like a step back to the early fifteenth century, lettercutters reverted to the use of wood, producing a wealth of decorative faces

in a wide variety of sizes. The St Bride Library in London contains numerous examples of this work both as letters and as specimen books embracing almost any conceivable style and size right up to letters of some 20 odd inches in height (effectively 1440 point size by modern standards). Originally these were hand cut by specialist manufacturers, though it was not at all uncommon to find individual letters or even ornaments run up by those skilled enough in the printing house.

By the middle of the nineteenth century, 'fat face' had become all the vogue for display lettering. The variety was almost bewildering: thick squat letters, ornamented designs of great complexity, three-dimensional faces produced from several interlocking parts and designed to be printed in different colours, floriated, chiselled and shaded faces together with the emergent sans serif style, then referred to as 'grotesque'. Sometimes they were used with restraint, but usually they are thrown together in a heady riot of colour and style which typifies the confidence of high Victorian printing.

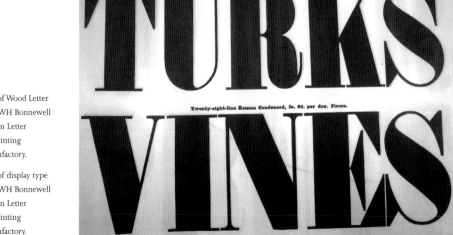

5

Twenty-six-line Roman Condensed, 5s. 6d. per doz. Pieces.

Twenty-eight-line Roman Condensed, 5s. 9d. per doz. Pieces.

5 Specimens of Wood Letter published by WH Bonnewell and Co, Caxton Letter Works, and Printing Material Manufactory.

6 Specimens of display type published by WH Bonnewell and Co, Caxton Letter Works, and Printing Material Manufactory.

Photography by Matthew Pull

As with much of the printing trade, mechanisation soon came to replace hand-crafted letters with the knife and specialist chisels of the wood letter cutter giving way to routing machinery by the mid-nineteenth century. Display types in various forms maintained a place at the compositor's desk well into the twentieth century, with some faces changing very little throughout the duration. Slab and modern faces seem to be associated with a return to prosperity after periods of austerity. In the late 1920s and early 30s they were re-invigorated with designs such as Memphis (in 1930) and in the lettering designed by Charles Hasler for the Festival of Britain in the 1950s.

In some provincial printers, wood display types continued to be used in jobbing work for estate agents notices and local announcements until such businesses ceased trading with the rise of the modern print and photocopy shop. The last commercial manufacturer of wood display type, DeLittle of York, remained in business until the mid-1990s, before closing down and passing remaining stock and machinery to the Type Museum in London.

6

Published by W. H. BONNEWELL & Co. Caxton Letter-Works, 75, West Smithfield, London.

CAN BE CUT TO ANY SIZE REQUIRED.

Published by W. H. BONNEWELL & CO., CAXTON LETTER WORKS, and Printing Material Manufactory,
16, OLD BAILEY, and 169, FLEET STREET, LONDON, E.C.
REMOVED from 85 & 87, Holborn Hill, E.C.

4
PENTAGRAM
A Conversation with Domenic Lippa

1 Poster designed by Domenic
Lippa to promote issue 15 of
Circular, the magazine of the
Typographic Circle. *Circular*
is available free of charge to
members of the Circle only. Each
issue is designed by Domenic
from scratch with its own size,
choice of papers, typefaces and
layout. For issue 15 Domenic
developed a new logo, creating
a roundel resembling a 'C' out
of the words "Circular Fifteen".
This roundel forms the basis for
the poster.

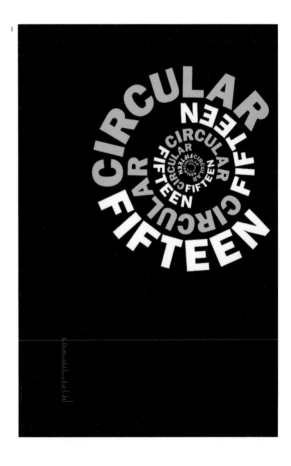

PENTAGRAM
A Conversation with Domenic Lippa

What makes a good font? What makes a bad font?

For me, a good font is one with balance and beauty. This applies equally to serif, sans serif or display fonts. A good font is well thought-out in terms of the form of the individual characters, but just as important is how those characters work together in lines of text.

I dislike fonts that are designed to express a personality, which I think is the role of the design and layout itself. Bad fonts try too hard to be different and idiosyncratic. A font like Comic Sans, which is the classic example of a font designers love to hate, is the typographic equivalent of a one-liner; you might smile at first but the joke stops being funny very quickly, especially when it's repeated ad nauseam thousands of times in a piece of text.

Are fonts a matter of fashion, or progression?

Even the oldest, most revered fonts still swing in and out of fashion. I think 90 per cent of the best fonts have existed for many years, but typography will inevitably progress as tastes and fashions develop.

How do you go about choosing a typeface for a new project?

I really don't have a rulebook for this. It comes down to the visual direction I want to take the design into. If I want to be aggressive with my design, I might choose something that is bold and robust, for example, but it will still come down to how I use it. I sometimes like the contradictions you can achieve by using a font you wouldn't think was appropriate.

What is the perfect font, if there is such a thing?

I don't think there is a perfect font—that's the beauty of it. I tire of some font designers who seem to need to re-invent the wheel. No matter how much I try to like certain 'new' fonts they often let me down. The fonts I most use are Akzidenz Grotesk, Clarendon, Franklin, Gothic 13, Didot, Baskerville and De Vinne. Some of the newer fonts I like are Champion (Knockout), Interface, Gotham, Shaker and Enigma.

Is there a type revival you would like to see developed?

If you're talking about type design—I can't think of one instantly. I think there have been some pretty good ones over the last 20 years. The only area I think that I'd like to see more exploration of is in script fonts. Most of these tend to be the sort of fonts that get constantly used on wedding invitations. It's a bit of a niche area and one that needs to be handled with sensitivity because it probably isn't that easy to tackle. If we're talking about typography in general, then 'revivals' such as bringing back Swiss typography tend to be too nostalgic. Typography ought to be respectful of the past but always needs to stretch itself.

How many different fonts should one use on a page?

No more than two fonts. On the whole, I prefer to try using one font in two weights and maybe two sizes. I think it's just too easy and too much of a shortcut to try and solve a problem by using too many fonts.

How would you approach the design of a typeface based on typography and graphic design of the recent past?

Well, I'm not a type designer so I haven't really had to try and do this. I think in comparison to ten years ago, when type designers were trying too hard to make a statement, tastes today are far more economical and there's a simplicity to design at the moment that allows for individual expression. I'm happy for hand written or quite elaborate expressions to exist, but I only really enjoy them when I see that the designer of the work feels it's an extension of their design philosophy.

Is typography culturally-specific? Can you determine the county of origin of a particular typeface just by looking at it?

This is quite complex and I don't think there's an easy answer. I suppose to an extent you can see regional characteristics in the history of typography, the Swiss school being a classic example, but I think that the age of that style of design has passed us now. The movements that created those national styles are now only interesting as historical influences, but what is interesting is the way these styles are being employed by designers today as elements of an educated and culturally-aware design language. I think that in the last couple of decades, typography has become more globalised, as with most other areas of design, which is a little bit of a shame because those unique pockets of influence have become fragmented and harder to find.

In your opinion, what is the most critical aspect of type design today?

I think the mood of type design today is quite restrained, which I like. There seems to be a more pragmatic and measured approach these days. When you compare contemporary typography to the excesses of the 1980s and 90s, I think it's far more thoughtful. Of course, I'm totally ignoring the myriads of silly and playful fonts that have existed during any period. These are the fonts that will not last or stay the course.

What is the future of type design?

If I knew that I'd be doing it myself! Every now and then a font does come along that defines a period but these often pass and again it's only fonts that are well crafted that come out of these periods and last.

5 MOVE TO THE MODERN

MOVE TO THE MODERN

This is the point in the story of type where the legacy of the hand-written letter is finally left aside in favour of new ideas and forms. The roman types favoured by Caslon and his predecessors had derived their shape from the strokes (of varying thicknesses) generated by a broad-nibbed pen, manifesting itself as 'oblique shading'—the thicks and thins as the writer moved the pen from vertical to horizontal line. With Baskerville—and then Didot—came a move away from this oblique shading to a style where the shading is more vertical and the serifs defined by the thinnest of lines, marking the arrival of the modern face.

It was not, though, as if the manuscript tradition disappeared overnight. Indeed, both printed and hand-written books existed side by side for many years, but their paths were diverging. Where the Gutenberg Bible and the productions of Caxton and his contemporaries owned much to the old tradition, those of the early sixteenth century printers looked to the future by throwing off the shackles of the past half a millennium. Suddenly, books were alive with the shock of the

1, 2 Pius II, Pont. Max, *Bulla cruciata contra turches*. Johann Fust and Peter Schoeffer, 1463. This is often referred to as the first title page.

3, 4 A manuscript title page dating from approximately 1485.

new. Title pages, which had been rarely (if ever) employed in the literary tradition, suddenly became a standard feature of the printed book, embodying all the possibilities for self-proclamation that are well known today. These new components provided the space for the printer and publisher—the two frequently being the one and the same—to not only include details of the author and title but also to advertise themselves as the craftsman who created the physical object of the work, often with a characteristic mark or emblem. This is in direct contrast to the medieval manuscript tradition of the colophon, which hid the artisan's details away in the depths of the final leaves. The advent of the title page also presented the printer with a tabula rasa upon which to exercise typographic creativity. This opening page did not require vast bodies of serifed letters adhering to the author's text. Instead titles, often set in large elegant lettering and contained within decorative borders, could show off the printer's craft to best advantage. It soon became apparent that printed decorations and illustrations could be added throughout the body of the book without the need

for a scribe, though it would take the invention of chromolithography in the mid-nineteenth century to finally shake off the last remnants of the colourist's brush and pen. Truly, then the age of the printer had arrived.

If Germany had given the Western world the printed book, it was the French, Swiss and Italian printers who were fully embracing those possibilities. They strove to perfect the medium throughout the fifteenth century, establishing many of the ground rules that are still used in typography today and creating some of the best-known typefaces in history. Step to the fore men like Aldus Manutius, the di Giuntas, Claude Garamond, Robert Granjon, Jean de Tournes, the Estiennes, Geofroy Tory and Johannes Froben. Honourable mention should also be given to Plantins at Antwerp and to the Elzeviers in Haarlem, both families for whom fine printing formed a long tradition.

If the Continental printers led the way in the sixteenth and seventeenth centuries, then the eighteenth century saw the coming of age of type design in Britain.

3

4

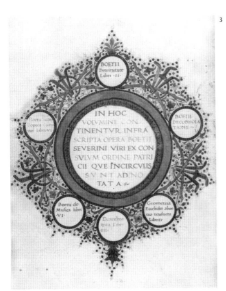

5

A SPECIMEN

By WILLIAM CASLON, Letter-Founder, in Chiſwell-Street, LONDON.

ABCD
ABCDE
ABCDEFG
ABCDEFGHI
ABCDEFGHIJK
ABCDEFGHIJKL
ABCDEFGHIKLMN

French Cannon.

Quouſque tan-
dem abutere,
Catilina, pati-
Quouſque tandem
abutere, Catilina,
patientia noſtra?

Two Lines Great Primer.

Quouſque tandem
abutere, Catilina,
patientia noſtra?
quamdiu nos etiam
Quouſque tandem a-
butere, Catilina, pa-
tientia noſtra? quam-
diu nos etiam furor

Two Lines English.

Quouſque tandem abu-
tere, Catilina, patientia
noſtra? quamdiu nos e-
tiam furor iſte tuus elu-
Quouſque tandem abutere,
Catilina, patientia noſtra?
quamdiu nos etiam furor

DOUBLE PICA ROMAN.
Quouſque tandem abutere, Catilina, patientia noſtra? quamdiu
nos etiam furor iſte tuus eludet?
quem ad finem ſeſe effrenata jac-
ABCDEFGHJIKLMNOP

GREAT PRIMER ROMAN.
Quouſque tandem abutere, Catilina, patientia noſtra? quamdiu nos etiam furor iſte tuus eludet? quem ad finem ſeſe effrenata jactabit audacia? nihilne te
nocturnum praeſidium palatii, nihil urbis vigiliae, nihil timor populi, nihil con-
ABCDEFGHIJKLMNOPQRS

ENGLISH ROMAN.
Quouſque tandem abutere, Catilina, patientia
noſtra? quamdiu nos etiam furor iſte tuus eludet?
quem ad finem ſeſe effrenata jactabit audacia?
nihilne te nocturnum praeſidium palatii, nihil
urbis vigiliae, nihil timor populi, nihil conſenſus
bonorum omnium, nihil hic munitiffimus
ABCDEFGHIJKLMNOPQRSTVUW

PICA ROMAN.
Melum, novis rebus ſtudentem, manu ſua occidit.
Fuit, fuit iſta quondam in hac repub. virtus, ut viri
fortes acrioribus ſuppliciis civem pernicioſum, quam
acerbiſſimum hoſtem coercerent. Habemus enim ſenatuſconſultum in te, Catilina, vehemens, & grave:
non deeſt reip. conſilium, neque auctoritas hujus ordinis: nos, nos, dico aperte, conſules deſumus. De-
ABCDEFGHIJKLMNOPQRSTVUWX

SMALL PICA ROMAN. No 1.
Nerum ego hac, quod jampridem factum eſſe horum
autoritatis. habemus enim hujuſmodi ſenatuſconſultum, verumtamen incluſum in tabulis, tanquam gladium in vagina
reconditum: quo ex ſenatuſconſulto confeſtim interfectum te
effe, Catilina, convenit. Vivis: & vivis non ad deponendam, ſed ad confirmandam audaciam. Cupio, P. C., me
effe clementem: cupio in tantis reipub. periculis non diffolu-
ABCDEFGHIJKLMNOPQRSTVUWXYZ

SMALL PICA ROMAN. No 2.
At vos vigeſimum jam diem patimur hebeſcere aciem horum
autoritatis. habemus enim hujuſmodi ſenatuſconſultum, verumtamen incluſum in tabulis, tanquam gladium in vagina
reconditum: quo ex ſenatuſconſulto confeſtim interfectum te
effe, Catilina, convenit. Vivis: & vivis non ad deponenda,
ſed ad confirmandam audaciam. Cupio, P. C., me effe
clementem: cupio in tantis reipub. periculis non diffolutum
ABCDEFGHIJKLMNOPQRSTVUWXYZ

LONG PRIMER ROMAN No 1.
Verum ego hac, quod jampridem factum effe oportuit, certa de
cauſa nondum adducor ut faciam. tum denique interficiam te, cum
jam nemo tam improbus, tam perditus, tam tui ſimilis inveniri poterit, qui id non jure factum effe fateatur. Quamdiu quiſquam erit
qui te defendere audeat, vives; & vives, ita ut nunc vivis, multis
meis & firmis praeſidiis obſeſſus, ne commovere te contra rempub.
poſſis. multorum te etiam oculi & aures non ſentientem, ſicut adhuc
fecerunt, ſpeculabuntur, atque cuſtodient. Etenim quid eſt, Cati-
ABCDEFGHIJKLMNOPQRSTVUWXYZÆ

LONG PRIMER ROMAN No 2.
Verum ego hac, quod jampridem factum effe oportuit, certa de
cauſa nondum adducor ut faciam. tum denique interficiam te, cum
jam nemo tam improbus, tam perditus, tam tui ſimilis inveniri poterit, qui id non jure factum effe fateatur. Quamdiu quiſquam erit
qui te defendere audeat, vives; & vives, ita ut nunc vivis, multis
meis & firmis praeſidiis obſeſſus, ne commovere te contra rempub.
poſſis. multorum te etiam oculi & aures non ſentientem, ſicut adhuc
fecerunt, ſpeculabuntur, atque cuſtodient. Etenim quid eſt, Catili-
ABCDEFGHIJKLMNOPQRSTVUWXYZÆ

BREVIER ROMAN.
Nerum. C. Manlium audaciæ facillimo mque adminiſtrum eſſe? non una facilitas,
Catilina, non modo nec tam tam avare, tam incredibili, verum, & quod modo
magis eſt admirandum, dico? Dici qui idem in iſtum, eadem te optimum exit-
nibili: in non effes a Kalend. Novemb. tum omnium proficiſcentur conſtituit Rom-
tum tum fit onmiravadi, quam horum conſiliorum exptuimiatem eaede prædu-
ta ille qui meis praeſidiis, ne ille tpſo dic meis periculis, mea diligentia circumcluſum, conniver in aratam neutra potui, in omnibus meis conſiliis ſtabilius, inlu-
mibis tanera, qui nonaniffimam, eade conventatum in tile duobus? Quid? cum te
ABCDEFGHIJKLMNOPQRSTVUWXYZ

DOUBLE PICA ITALICK.
Quouſque tandem abutere, Catili-
na, patientia noſtra? quamdiu
nos etiam furor iſte tuus eludet?
quem ad finem ſeſe effrenata jac-
ABCDEFGHJIKLMNO

GREAT PRIMER ITALICK.
Quouſque tandem abutere, Catilina, pa-
tientia noſtra? quamdiu nos etiam fu-
ror iſte tuus eludet? quem ad finem ſe-
ſe effrenata jactabit audacia? nihilne te
nocturnum praeſidium palatii, nihil ur-
bis vigiliae, nihil timor populi, nihil con-
ABCDEFGHIJKLMNOPQR

ENGLISH ITALICK.
Quouſque tandem abutere, Catilina, patientia noſ-
tra? quamdiu nos etiam furor iſte tuus eludet?
quem ad finem ſeſe effrenata jactabit audacia?
nihilne te nocturnum praeſidium palatii, nihil ur-
bis vigiliae, nihil timor populi, nihil conſenſus bo-
norum omnium, nihil hic munitiffimus habendi
ABCDEFGHIJKLMNOPQRSTVU

PICA ITALICK.
Melium, novis rebus ſtudentem, manu ſua occidit.
Fuit, fuit iſta quondam in hac repub. virtus, ut viri
fortes acrioribus ſuppliciis civem pernicioſum, quam
acerbiſſimum hoſtem coercerent. Habemus enim ſenatuſ-
conſultum in te, Catilina, vehemens, & grave: non deeſt
reip. conſilium, neque autoritas hujus ordinis: nos, nos,
dico aperte, conſules deſumus. Decrevit quondam ſenatus
ABCDEFGHIJKLMNOPQRSTVUWXYZ

SMALL PICA ITALICK. No 1.
At vos vigeſimum jam diem patimur hebeſcere aciem horum
autoritatis. habemus enim hujuſmodi ſenatuſconſultum, verum-
tamen incluſum in tabulis, tanquam gladium in vagina recon-
ditum: quo ex ſenatuſconſulto confeſtim interfectum te effe, Ca-
tilina, convenit. Vivis: & vivis non ad deponendam, ſed ad
confirmandam audaciam. Cupio, P. C., me effe clementem:
cupio in tantis reipub. periculis non diffolutum videri: ſed jam
ABCDEFGHIJKLMNOPQRSTVUWXYZ

SMALL PICA ITALICK. No 2.
At vos vigeſimum jam diem patimur hebeſcere aciem horum au-
toritatis. habemus enim hujuſmodi ſenatuſconſultum, verumtamen
incluſum in tabulis, tanquam gladium in vagina reconditum:
quo ex ſenatuſconſulto confeſtim interfectum te effe, Catilina, con-
venit. Vivis: & vivis non ad deponendam, ſed ad confirman-
dam audaciam. Cupio, P. C., me effe clementem: cupio in tantis
reipub. periculis non diffolutum videri: ſed jam me ipſe inertiae
ABCDEFGHIJKLMNOPQRSTVUWXYZ

Long Primer Italick. No 1.
Verum ego hac, quod jampridem factum effe oportuit, certa de cauſa
nondum adducor ut faciam. tum denique interficiam te, cum jam nemo
tam improbus, tam perditus, tam tui ſimilis inveniri poterit, qui id
non jure factum effe fateatur. Quamdiu quiſquam erit te te defen-
dere audeat, vives: & vives, ita ut nunc vivis, multis meis & firmis
praeſidiis obſeſſus, ne commovere te contra rempub. poſſis. multo-
rum te etiam oculi & aures non ſentientem, ſicut adhuc fecerunt,
ſpeculabuntur, atque cuſtodient. Etenim quid eſt, Catilina, quod
ABCDEFGHIJKLMNOPQRSTVUWXYZÆ

Long Primer Italick. No 2.
Verum ego hac, quod jampridem factum effe oportuit, certa de cauſa
nondum adducor ut faciam. tum denique interficiam te, cum jam nemo
tam improbus, tam perditus, tam tui ſimilis inveniri poterit, qui id non
jure factum effe fateatur. Quamdiu quiſquam erit te te defendere
audeat, vives: & vives, ita ut nunc vivis, multis meis & firmis
praeſidiis obſeſſus, ne commovere te contra rempub. poſſis. multo-
rum te etiam oculi & aures non ſentientem, ſicut adhuc fecerunt,
atque cuſtodient. Etenim quid eſt, Catilina, quod jam amplius expectes,
ABCDEFGHIJKLMNOPQRSTVUWXYZÆ

Brevier Italick.
Nerumh. C. Manlium audaciæ facillimo mque adminiſtrum eſſe? non una facilitas,
Catilina, non modo nec tam tam avare, tam incredibili, verum, & quod modo magis
eſt admirandum, dico? Dici qui idem in iſtum, eadem te optimum exit non eſſe a
Kien e Kalend. Novemb. tum omnium proficiſcentur conſtituit Romam, cum fit on-
niravadi, quam horum conſiliorum exptuimiatem eaede prædita ille qui meis præ-
fidiis, ne ille tpſo dic meis periculis, mea diligentia circumcluſum, conniver in aratam
neutra potui, in omnibus meis conſiliis. Quid? cum te Praeridie Kalend. ipſas
Novemb. curiquonam conventatum. Quid? cum te Praeridie Kalend. ipſas Novemb.
ABCDEFGHIJKLMNOPQRSTVUWXYZÆ

Pica Black.
And be it further enacted by the Authority
aforeſaid, That all and every of the ſaid Exchequer Bills to be made forth by virtue of
this Act, or ſo many of them as ſhall from
ABCDEFGHIJKLMNOPQRSE

Brevier Black.
And be it further enacted by the Authority aforeſaid, That all and every
of the ſaid Exchequer Bills to be made forth by virtue of this Act, or ſo
many of them as ſhall from time to time iſſue remaining not uncan-
celled, until the diſcharging and cancelling the ſame purſuant to this Act,

Pica Gothick.
ᚪᛏᛏᚪ ᚢᚾᛋᚪᚱ ᚦᚢ ᛁᚾ ᚻᛁᛗᛁᚾᚪᛗ ᚢᛖᛁᚻᚾᚪᛁ
ᚾᚪᛗᚩ ᚦᛖᛁᚾ ᚢᛁᛗᚪᛁ ᚦᛁᚢᛞᛁᚾᚪᛋᛋᚢᛋ ᚦᛖᛁᚾᛋ
ᚢᚪᛁᚴᚦᚪᛁ ᚢᛁᚪᚷᚪ ᚦᛖᛁᚾᛋ ᛋᚢᛖ ᛁᚾ ᚻᛁᛗᛁᚾᚪ

Pica Coptick.
Ⲇⲉⲛ ⲟⲩⲁⲣⲭⲏ ⲁ⳿ϯ ⲟⲁⲙⲟ ⲁⲧⲫⲉ ⲛⲉⲙ ⲡⲕ-
ⲁϩⲓ· ⲡⲕⲁϩⲓ ⲇⲉ ⲛⲉ ⲟⲩⲁⲧⲟⲁⲧ ⲉⲃⲟⲗ ⲛⲉ ⲟⲩⲟϩ
ⲛⲁⲧⲥⲟⲃϯ ⲟⲩⲭⲁⲕⲓ ⲛⲁϣⲭⲛ ⲉⲭⲉⲛ ⲫⲛⲟⲩⲛ ⲟⲩⲟϩ
ⲟⲩⲡⲛⲁ ⲁⲧⲉⲫϯ ⲛⲁϣⲫⲟⲣ ϩⲓϫⲉⲛ ⲛⲓⲙⲱⲟⲩ ⳽⳿ ⳽⳿

Pica Armenian.
Որովհետեւ մեք եզր եմ, ու ճաշ, որ աշ
մ աշակերտ որդան ե ե եսք ոու Ատանաք
ոստ ոսմամ ե գարումառէ ֆ մե գործ գու գ
Զապառապ, ե Հատու ոարձումտ,ձ, արդ մ

English Syriack.
ܐܕܠܐܝܐ ܐܣܐܠܕ ܐ܂ ܠܚܕܐ ܐ܂܀ ܐ ܟܕ ܒܐܢܚܕ
܂ܐܒ ܚܕܘ ܢ ܒܟܒ ܥܕ ܐ܂ ܒ ܡܪܐ ܐ܂ ܒ ܚܕ
ܐ܂ ܒ ܐܚܕ ܟܐ ܐ܂ ܐ܂ ܂ ܐܟܕ ܟܕ ܚܕܪܕ

Pica Samaritan.
ࠁࠓࠀࠔࠉࠕ ࠁࠓࠀ ࠀࠋࠄࠉࠌ
ࠀࠕ ࠔࠌࠉࠌ ࠅࠀࠕ ࠄࠀࠓࠑ ࠅࠄ
ࠀࠓࠑ ࠄ ࠕࠄ ࠕࠄࠅ ࠅ ࠉ ࠄࠅ

English Arabick.
أَوّلَ مَا أَنَّ ثُمَّ يُخْرِجُ وَ لَا تَكْلِفُ أَنْ تَصْبِرَ فَ
لِلَّهِ السَّمَا مِنْ فَوْقُ وَ مَا فِي الأَرْضِ مِنْ السَّفَلَ وَ لَا مَا فِي
المَا وَ مِنْ تَحْتَ الأَرْضِ وَ لَا تَعْبُدُ آلِهَ وَ الرَّبُّ السَّمَا الْرَبُّ الَّذِي

Hebrew with Points.
בְּרֵאשִׁית בָּרָא אֱלֹהִים אֵת הַשָּׁמַיִם וְאֵת הָאָרֶץ ׃ וְהָאָרֶץ
הָיְתָה תֹהוּ וָבֹהוּ וְחֹשֶׁךְ עַל־פְּנֵי תְהוֹם וְרוּחַ אֱלֹהִים
מְרַחֶפֶת עַל־פְּנֵי הַמָּיִם ׃ וַיֹּאמֶר אֱלֹהִים יְהִי אוֹר וַיְהִי־אוֹר ׃
וַיַּרְא אֱלֹהִים אֶת־הָאוֹר כִּי־טוֹב וַיַּבְדֵּל אֱלֹהִים בֵּין הָאוֹר
וּבֵין הַחֹשֶׁךְ ׃ וַיִּקְרָא אֱלֹהִים לָאוֹר יוֹם וְלַחֹשֶׁךְ קָרָא לַיְלָה

Hebrew without Points.
בראשית ברא אלהים את השמים ואת הארץ ׃ והארץ
היתה תהו ובהו וחשך על פני תהום ורוח אלהים
מרחפת על פני המים ׃ ויאמר אלהים יהי אור ויהי אור ׃
וירא אלהים את האור כי טוב ויבדל אלהים בין האור
ובין החשך ׃ ויקרא אלהים לאור יום ולחשך קרא לילה

Brevier Hebrew.
בראשית ברא אלהים את השמים ואת הארץ ׃ והארץ היתה תהו
ובהו וחשך על פני תהום ורוח אלהים מרחפת על פני המים ׃ ויאמר
אלהים יהי אור ויהי אור ׃ וירא אלהים את האור כי טוב ויבדל
אלהים בין האור ובין החשך ׃ ויקרא אלהים לאור יום ולחשך

English Greek.
Πρόκλος ὁ σοφὸς ἐκ τῶν συγγράμματων τοῦ Ἡρακ-
λέιτος (ὥσπερ δὲ τὶς ἐφήσεν) ἐνδὑομένος) ἀπος καμὲ τὰν
ἀπὸ τοῦ Ἡρακλῆς, ἐπὶ τὸ παιδὸν ἐκ τῶν ἀφοράτων ἐχθρῶν σὺν Ἡρακλᾶι, ἐπὶ τὰ παιδία ἐπὶ τινος ἀρετῆς ἀξιώσεως καὶ

Pica Greek.
Πρόκλος ὁ σοφὸς ἐκ τῶν συγγράμματων τοῦ Ἡρακλῆς
(ὥσπερ δὲ τὶς ἔφησεν) ἐνδυομένος, ἀπὸς καμὲ τὰν ἀπὸ
τοῦ Ἡρακλῆς, ἐπὶ τὸ παιδὸν ἐκ τῶν ἀφοράτων ἐχθρῶν
σὺν Ἡρακλᾶι, ἐπὶ τὰ παιδία ἐπὶ τινος ἀρετῆς ἀξιώσεως
καὶ

Long Primer Greek.
Πρόκλος ὁ σοφὸς ἐκ τῶν συγγράμματων τοῦ Ἡρακλῆς (ὥσπερ δὲ τὶς ἔφησεν) ἐνδυομένος, ἀπος καμὲ τὰν ἀπὸ τοῦ Ἡρακλῆς, ἐπὶ τὸ παιδὸν ἐκ τῶν ἀφοράτων ἐχθρῶν σὺν Ἡρακλᾶι,
ἐπὶ τὰ παιδία ἐπὶ τινος ἀρετῆς ἀξιώσεως

Brevier Greek.

Pica Saxon.
Ða he þa mid þumman
þpiðum } þeaprena heopa
cð þæt } he eaðe ða pica

Long Primer Saxon.

This SPECIMEN to be placed in the Middle of the Sheet 5 U u, Vol. II.

Appalled by the poor quality of type used by the majority of printers, Bishop John Fell of Oxford and Vice-Chancellor of Oxford University, imported type from Holland in the 1670s and then set up a foundry for the University Press, subsequently re-branded as the Clarendon Press. The resulting types came to be highly regarded by the twentieth century revivalists such as Stanley Morison, who prized them for their clarity and precision, exactly the qualities that Dr Fell had striven to execute some two centuries previously when he had issued the faces.[1]

Like Fell, William Caslon was not first and foremost a printer. He had started out as an apprentice engraver of gunstocks in Vine Street near the Tower of London. From the cutting of decorations and the like into the hard metal of these weapons, it was only a short jump to designing and engraving of letters and ornaments for bookbinders' tools. It was probably through these tools that he came to the attention of two printers, William Bowyer and John Watts, who would later nurture another visionary figure in the history of printing, the young Benjamin Franklin.

Both Bowyer and Watts had reached much the same conclusion that Fell had over the state of English typefounding, namely that it was at a pretty low ebb. Most type was bought in from Holland and was of the cheaper kind of quality. That which was not imported was cast from Dutch matrices with a poverty of skill and little attention to detail. This was the state of affairs that set the stage for Caslon's emergence onto the typographic scene. Various romantic stories exist concerning the Caslon's induction into the printing trade but the undoubted result was that by 1720, he was able to set up business as a type founder in Helmut Row.[2]

Cutting the punches for restrained roman letters must have seemed dull work to a man who had excelled at Rococo decorations for gunstocks. It is little surprise then that he readily accepted a commission to cut an Arabic fount for the Society for the Promotion of Christian Knowledge. Indeed, he went on to cut Coptic, Armenian, Etruscan and Ethiopic faces as well as a blackletter Old English and the roman for which he has become

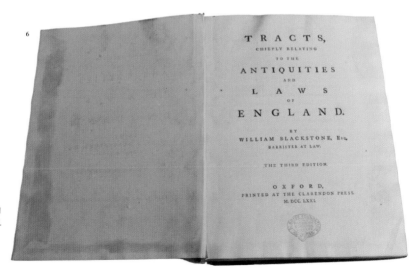

6

5 William Caslon's 1734 specimen sheet, showcasing some 38 founts.

6 The title page from William Blackstone's *Tracts, Chiefly Relating to the Antiquities and Laws of England.* Printed in Oxford at the Clarendon Press.

Photography by Matthew Pull.

T R A C T S,
CHIEFLY RELATING
TO THE
ANTIQUITIES
AND
L A W S
OF
E N G L A N D.

BY
WILLIAM BLACKSTONE, ESQ.
BARRISTER AT LAW.

THE THIRD EDITION.

O X F O R D,
PRINTED AT THE CLARENDON PRESS.
M. DCC. LXXI.

best known. These are shown in a variety of sizes ranging from non-pareil up to three-line pica in his 1734 specimen sheet—a grandly executed affair displaying some 38 founts, accompanied by the proud declaration "the above were all cast in the foundry of Mr W Caslon, a person who, though, not bred to the art of letter foundry has, by dint of genius, arrived at an excellency in it unknown hitherto in England, and which even surpasses anything of the kind done in Holland or elsewhere". This was no idle boast, for Caslon could be said to have almost single-handedly turned around the fortunes of the British typefounding industry, so that by the time of his death in 1766, fonts of his type were being exported all over the Continent, including Holland. Indeed his faces had spread even to the New World, where in perhaps their most famous and most enduring exposure; Benjamin Franklin chose to set the American Declaration of Independence in a Caslon roman.

With success came strife. In 1757, following a disagreement over pay, Joseph Jackson, one of Caslon's apprentices, left to set up a rival foundry. Co-incidentally, it was in this same year that the other great English letterfounder of the eighteenth century came to public attention. John Baskerville also came from a background somewhat, but not completely, outside of the printing trade. Starting as a writing master, he had subsequently made a profitable career as a japanner in Birmingham. Like Fell and Caslon, he felt that British printing had fallen into the doldrums and so set about seeking improvements. In the mid-eighteenth century, Birmingham was gearing up to the Industrial Revolution and the next 50 years would see it develop into an economic powerhouse—truly a city of a thousand trades. Both of Baskerville's early interests would have a bearing on the way he was to approach the craft and art of printing. As a writing master, he had a keen eye for the correct formation of letters, whilst his background in japanning engendered an appreciation of the quality of materials and finish. From the start, then, his ambition was aim to improve upon not only the design of the type but to make substantial advances in the quality of the inks and papers themselves.

7

8

7 William Caslon, A specimen sheet of typefaces and languages, in *Cyclopaedia*, 1728.

9 Lock of a musket engraved in 1718 for the Board of Ordnance, possibly by William Caslon. The Armouries, Tower of London.

10, 11 Baskerville specimen sheet and detail.

At a basic level, printing had altered little since Gutenberg's day. Good as Caslon's typefaces were, they were often let down by shoddy pressmanship and poor quality papers. Like Gutenberg, Baskerville realised that a good quality ink was crucial to the appearance of the finished piece so he set about perfecting an ink that was more black and slightly more glossy than usual. Even some 70 years later, the Birmingham japanners Joseph Hardy & Co were still advertising that as well as their main line in goods, they were also "manufacturers of superior printing ink…".[3] Baskerville also experimented with paper technology, developing techniques borrowed from the japanning trade. The idea was to obtain a finely polished white surface to each page which would further extenuate the glossy blackness of the inks and allow his types to stand out with greater contrast. This was achieved by a process of passing the paper between heated copper plates or cylinders and then finishing the surface off with a smooth varnish. The result was a paper of unparalleled quality which he used to startling effect in his

first major book production, an edition of Virgil's *Bucolica, Geogica, et Aeneis* which appeared in 1757.

The book certainly has a revolutionary feel to it. The title page is full of white paper with no sign of any ornamentation. Instead the type is allowed to stand to full effect—centred, widely-spaced and printed with that black glossy ink; there is an elegance of classical proportions that was lacking in even the best of contemporary productions. That the correct spacing and layout of pages with perfectly scaled lettering was of crucial importance to Baskerville is evidenced by the comments in the preface to an edition of Milton's *Paradise Lost* which he printed the following year, where he claims to have "endeavoured to produce a Sett of Types according to what I conceived to be their true proportion".[4]

The Virgil was a success, with several hundred subscribers being listed on record, including printers John Hughs, William Faden and Benjamin Franklin of Philadelphia who ordered no less than six copies.

9 10

11

BASKERVILLE

ROMAN *ITALIC* **BOLD**

SIZES - ROMAN 6-36 pt ITALIC 6-36 pt
BOLD 6-36 pt

A
SPECIMEN
OF
PRINTING TYPES

CAST AT

BELL & STEPHENSON's

ORIGINAL

British Letter Foundry,

FROM

Punches and Matrices

EXECUTED UNDER THEIR DIRECTION.

By William Colman, *Regulator*,
And Richard Austin, *Punch-Cutter*.

In the
SAVOY, LONDON.
1789.

However, not all of Baskerville's contemporaries approved. For some, the paper was too white and the impact of the type—with its differentiated thicks and thins—too 'sharp'. Today Baskerville's face is described as transitional, where the letters demonstrate a vertical axis, or are slightly inclined to the left. Serifs are less heavily bracketed and are more refined than in Caslon's Old Face and there is a greater contrast between the thicks and the thins. Unsurprisingly, given his background, many of these characteristics are seen in the letterforms used by copperplate engravers of the period. And yet, whilst it was deemed acceptable practice on the engraved plate, these defined contrasts appeared to annoy many commentators. The result was that although he continued to produce very laudable books, including the imposing folio Bible, Baskerville never enjoyed the same success as Caslon did. While the typographer himself died in 1775 (leaving instruction to be buried upright in a coffin overlooking his garden), his designs have endured, providing the inspiration for countless typographic revivals. His legacy lived on in Fry's

Baskerville, a version of the face first used in the Virgil and marketed by the Fry and Pine type foundry from the 1760s. Later, the printer John Bell was to produce a face of a similar design using it extensively in some of his own publications.

Some of Baskerville's punches even made their way to Paris, where in the fevered years of the French Revolution, they were used to print the *Gazette Nationale*, the official organ of the nascent French Republic. Like Caslon, Baskerville's type, so revolutionary as lettering, had found voice as the print medium of a world changing document.

It is curious that the French should have in the end adopted Baskerville when they had a savant of letters of equal worth produced by Pierre Simon Fournier le Jeune. Fournier had printing in his blood, indeed it was at his brother's type foundry that he learnt his craft. In 1742, he published one of the most notable specimen books of the eighteenth century, *Modèles des Caractères de l'Imprimerie*, which was followed some 20 odd years later by the seminal *Manuel Typographique*.[5]

13

12 Title page from *A Specimen of Printing Types*, Bell and Stephenson's British Letter Foundry, 1789.

13, 14 Cases containing sorts of lead for spacing.
Courtesy of St Bride Library.
Photography Jarek Kotomski.

14

Both Baskerville and Fournier's faces are described as transitional in that there was been a move away from the oblique shading of Caslon and his predecessors. The final rejection of the last vestiges of the penned letter came with the introduction of modern face. Here the alignment is more vertical and the serifs are defined by the thinnest of lines— a style inexorably associated with Firmin Didot. The vogue for hairline unbracketed serifs swept through the Continent adding a breath of cool elegance to even the most humble printed artefact.

Meanwhile, in Parma there was to be a still greater exponent of modern face. Giambattista Bodoni was heavily influenced by both Fournier and Didot. He too had been born into a printing family, starting his life as a compositor at the Propaganda Fide, the Catholic Church's printing house in Rome. When only 28 years old, he was invited to set up a printing house for the Duke of Parma. Bodoni would remain there for the rest of his life, creating some of the most grandiose books of the era. To begin with, he favoured books in the smaller

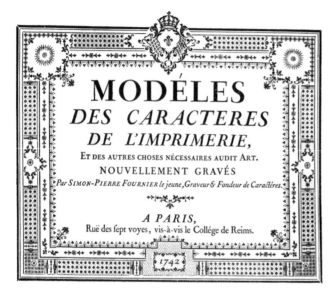

15

16

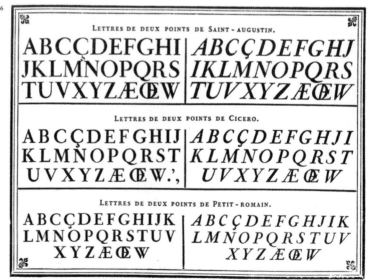

15 Title page from Pierre Simon Fournier's, *Modèles des caractères de l'imprimerie*, 1742.

16 Pierre Simon Fournier, Comparative illustration of Saint-Augustin, de Cicero and Petit-Romain typefaces.

17 Giambattista Bodoni, *Manuale Tipografico*, first volume, 1818.

sizes often printed using Fournier's types, but from 1791 he came (like Baskerville) to emphasise open spacing, wide margins, and the play of richly black ink against white paper. To enhance the effect, he often used a large folio format against which his splendidly contrasting types could fully resound. Bodoni's types are defined as didone or modern face, but can trace their origins back to the romans du Roi of Louis XIV's printing house. In Parma, he took the process even further, reducing the serif to the finest of strokes.

At his death in 1813, Bodoni was working on the codification of his types in the magnificent *Manuale Tipografico*. This was eventually published by his widow posthumously, and remains a testament to the vision of the Parma printing house. For the remainder of the nineteenth century, though, didone or modern face, rarely achieved its full potential. In Britain, it became transmuted into the slab serifed advertising faces and equally weighty Egyptians. Principal amongst the early exponents of this bold typographic foray was the typefounder Robert Throne who produced a type specimen sheet in

1820, heavy with slab serifs that could be seen shouting from posters and billboards all over the country for most of the nineteenth century.

17

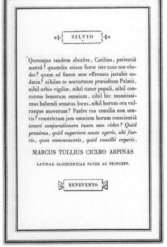
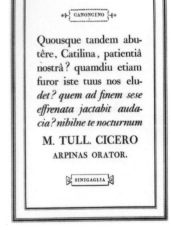

5
ED FELLA
Visual Essay

This two-sided piece might demonstrate the relationship
between graphic design and 'art' in a semi-satirical way.
The front is typography and lettering and is clearly
a somewhat challenged, but readable, text announcing
a lecture and exhibition with all the information
necessary; name, time, title, date, place, etc. It also
refers, again in a somewhat challenging postmodernist
skewing, to a variety of twentieth century historic
styles from Dada to the commercial art vernacular.

Even though the back is pure image, the underlying
structure it sets in is a 'mailer', stamp placement, address
and return address blocks. The images are related to fine
art, from non-objective abstraction to representation,
with techniques of gestural marks, photography and
collage. It is meant to look like 'art' with an artist's
signature or a little actual touch of the artist's hand.
The white windows are not part of the printing,
but hand-painted on each copy.

FEB 21–APR 6
═ TWO LINES ALIGN: ══
DRAWINGS & GRAPHIC DESIGN ⓑ ED FELLA & GEOFF MᶜFETRIDGE
CURATED BY
MICHAEL WORTHINGTON

1

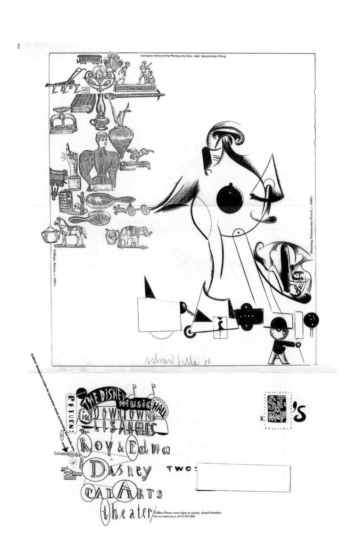

2

1, 2 Poster for *Two Lines Align: Drawings and Graphic Design* by Ed Fella and Geoff McFetridge, Redcat Gallery, 2008.

3, 4 Poster for Ed Fella's
talk at Roski School of Fine
Arts, University of Southern
California, 2008.

4

6

5, 6 Poster for *Many Happy Days,*
designed by Ed Fella, 2008.

7

7, 8 Poster for Ed Fella's lecture
at the Minneapolis Walker Art
Centre, 2008.

6 MECHANISATION

MECHANISATION

The nineteenth century was a time of technological advance, in which many of the old practices in typography were swept away in favour of experimentations in method. New presses permitted faster and more efficient printing, whilst wood engraving—along with lithography—added to the printer's repertoire of illustrative techniques. Even the lot of the typefounder was not immune to change as the first Linotype and Monotype machines appeared, enabling even the smallest printing house to cast hot metal type on their own premises. Designers were continually revising and re-inventing old faces as well as designing altogether new ones. Caslon Old Face was re-jigged for the discerning printer Charles Whittingham, whilst Linn Boyd Benton and the younger Morris Fuller Benton headed the move to more modern faces for the twentieth century with designs such as Century, News Gothic and Franklin Gothic, the latter clearly another revival of the nineteenth century grotesques.

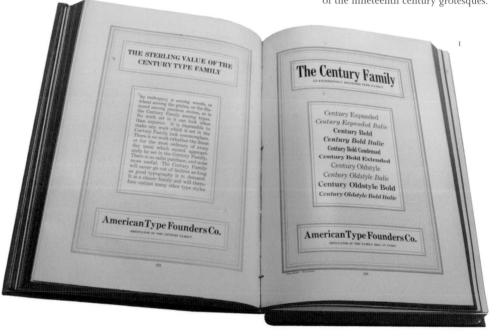

2

At the beginning of the nineteenth century, books were produced in much the same way as they had been in Gutenberg's day. The wooden press, sometimes called the 'common press' because of its ubiquitous employment, together with moveable type, printed numerous books, journals, newspapers and all manner of ephemeral posters, broadsides and squibs. The single sheet broadside, usually printed on one side and hawked door to door by itinerant traders, was aimed at the lower classes of society. Produced by the smaller printers in every part of the country they were, from the mid-seventeenth century onwards, the staple fare of the poor and the semi-literate. Broadsides were also often used to publicise local notices such as advertisements for sale, elections or trials and because they were sold, read and occasionally even printed in the open air, they are often grouped under the collective term of 'street literature'. Illustrations were either cut on wood and printed alongside the type, or engraved onto copper plates, in which case they had to be printed on a separate rolling press. But the Industrial Revolution was

1 Century typeface specimen from the *American Specimen Book of Type Styles*, American Type Founders Company, 1912.
Photography by Matthew Pull.

2 An albion printing press
Illustration by Emma Gibson.
Image Courtesy of the artist.

taking hold, and change was in the air. Old cardinalities were being dissolved and the printing trades were by no means immune. Cast iron was at the heart of the Industrial Revolution, and it was not long before this material was applied to press technology. The first iron printing press was the Stanhope press, created in 1800 and first employed at the Shakespeare Press.[1] Stanhope failed to patent his design, leading other iron press innovators to follow hot on his heals, giving rise to the Russell, Gogger's Press, the Imperial Press and the showy Columbian Press, with a decorative eagle that rose and fell as each impression was taken. In 1838, Timperely observed that "the advantages of the iron presses in working are very considerable, both in saving labour and time. The first arises from the beautiful convenience of the levers, the power of the press being almost incalculable at the moment of producing an impression; and this is not attended with a correspondent loss of time, as is the case in all other mechanical powers, because the power is only exerted at the moment of pressure, being before that adapted to bring down

3

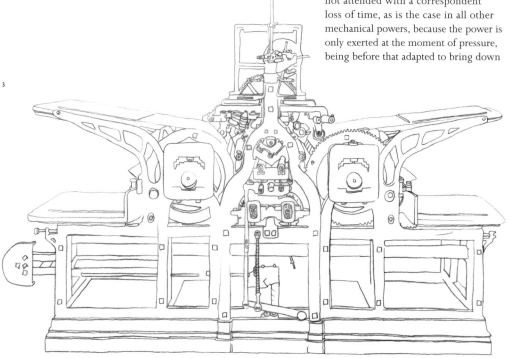

the plattin as quickly as possible."[2] What Timperely fails to mention is that the real advantage of the new presses over their wooden predecessors was that only a single pull was required to take an impression. Due to the size of the platen, the wooden press required the pressman to make a double pull—first on the upper and then another to take an impression of the lower portion of the forme. Due to the greater strength and power of the iron presses, a single pull was all that was required to produce an impression of the whole forme. So impressive was this new technology that the typefounder Ambroise Firmin Didot bought a Stanhope press for his office in Paris and later imported a Columbian as well. The resulting gains in efficiency and time would go a long way to feeding the new age of mass literacy.

It was not long before the presence of that other great invention of the Industrial Revolution—the steam engine—was felt in the print workshop. The first truly practical steam engine was designed by Thomas Newcomen in 1712, and further developed by the Scottish instrument maker James Watt, who obtained a patent for his design of a rotary gearing system known as the 'sun moon' system in 1782. Before long, most of the machinery in Watt's Birmingham Factory was powered by steam, and by 1800, seven such machines were to be found elsewhere in the city.[3] At that same time, Richard Trecithick was working on a small engine, powered by high-pressure steam, producing the first steam locomotive in 1802. Other steam locomotives followed in quick succession, most notably George Stephenson's Rocket, the first vehicle to travel faster than a horse.

As John Johnson points out, "In 1814, The Times newspaper was first printed by a steam engine, consequently, from its being a cylinder power, rollers were indispensably necessary."[4] Newspapers were the first publications to make use of emerging printing technologies, as speed of production was of the essence, where books could still be produced at a more leisured pace. Throughout these innovations, type still continued to be cast and set by hand, in much

3 Illustration of the first generation of steam presses used in commercial printing.
Illustration by Emma Gibson.
Image courtesy of the artist.

4 Page from The Times newspaper, 1932. The Times was the first newspaper to be printed using a steam press.

the same way as it had been at the workshops in Mainz three and a half centuries previously. There were some notable attempts at improvement, one of which gave rise to the 1840 Pianotype, manufactured by Young and Delcambre. The Piantoype functioned with an operator working a type keyboard, which opened flaps to release requisite pieces of type down a shute and into a setting stick. A second operator then inserted pacing material between the words and justified the set lines if necessary. Although a considerable move forward, the whole enterprise floundered when advertisements were released depicting women using the apparatus. The idea behind the advertisement was presumably to demonstrate that there was only slight labour involved in the working of such a machine, but the ruse apparently backfired when the male-dominated industry saw such a suggestion as a threat to their position in the workplace. Some 200 experimental models of such machines were patented in the 60 years after 1820, most of which coming out of America, and nearly all failing to reach success. The most successful typesetting machine was

constructed in 1880 by Joseph Thorne, and sold under the name of the Simplex Setter. In 1898, an improved spacing system was incorporated into Thorne's invention, then renamed the Unitype, on which a skilled operator could set up to 10,000 types an hour.

Illustrative techniques developed in tandem with advances in type technology. Up until the end of the eighteenth century, the majority of book illustration was divided up between two methods that both predated Gutenberg. Fine illustrative work was applied using engraved or etched plates, with colour added by teams of painters directly to the printed sheets. The publisher Rudolph Ackermann, who specialised in high quality books often illustrated with a sophisticated form of tonal etching (aquatints) claimed to have many of the women and children from the dispossessed aristocratic families of Europe working at colouring such plates, in what he kindly referred to as his 'drawing school'. Coarser decoration was added to the cheaper kind of book by woodcut illustration, using wooden

5, 6 Examples of some of the first illustrations from wood engraving in *A History of British Birds*. Wood Engravings by Thomas Bewick, Printed by Edward Walker, 1816.

7 Example of an early lithographic printing of D Capranica's *Scena e duetto 'Che dicesti? Il figlio?'*, Litografia delle Belle Arti, Rome, 1855.

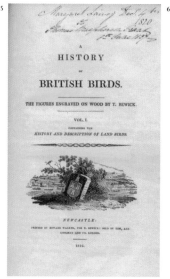

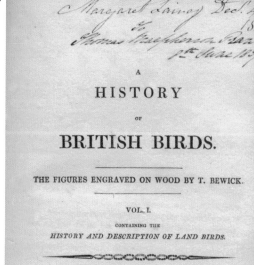

blocks cut from the plank in a method that can trace its lineage back to the Diamond Sutra a millennia before.[5]

However, illustrative techniques were also set to change drastically directly preceding and during the Industrial Revolution. Indeed, several new methods emerged in the 1790s that were to define book illustration for the next hundred years. One such innovator was Thomas Bewick of Newcastle, who began to apply some of his copper engraving techniques to the hard end grain of boxwood. In so doing, he produced some of the first wood engravings, which had the advantage of being both finely detailed and created according to the same relief principles as type, meaning that the resulting illustrations could be produced on the letterpress, eliminating the need for the more labour intensive rolling press required for copper plates. In 1798, the Bavarian Alois Senefelder forged another radical shift in the printing process. In Senefelder's approach, "the image to be printed was produced on compact limestone with a greasy substance which had an antipathy to water. When the stone was dampened, the water was rejected by the greasy marks, but attracted by the porous stone. The reverse was the case when greasy printing ink was applied to the dampened stone. This capacity of grease and water to repel one another was the essence of Senefelder's process, which he originally called 'chemical printing', though, before long the word lithography and its foreign-language variants (mostly derived from the Greek word for stone) were being widely used to describe the process". Senefelder published his findings in Munich and Vienna in 1818, and then in an English edition a year later where it appeared as *A Complete Course of Lithography Containing Clear and Explicit Instructions in all the Different Branches* accompanied by 14 plates in lithography. This new process allowed both artists and commercial printers to produce images and complex letterforms with relative ease. For the first time the printing of music—which had always presented a thorny problem when utilising musical type—could be achieved with little difficulty, as could

7

letterheads, forms, stationary, advertising labels and countless other items required by an increasingly industrialised society.

Eventually, lithographic printing was also applied to the problem of producing cheap colour images. Lithographic stones, one for each colour were over printed one on top of the other onto a single sheet to produce vibrant images. Owen Jones, one of the foremost exponents of the craft, used this method to produce his lavish folio volume on the *Alhambra* in 1836. If this wasn't revolutionary enough, another great illustrative process—photography—was to develop within a decade from the advent of lithography. William Henry Fox Talbot issued the first book to be illustrated by photography in 1844. In 1852, he proposed the idea of the half-tone screen, which broke the photographic image down into a series of light and dark dots of varying intensity. Using this method, illustrations of greater or lesser quality could be produced, depending upon the graduation of the screen. By the beginning of the twentieth century, photographic illustrations were common,

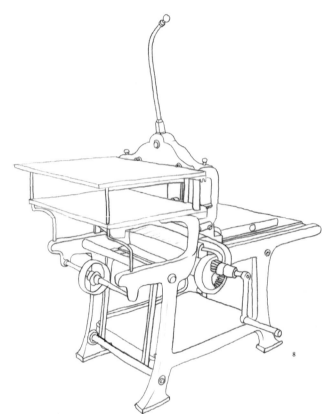

8

9

8, 9, 10
Early lithographic printing.
Illustrations by Emma Gibson
and Luke Waller.
Images courtesy of the artists.

11 A first edition of
*The First Six Books of The Elements
of Euclid* by mathematician
Oliver Byrne, 1847.

appearing regularly in books, newspapers and catalogues of all kinds.

This was a period of proliferation—if not complete revolution—in the printing process, with new ideas of increasing complexity emerging nearly every year. Some remained a niche market, such as nature printing (where impressions were taken, via several processes, from actual plants) and anaglyptography, a method of imitating the three-dimensional surface of a coin or medal. Others, like heliogravure and photogravure achieved a more widespread distribution for high quality reproductions of photographs. To showcase these new innovations in printing technology, William Stannard rounded up some 156 different printing methods, which he put together into a vast volume published in 1859 as *The Art Exemplar*. Even in Stannard's own day many of these methods would have seemed strange. Today, when printing is dominated by offset lithography—where the lithographic image is set off onto an intermediate roller in the printing press—some of these nineteenth century inventions seem downright curious.

Though printing technology was vastly improving, the explosion in the demand for printing engendered a proportional decrease in quality. In some ways, it was a return to the early years of the eighteenth century, with poorly rendered and bastardised faces being peddled on the cheap, a problem that has re-surfaced in the present age where the democratising influence of the computer revolution has seen the return of ill-constructed DIY graphics and shoddy digital types. In the early years of the nineteenth century, very few firms maintained the high standards of Caslon, Baskerville, Foulis or Bodoni, preferring instead to cater for a popular culture of mass production. There were, however, some notable exceptions, for example, the founder of the Chiswick Press, Charles Whittingham. Founding his press in 1811 (and later handing it over to his nephew, also Charles Whittingham) the Whittinghams quickly gained a reputation for being the finest printers in the country, leading to a long association with the publisher William Pickering. This relationship resulted in some of the most beautifully produced books of the era, including the Aldine Poets series.

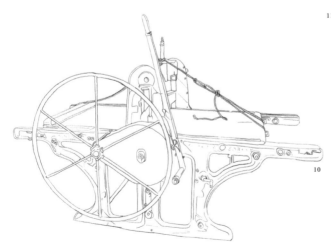

10

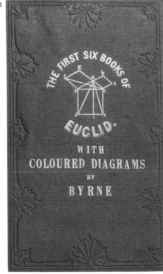

11

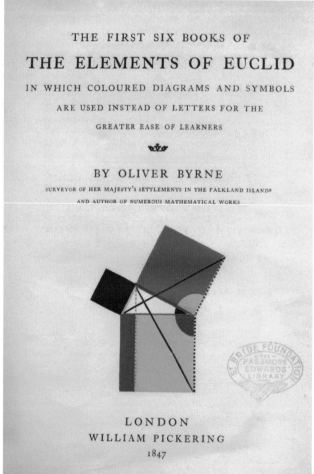

THE FIRST SIX BOOKS OF

THE ELEMENTS OF EUCLID

IN WHICH COLOURED DIAGRAMS AND SYMBOLS

ARE USED INSTEAD OF LETTERS FOR THE

GREATER EASE OF LEARNERS

BY OLIVER BYRNE

SURVEYOR OF HER MAJESTY'S SETTLEMENTS IN THE FALKLAND ISLANDS

AND AUTHOR OF NUMEROUS MATHEMATICAL WORKS

LONDON
WILLIAM PICKERING
1847

12

Both in name and in attention to typographic detail, these volumes hark back to the ideals of the great Venetian printer Aldus Manutius, who had been one of the first to produce a series of popular pocket classics. The printer did not go so far in his homage as to use an Aldine face, instead favouring the antique in deploying Caslon's Old Face. "In fact", as Updike says, "the chief typographic event of the mid-nineteenth century was this revival of the earliest Caslon types in the competent hands of Pickering and Whittingham."[7] However historically conscious, Pickering and Whittingham's work was not at all retrospective. The edition of Oliver Byrne's *First Six Books of the Elements of Euclid*, printed by Pickering in 1847, was highly revolutionary, "coloured diagrams and symbols are used instead of letters for the greater ease of learners" with the intention (according to the Preface) that "the *Elements of Euclid* can be acquired in less than one third the time usually employed, and the retention by the memory is much more permanent". As the typograher R McLean notes: "each proposition is set in Caslon italic, with a four line initial engraved

13

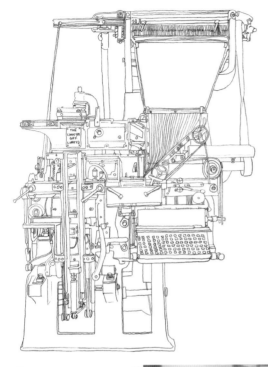

on wood by Mary Byfield: the rest of the page is a unique riot of red, yellow and blue: on some pages letters and numbers only are printed in colour, sprinkled over the page like tiny flowers, demanding the most meticulous register: elsewhere, solid squares, triangles, and circles are printed in gaudy and theatrical colours, attaining a verve not seen again on book pages till the days of Dufy, Matisse and Derain".[8] With this combination of revolutionary spirit and careful typography, it was natural that William Morris should choose Whittingham to print his own writing, prior to the creation of the Kelmscott Press.

This period also saw the emergence of American type designs and printers onto the world stage. In the years following the Civil War, the country had expanded rapidly and was now bustling with creative energy. One of the most notable typographic relationships of this period emerged with the father and son duet of Linn Boyd Benton and the younger Morris Fuller Benton. The elder Benton had been involved in setting up one of the companies that would, in 1892,

14   15

12 Title page from Oliver Byrne's *First Six Books of the Elements of Euclid*, printed by William Pickering in 1847.

13 Calson Old Face Monotype, printed by The Monotype Corporation Ltd.

14 A linotype machine.
Illustration by Emma Gibson.
Image courtesy of the artist.

15 Linotype machines in use at a New York printing room, 1909.

merge to create the typographic giant American Type Founders (ATF). However, Benton's most important contribution was on the technical side of things, indeed he almost single-handedly revolutionised the way type was to be made in generations to come. In spite of a few curious experiments, type was still being produced by a foundry before being distributed to the printer for setting by hand. This all changed with the appearance of Otto Merganthaler's Linotype Machine. First installed by the *New York Herald Tribune* in 1886, this new machine produced a slug of type metal on which appeared a complete line of type raised up—literally a 'line-o-type'. A competing model, the Monotype machine of the Talbot Lanston Corporation, produced just a single piece of type at a time. With both processes, type was hot cast by the machine in the actual printing office, the system was referred to as 'hot metal' in contrast to the 'cold metal' type, which was supplied ready cast from the foundry. Typecasting was now fast and accurate and could be carried out by anyone in possession of one of these machines, and once the

word got out, everyone wanted one. The problem for Merganthaler, though, was there weren't enough matrices to satisfy the demand for these machines. This is where Benton senior came in, for he had just invented an automatic punch cutter from which matrices could be generated at speed, supplying the missing piece of the puzzle, and forever changing the way type was made. The new machinations of the typefounding industry set the stage for a new breed of typefaces, inspired by the wider world of art, design and architecture. One of the first of these was Cheltenham, designed by the architect Bertram Grosvenor Goodhue for the Cheltenahm Press in New York. Its short descenders permitted a wider line spacing, creating an airy and clean look that ultimately promoted greater legibility. Meanwhile, Benton was collaborating with the renowned letterpress printer Theodore Lowe De Vinne to produce the eponymous Century typeface, first employed in the magazine of the same name during1895, and now widely used in its revised form, Century Schoolbook as cut by Monotype. The younger Benton was no less inventive

16

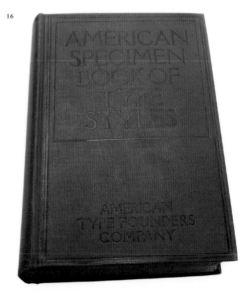

16 Cover of *American Specimen Book of Type Styles*, American Type Founders Company, 1912.
Photography by Matthew Pull.

17 Illustration of an automatic punchcutter.
Illustration by Emma Gibson.
Image courtesy of the artist.

18 Pages from *American Specimen Book of Type Styles* depicting Franklin Gothic. American Type Founders Company, 1912.
Photography by Matthew Pull.

than his father, designing a huge range of typefaces in his own right. Cheltenham became a complete family in 1904, Century turned into Century Expanded and Century Italic and in 1907 the younger Benton designed Clearface and a Bodoni revival. He also oversaw a reprise of Baskerville, Garamond and the much vaunted News Gothic. With the energy of Modernism coursing through the 1920s, the younger Benton released fresh display types such as Broadway and Parisian. His Century Expanded is particularly redolent of the period where it was used extensively for advertising, making use of a large x height and simple letterforms in an exceedingly legible face. News Gothic and its stable mate, Franklin Gothic are both very serviceable sans serifs, rooted in the nineteenth century display faces, but still modern and outward looking. If anything the younger Benton was a man before his time, indeed it is often Gill Sans or Univers that are considered groundbreakers in the modern typographic age, but Benton was busy mapping these new grounds some two decades in advance of either Gill or Frutiger.

17

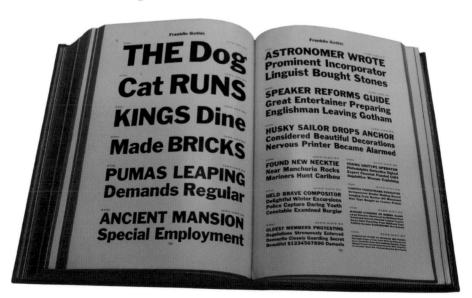

18

6
TEAL TRIGGS

Great Women Typographers: Where are They?
Teal Triggs asks Sibylle Hagmann

A battalion waiting
à l'hôtel Odéon
ſpilled black seeds
un día más de calma atmosférica
Schiffskapitänin
some offbeat single fittings
el árbol pequeño
Les chansons téléchargées
Acting ſtrangely

Font family Odile, designed by
Sibylle Hagmann in 2006.

ODILE ROMAN AND BOLD

Art historians have long bemoaned the lack of representation of women's work in the history books and in gallery and museum collections. The question was first posed by Linda Nochlin in her analysis "Why Have There Been No Great Women Artists?", written during the rise of feminism in the 1970s. This is a question still resonating today, particularly when considered within the context of women working in typography and graphic design. Design writers and historians have attempted to redress the balance, but the problem remains.

The following email interview between Sibylle Hagmann and Teal Triggs attempts to shed some light. Sibylle Hagmann is an emerging figure in type design. She completed the typeface family Cholla in 1999, originally commissioned by Art Centre College of Design and released by the digital type foundry Emigre in the same year. Cholla was among the winning entries of bukva:raz!, the type design competition of the Association Typographique Internationale (ATypI) in 2001. The typeface family Odile was released in 2006 and was awarded the Swiss Federal Design Award in the same year.

Teal Triggs: Nochlin writes in her essay: "There are no great women artists (read typographers) because women are incapable of greatness". She begins with this premise in order to provoke the reader to reflect on the assumptions and perceptions of women artists made by her contemporaries. How might you respond to this statement today and in relationship to the field of typography?

Sibylle Hagmann: It could be argued that women have been part of the field of the fine arts a great deal longer and in bigger numbers than in the field of typography, or type design. Among other reasons, one of them is that only by 1980 the industry experienced the end of the dirty, physically strenuous work involved in the production of eg metal type. The type setting industry was traditionally a male-dominated field of expertise and craft, partly because it took place in the context and trade of mass communication. Manufactured items, produced with a mechanical process are more firmly placed in a patriarchal and industrial background. Given this history, females, although few, intermingle on the list of major typographic accomplishments and contributions. But design and typography history are mostly presented and illustrated through the canon of art history—glorifying famous work and equally celebrated creators. After roughly a quarter of a century of women participating in the digital typographic métier, we have yet to see a monograph discuss female accomplishments.

Nochlin's essay raises other interesting questions, for example: who has a problem with the fact that there are less females working in a particular field—men or women? Most likely the lack of female participation is less perceived as a 'problem' by the outnumbering male practitioners. This question can be formulated differently: what would the profession gain, if typographic culture reflected insights and sensibilities from a more balanced and diverse pool of typographic practitioners? Attracting and including minorities of all kinds is a distant goal. As universal history proves, disadvantaged groups cannot expect that those with privileges one day see the light and grant complete access to the historically less powerful, including—to borrow from a statement from the 1970s—everybody who deviates from being male, white and middle class. Structures perceived as 'normal'—such as for example, how a society distinguishes gender roles—are extremely difficult to turn up. Does that mean we should sit and wait for the next 60 or so years, to find us being content by the fact that a greater number of women are working in the field of typography by 2080?

One comment I received from a male typographer about the essay I wrote ("Non-existent design: women and the creation of type" for The New Typography, was that what (females) mainly need to do is networking (with males) in order to gain recognition. Networking is another way of making oneself visible to others, but it doesn't 'overthrow' the established structures in place. True, and there is no doubt, women have to be willing to make efforts to be visible and to reach the top in order to be competitive. Do women up to the present time shy away from the opportunity to speak at typographic conferences? Some of these symposia may suffer under remnants of elitism and 'old boys' club-like auras, notwithstanding, women need to stake out new territories and surface in public. I believe that women working in the field of typography and type design generally conceive themselves as equal and I doubt that they are blocked by a refusal to look the facts in the face. Female type lovers do not suffer under self-pity, but can't deny the fact that they are few. They realise that they are, and indeed must, be measured by the same criteria as everybody else, in order to succeed, including a considerable emotional—and intellectual—commitment.

Women on higher levels are a niche, no matter what kind of field one examines—CEOs, symphony lady maestros, even leading female roles in movies are currently meager, as a New York Times article "Is there a real women in this multiplex?" suggests.[1] The problem I conclude lies much deeper than in individual industry structures. I'm thinking, for example, of how society assists women pursuing to devote themselves to both family and a career. In the end it becomes a sociological, societal and cultural issue. Delegating the responsibilities of nourishing and nurturing a child becomes a major economical and, again, societal issue.

Linking it back to the fine arts, perceived value structures presently evaluate male art much higher than art created by females. Jackson Pollock's painting titled No 5, 1948, was sold in 2006 for 140 million dollars, whereas the most expensive female art object ever sold, a marble sculpture by Louise Bourgeois, auctioned off for four million dollars in the same year.

TT: In your essay "Non-existent design: women and the creation of type" you explore the relationship between gender, stereotyping and industry-accepted typographers. Part of your argument attributed this lack of a female presence to a perceived women's 'fear' of technology, but also to educational contexts and the lack of female role models. Do you feel that even today with technology firmly embedded within design practice and process, this is still the case? How might we ensure our students are more aware of women working in the field without putting women on a pedestal?

SH: With new font formats in demand, the production of digital typefaces can quickly demand a greater involvement with technology. Exploiting OpenType technology requires scripting for example. The engineering of fonts is, by today's standards, a predominantly male activity. Professional education of type design, offered in several institutions with a concentration in Europe, foster the students' involvement in font technology which in turn may cultivate women specialising in this area.

La terre battue

a flower shop fragrance

Fliegen & Wespen

El gatito se movía adelante

What a nice breeze

Efficiency is the key to success

an der Ostküste der Insel

C'est ma mère!

Geschnetzeltes mit Rösti

Prix Nobel d'économie

TODO EL MUNDO

Repräsentantenhaus

Binoculars

Olympische Spiele 2008

EL AÑO PASADO

The Great American Dust Bowl

qui n'hésite pas à s'affranchir?

Universität

ODILE ITALIC AND BOLD ITALIC
ODILE SMALL CAPS AND SMALL CAPS ITALIC

A list of books currently on the market discussing the lack of women in technology, lets me conclude that this is a burning issue: *Women and Information Technology: Research on Underrepresentation*, 2008; *Gender and Computers: Understanding the Digital Divide*, 2003; or *Reconfiguring the Firewall: Recruiting Women to Information Technology across Cultures and Continents*, 2007. Numerous efforts are under way addressing the deficiency of women in, for example, engineering. According to a statement from the University of Houston of May 2006, "females make up only 20 per cent of engineering undergraduates, and women hold less than a quarter of jobs in all technical fields".

Given the relatively brief history of women being actively involved in the practice of typography, I believe that the females currently at the peak of their careers almost entirely lacked personal role models, mothers, or close female relatives who were type designers, typographers, or women making a living from design or art. This generation grew up during a time when it was still common for sons to follow in their fathers' footsteps. It would actually be interesting to find out how many male typographers and type designers had close family, or friends who inspired them to work in the professional field of typography or type design. Matthew Carter, humorously emphasised in one of his talks that his father was a typographer and that he chose the least resistance in following his father's footsteps. No doubt the world is delighted he did.

Within educational institutions, providing female mentors working in the field of typography—or mentors aware of female accomplishments in design history—could help raise the awareness of women designer contributions. Educators should address the issue of gender when introducing design and typographic history. Institutions could create an educational methodology with design history modules incorporating the work of women. Such efforts would make the student familiar with female names and achievements within the field.

Further, departments and design schools could invite experts in sociology or womens' studies, who can lend a feminist approach to teaching design history. One could also consider initiating a female speakers series. I believe students are best exposed to visible traces of females working in the field of typography and type design in order to inspire and manifest a strong participation, as opposed to putting women on a pedestal.

TT: So far the majority of key texts on graphic design history and typography have been written by men. While specific mention is made by female historians Drucker and McVarish (2009) of women working within the graphic design profession (Pineless, Greiman, Licko and McCoy) there is little new historical information about them or the inclusion of other female typographers. And, in terms of published monographs, we are still seeing the usual suspects (eg Barnbrook, Carson, Fuel, Tomato, to cite just a few). Is the perception that there aren't many women in typography due to the fact that design historians have not necessarily addressed this issue in terms of how typography has been written about in the history books?

SH: Just as the issue remains unaddressed within the industry itself, design historians have largely under-recognised the contributions of women in typography. Since textbooks on design are mostly written by males, educators ought to push for un-closeting women typographic designers, giving them the appropriate place in graphic design history texts. Monographs and the publishing of material about women concerned with typography would feed back into an effort to recover women previously lost in history. Citing Ellen Lupton in *Women Designers in the USA, 1900–2000*: "During the last quarter of the twentieth century, women played a central role in building the discourse in graphic design. [...]. Women were no minority among the educators, critics, editors, and curators who defined the theoretical issues of the time."

TT: Over the years arguments have been made about there being a 'definable female aesthetic' in graphic design/typography which draws upon stereotypical components such as being described soft, round, smooth and pink! Do you feel that the outcomes of your own typographic practice may be described as such? How does your own design process ensure you don't fall into expected or stereotypical forms?

SH: Aesthetic outcomes are easily categorised in stereotypical terms as male or female, but generally I believe that style should not be used as a gauge for artistic and visual criteria. Aesthetic preferences underlay movements of visual fashions arriving in waves and disappearing again shortly thereafter, only to resurface within a novel and future style cycle. The Jugendstil or Art Nouveau that peaked in popularity at the turn of the twentieth century and which could fit the vague criteria of short, round, smooth and pink, followed out of the British Arts and Craft Movement with major contributions by Otto Eckmann, Josef Sattler, Peter Behrens, or Henry van de Velde, had a minor contribution from women. Earlier, Rococo, a flowery and luscious style with representatives such as the painter François Boucher, or the architectural designs of Nicolas Pineau in eighteenth century France, found popularity with minute women designers' contributions. Furthermore, during the eighteenth century most French art academies didn't admit women, representing a setback for female artists. These examples show that the choice of a form language or subject matter will not necessarily tell about the creator's gender. Undeniable though are the influence of a designer's context and culture he or she identifies with.

For the above reasons, the artistic or typographic work of women should not be judged by a style criteria, after "a distinct and recognisable feminine style", based on "the special character of women's situation and experience", as mentioned in Nochlin's essay and

Herbstliches Angebot

CASSIOPEIA

An affirmative answer

Gelehrte ❀ Minerva

Apparent in the finest detail

L'ÉCHO LUMINEUX

La producción del maestro francés

DAS GESICHT DER FRAU

THEATRICAL MAGIC

ODILE UPRIGHT ITALIC, SMALL CAPS, INITIALS,
DECO INITIALS AND ORNAMENTS

proposed by some contemporary feminists, but by the quality and inventiveness of the form language, concept and methods of the creative process, intellectual involvement, and experimentation. I think there is a certain temptation to critique form by styles seemingly approved by the (design) establishment. Modernism became another visual style, despite its initial goal of maintaining complete objectivity over how content is presented in order to separate itself from an illusive, subjective and illustrative communication method.

My own practice is not interested in producing an aesthetic definable as typical female, but I can't deny that I'm female and my upbringing, perception, and reasoning are those of a woman designer. I can't get rid of that, nor should I have to. My design process follows conclusions which may not have much to do with style or being female in the first place, but rather weighed with intellectual considerations which then lead to an employment of a particular form language. The font family Odile, 2006, includes four weights, Odile Upright Italic, Initials, Deco Initials and Ornaments, which could probably be described as rather female. However, this was not the key intention. Rather, its visual outcome is the result of an experiment I assigned myself to find out how far I can push, and if I could produce forms which are ornate in nature. My educational background consists of a degree from the Basel School of Design and from CalArts, two institutions with rather opposing philosophies and methodologies. While my first education was based on Modernism and the Bauhaus, the latter rejected categorisations alltogether and still follows an interdisciplinary approach. Odile Initials, Deco Initials and Ornaments became an experiment initiated on a personal level to overcome the deeply imbedded— partly imposed by education—inhibition for intricate, elaborate and ornate forms. In addition, it seemed appropriate to explore this idea within the context of the design of this particular typeface family.

In *Eye* magazine Odile was one of ten typefaces reviewed by Deborah Littlejohn, Jan Middendorp, Petra Cerne Oven and Mark Thomson in the article titled "Lust and Likeability". The introduction states: "Deborah Littlejohn contacted 95 fellow designers by email, asking them to rank and rate a (slightly longer) list of typefaces, and compiled a fascinating (if non-scientific) survey, paying attention to preferences by gender, and what she terms the 'likeability factor', testing her own opinions with those of her peers." Littlejohn's survey documents women ranking the Odile typeface family rather high, while males' ratings were somewhat lower. Littlejohn's accompanying assessment discloses: "Odile is […] so darn feminine and almost painfully sweet and decorative." The survey illustrates that taste varies between genders, just as gender and its cultural context influence form-making.

TT: In 1994, Martha Scotford defined women's involvement in graphic design by categories which broadly include women practitioners, women in education, women as critics, historians and theoreticians. I would also add women in industry—those who are not necessarily typographers themselves, but are

champions for the discipline. I am thinking of women such as Beatrice Warde, 1900–1969, the publicity manager at Monotype, who also as a writer and critic, played a significant role in defining 'good typography'. Who would you say are today's women role models and champions of the typographic profession?

SH: Women like Beatrice Warde give us the confidence that we are on the right track. In my personal view the most influential role models are those who are still with us. Keeping the active women of my time in mind gives me a sense of community, despite its rather small size. My list includes many of the usual suspects: Zuzana Licko, Carol Twombly, Lorraine Wild, Paula Scher, Ellen Lupton, Sheila de Bretteville and so forth, but also contemporaries like those very loosely coming together in a forum named Typeladies (www.typeladies.org).

TT: Are there any further questions you would like to raise and /or address?

SH: Patience. I'm convinced that each successive generation of women typographers will find the playing field slightly more even, just as there is an increased gender balance perceivable in the graphic design profession. It will take patience and continuous efforts to raise consciousness. There is no discernible resistance, yet how can we foster strategies pushing for awareness, collaboration, opportunities, and achievements in becoming one forward-thinking, all-inclusive typographic niche.

7 ART AND STYLE

ART
AND STYLE

In 1844, the Englishman William Henry Fox Talbot published *The Pencil of Nature*, the world's first book to be illustrated entirely by photographs. Inspired by Emery Walker's now famous 1888 Arts and Crafts lecture on the history of type design, William Morris then set out to create the first photographically-inspired types. It was to be the dawn of a new era in which even the conventions of relief typefaces would be replaced with filmsetting and, eventually, digital typography. And with new technologies came new ideas; the reverence for the past that inspired Morris and the typographers of the private press movement would be replaced by the forward-looking ideas of the Dadaists and the Futurists, who believed in breaking down the old rules of ordered typesetting. From this came a fresh outlook that would attempt to reconcile the demands of good design with those of modern industrialised production, resulting in such innovations as the sans serifed alphabets, and at one stage, the rejection of upper case letters altogether.

1

By the end of the nineteenth century, changes in technology were being felt in the everyday lives of ordinary people. Gas lighting was being replaced by electricity and the first horseless carriages—petrol driven motor cars—could be seen travelling on the roads, albeit at limited speed. Illustrators and designers such as Aubrey Beardsley in Britain and Alphonse Mucha, Gustav Klimt, Koloman Moser and Victor Horta on the Continent were experimenting with new techniques and letterforms of rounded lines which came to be known by the French term Art Nouveau and which were essentially derived from a Japanese style of woodblock illustration. The influence of the East on the whole field of artistic endeavour had been building since the opening up of Tokyo with trade agreements in the 1860s. Works by artists such as Hiroshige and Hokusai—with their vibrant views of seascapes, mountains and flowers—were available to far-flung audiences for the first time, inspiring artists, designers and typographers across the Western world. This reverence for the natural world can be seen reflected in the vegetative

2

1 Poster announcing the
Cincinnati Fall Festival,
Strobridge & Co
Lithography, 1903.

2 Aubrey Beardsley, Design
for the prospectus of the
Yellow Book, 1894.

border designs and luxuriant foliage in Beardsley's working of Oscar Wilde's 1894 *Salome*. Beardsley was highly influential and moved within a group of mostly radicalised practitioners, all of whom boasting a variety of styles, the breadth of which can be seen in *The Yellow Book*, a periodical that he edited for a time.

As a movement, Art Nouveau would be comparatively short-lived, but the influence of its essential tenets would survive well into the twentieth century. In 1933, the Adana specimen sheet included a face called Auriol Outline in a variety of sizes, which owes much to the Japanese-influenced display faces of the 1890s. It is entirely right that Adana—a firm who championed presses and equipment for the amateur and craft printer—should be offering up such a face. Indeed, in many senses the whole Art Nouveau movement was a reaction against the industrialisation of late nineteenth century Britain. At the same time, another group of young artists pledged themselves to resist what they saw as the advance of a burgeoning epidemic of bad taste promoted by

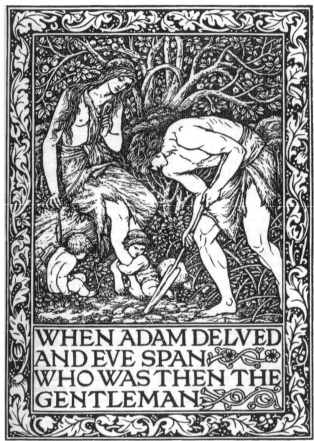

3

4

3 Frontispiece of *A Dream of John Ball*. Designed by Edward Burne-Jones, lettering and border design by William Morris.

4 Process drawings for William Morris' Golden Type design.

5, 6 The second edition of *The Story of The Glittering Plain*, printed by Kelmscott Press in 1894. Illustrated with engravings by Walter Crane.

mass production. These were the pre-Raphaelite brotherhood who sought to promote what they saw as the artistic ideals of the medieval craftsman, initiated by people such as William Morris. His company, Morris & Co produced a wide range of textiles, furniture and stained glass, designed either by himself or by other artists such as Burne-Jones and the Rosettis, all of whom subscribed to the Arts and Crafts aesthetic ideals.

William Morris came comparatively late to book design. By the latter part of the nineteenth century, the majority of books produced were seen by some as being denuded of vitality. It was not as if they were technically inept, there was just something wanting in terms of the kind of artistry which had been lent to the works produced by Jenson, the Plantins and even Baskerville. Some interest in a typographic re-appraisal had been promulgated by Selwyn Image and Herbert Horne in *The Century Guild Hobby Horse*, which had been founded as the mouthpiece for Arthur Heygate Mackmurdo's Arts and Crafts organisation—the Century Guild—in 1884.[1] William Morris had at first selected

Charles Whittingham at the Chiswick Press to print his works, yet he eventually felt strongly that something was lost in the mechanistic production of the changing printing industry. At an Arts and Crafts Society lecture, at the New Gallery in Regent Street, Morris heard Emery Walker speak on the early printers—of the Elzevirs, Caslon and Baskerville. This proved to be all the inspiration that he needed to change the way his work was produced, and before long he resolved to set up his own press in the spirit of those early print craftsmen. This would become the Kelmscott Press, issuing its first book in 1891, *The Story of the Glittering Plain*, written by Morris himself. Morris also set about designing his own typeface, which he based on those used in the Rubeus' *Historia Florentina* and Nicholas Jensen's Pliny. Morris' design method was quite basic, he had Walker supply photographic slides of pages from the works he wished to replicate, which he projected on paper and used as tracing forms. From these designs, he had punches cut and eventually a fount of type was cast which he named the Golden Type after Caxton's *Golden Legend*.[2] Coupled with wide decorative

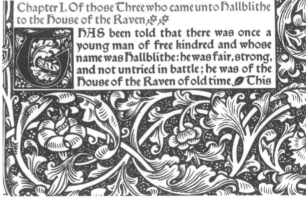

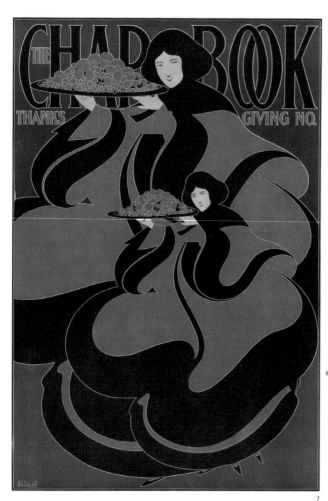

7

borders, Morris's pages are instantaneously recognisable for their Medievalism and dense body of blackly inked type.

Morris designed two further typefaces, the Troy type—specially cut for the Kelmscott Press edition of *Froissart's Chronicles*—and a blackletter, appropriately called Chaucer and used in the Press' most sumptuous publication *The Works of Geoffrey Chaucer*. His types are elegant when taken as individual letters but the *Chaucer* in particular is hardly readable, of course that was not the point, it was the look that mattered. What Morris had done was to rekindle a fascination with the works of the early practitioners—those books printed in the earliest years of the craft up to 1500. On the back of the 53 books put out by the Kelmscott Press, foundries both in Britain and America started to design their own Jensen-inspired faces. After Morris' death in 1896, the Chiswick Press printed a series of the author's works using a version of the Golden Type and bound in imitation of the cheaper board bindings used on the original Kelmscott volumes.

8

7 Will H Bradley, *The Chapbook*, Thanksgiving, 1895.

8, 9 Pages from *The Works of Geoffrey Chaucer, Now Newly Imprinted*, printed by William Morris at the Kelmscott Press, 1896.

In spite of his avowed intentions, Morris' books are profoundly Victorian; their heavy decoration and lavish use of densely inked type more closely allied to Beardsley or to the high Gothic of Owen Jones' pseudo-illuminated manuscripts, than to the simple refinement of Fust or Jensen. Yet, the attention to detail and promulgation of an adherence to the use of a single unified typeface over the ill-favoured homogeneity of the multifarious faces found in the books of the majority of his contemporaries heralded a new era of typographic design.

The most lasting and wide-ranging result of Morris's printing adventure was the initiation of what has become known as the private press movement. Some of the greatest names in twentieth century typography have been associated with this desire to follow Morris in creating limited edition works, renowned for their impeccable types and fine press work. The most notable example in America was Daniel Berkley Updike's Merrymount Press in Boston and Will Bradley's Wayside Press in Springfield, Massachusetts, where the spiritual tradition of the

Kelmscott Press was kept alive with books distinctively rendered with rich borders and decorative initials. Using his influence as art director of *Century Magazine* and editor of *The Chapbook* (issued by ATF) Bradley also managed to bring the philosophy of Arts and Crafts printing to commercial publishing for a time. Updike had learned his craft at the Riverside Press in Cambridge Massachusetts, succeeded there by another great name in the field, Bruce Rogers. His best-known creation is Centaur—another typeface based on a Jenson face, this time inspired by that used in the 1470 edition of *Eusebius*. It was used to great effect in the Oxford University Press edition of *The Odyssey of Homer* translated by TE Lawrence and printed for the first time in America in 1932.

During the great age of the private press, the proprietor of each establishment was seemingly striving for individuality by designing their own typeface. At the Ashendene Press, founded in 1894, St John Hornby first used Caslon and Fell types before commissioning Emery Walker to design the Subiaco type based on that

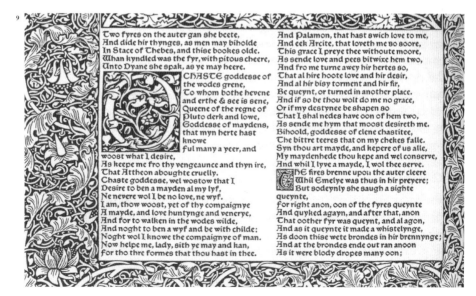

9

first used by Sweynheym and Pannartz in 1465 at Subiaco. Charles Ricketts cut the Vale type for his press of the same name and Lucien Pissarro designed the Brook type for his highly artistic books of the Eragny Press. Thomas James Cobden-Sanderson, proprietor of the Doves Press likewise commissioned an eponymous typeface which, like Morris' Golden Type was based on the Jenson original and cut by the same punchcutter, Edward Prince. If anything the Doves type is much closer to the original than Morris' creation as can be seen in the great multi-volume Doves Bible where it is presented on monumental pages unadorned aside from the occasional intercession of decorative letters designed by Edward Johnston. It is a pleasantly readable face of a fulsome x height and with flat unbracketed serifs.

The British private presses exerted a very strong design ethos over the whole of Europe and America throughout the early years of the twentieth century. Morris' revival of the fifteenth century typographic ideals was particularly successful in Germany where the Art Nouveau book style maintained a strong following. Indeed, it was in Germany that Emery Walker was commissioned by Insel-Verlag to design a series of titles based on their German classics. Eric Gill and Edward Johnston were also brought in to provide title pages for the series. Throughout much of the nineteenth century, America had been content to follow the old world. It is generally thought that the first type specimen book to be issued in America was put out by the Philadelphia foundry of Binny and Ronaldson, in which can be found one of the best of the early transitional types, named the Oxford, with a peculiar hankering for the historical associations of old time Britain.

Both the Bremer Press (which was founded in 1911) at Munich and the Cranach Press of Weimar followed the British lead with a reliance on strong typographic style. Harry Graf von Kessler had established the later press in the year before the outbreak of the First World War with the help and advice of Anton Kippenberg of the Insel-Verlag. The first book, eventually published in three editions between 1926 and 1927, was an

11

10

PRINTER'S NOTE

N writing a short introductory note to this first piece of printing in my Centaur type as now made in various sizes by the Lanston Monotype Corporation, it is, first of all, a pleasure to record my vivid recollections of the friendliness and forbearance with which, many years ago at the British Museum, Mr. Pollard met the importunities of an unintroduced American visitor who had then only recently decided to become a printer. The store-houses, not only of the British Museum Library but also of Mr. Pollard's own richly varied knowledge of books and printing, were readily thrown open to me; and they have always remained open during twenty-five intervening years— a standard by which to measure work done and a stimulus to new endeavour.

The type known as 'Montaigne,' for which I had been largely responsible, had met his warm approbation; for in those days we all liked heavier and cruder types than our reconsideration of the matter now leads some of us to prefer. It may be

edition of Virgil's *Eclogues*, illustrated with woodcuts by the French sculptor Maillol and set in the Cranach Textura type for which punches had been cut by Edward Prince and GT Friend, with initial letters provided by Eric Gill. The most famous book, and arguably one of the most distinctive publications of the twentieth century, was an edition of Shakespeare's *Hamlet*, which came out in a German edition in 1929 and in English a year later. It was strikingly illustrated with black figure woodcuts by the theatre designer Edward Gordon Craig.[3] For this work Johnston designed types based on those of Fust and Schoeffer, which were set in a text block bordered by a commentary.

France was experiencing something of an artistic revolution during the same period. The artist Henri Matisse had gathered together a band of like-minded individuals to form a group now known as the Fauves—literally the *Wild Beasts*. Their artistic expression was supposed to be untamed, much influenced by primitive sculpture. The Italians, by comparison, had embraced the Futurist movement, headed up by

the poet Filippo Tommaso. The Futurists expressed a widespread contempt for the past, which they took to be enshrined in a bourgeois cultural stereotyping. For them, all vitality lay in the future with its whorl of extreme creativity. Typographically, their publications sought to violate all the established laws of good practice by juxtaposing faces of all sizes and descriptions with seeming abandon, often set in anything but the expected place and direction. The impression is one of multifarious flux and confusion within which legibility and communication are only just discernable. The logical outcome was Marinetti's doctrine of *Tipografia in Libertà and Parole in Libertà*, which proposed the unfettered use of words and letters, releasing them from their hitherto defined places in sentences to become radicalised and self-contained expressive elements. Summarising this in, *The Destruction of Syntax/Imagination without Strings/Words-in-Freedom* of 1913, he proclaimed:

> The book must be the Futurist expression of our Futurist thought. My revolution is aimed at the so-

12

10, 11 The first printed example of Monotype Centaur, in Alfred W Pollard's, *The Trained Printer and the Amateur, and the Pleasure of Small Books,* 1929.

12 Page detail from TJ Cobden-Sanderson's *The Ideal Book or Book Beautiful,* set in Doves type and printed by Doves Press, 1901.

Illustration important question. The main question is the aspect which the illustration shall be made to take in order to fit it into and amid a page of Typography. And I submit that its aspect must be essentially formal and of the same texture, so to speak, as the letterpress. It should have a set frame or margin to itself, demarcating it distinctly from the text, and the shape & character of the frame, if decorative, should have relation to the page as well as to the illustrative content; and the illustrative content itself should be formal and kept under so as literally to illustrate, and not to dim by over brilliancy the rest of the subject matter left to be communicated to the imagination by the letterpress alone.

called typographical harmony of the page, which is contrary to the flux and reflux, the leaps and bursts of style that run through the page. On the same page, therefore, we will use three or four colours of ink, or even 20 different typefaces if necessary. For example: italics for a series of similar or swift sensations, boldface for violent onomatopoeias, and so on. With this typographical revolution and this multi-coloured variety in the letters I mean to redouble the expressive force of words.[4]

By 1916, it was not just the vocabulary of art that was dying. On the Western Front (and beyond) thousands were being slaughtered in the great conflict of the First World War. Increasingly sophisticated technology on the battlefield meant greater carnage and whilst Zeppelins bombed London and the Royal Flying Corps attacked German troops from the air, a new movement was beginning in Zurich. The Dadaists, like the Futurists, rankled at the old world order but instead of looking to the possibilities of a mechanised age, they railed against it. Their typographic philosophy was just as radical, proposing a rejection of what they saw as the needless conventions of upper case letters and punctuation. So works like *La Première Aventture Céleste de Mr Antipyrine* published in 1916, and set entirely in lower case by the leading Dadaist Tristan Tzara, are a kind of peon to a pared down typographic tradition devoid of superfluous elements.

This obsession would be a dominant theme of the artists and theoreticians associated with the Bauhaus where form and function were seen to be inextricably conjoined. Germany (defeated in 1918) was a broken nation cruelly treated by the victorious Allies at the Paris Peace Conference of 1919. Against this background of urgent exigency, the Weimar Arts and Crafts School and the Academy of Art were merged under the visionary Walter Gropius to create one of the first unified forums for the study of all the arts.

The Bauhaus tenet was once again an attempt to reconcile the demands of good design with those of modern industrialised production.

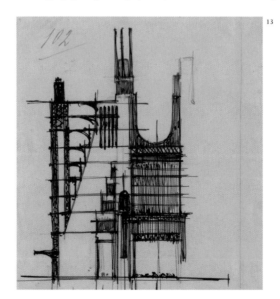

13

13 An example of Futurist architecture. Antonio Sant'Elia, Casa a gradinata con ascensori esterni, 1914.

14 Bauhaus syllabus, 1922.

das bauhaus in dessau

lehrplan

auskunft erteilt die geschäftstelle des bauhauses: dessau mauerstr. 36

zweck:

1. durchbildung bildnerisch begabter menschen in handwerklicher, technischer und formaler beziehung mit dem ziel gemeinsamer arbeit **am bau.**
2. praktische versuchsarbeit für hausbau und hauseinrichtung. entwicklung von standardmodellen für industrie und handwerk.

lehrgebiete:

1. **werklehre** für

    a. holz (tischlerei)
    b. metall (silber- und kupferschmiede)
    c. farbe (wandmalerei)
    d. gewebe (weberei, färberei)
    e. buch- und kunstdruck

    ergänzende lehrgebiete:

    material- und werkzeugkunde
    grundbegriffe von buchführung,
    preisberechnung, vertragsabschlüssen

2. **formlehre:** (praktisch und theoretisch)

    a. **anschauung**

      werkstoffkunde
      naturstudium

    b. **darstellung**

      projektionslehre
      konstruktionslehre
      werkzeichnen und modellbau für alle räumlichen gebilde
      entwerfen

    c. **gestaltung**

      raumlehre
      farblehre

    ergänzende lehrgebiete:

      vorträge aus gebieten der kunst und wissenschaft

lehrfolge:

1. **grundlehre:**

dauer: 2 halbjahre. elementarer formunterricht in verbindung mit praktischen übungen in der besonderen werkstatt für die grundlehre. im zweiten halbjahr probeweise aufnahme in eine lehrwerkstatt.
ergebnis: endgültige aufnahme.

In common with William Morris and the Arts and Crafts Movement, the progenitors of the Bauhaus recognised the dehumanising influence of mass production with the consequent want of quality in modern products. But there was none of the yearning for the manual craftsmanship of Morris, instead they attempted to offer a synthesis with the ideals of the Futurists, where the machine was accepted as a necessary element of modern production. Crucially, in the early years at least, the Bauhaus maintained a sympathy with the Dutch De Stijl movement, which sought to mediate life through art and architecture. This translated into the guiding principal of the Bauhaus where form was to follow function in all aspects of design.

This ethos permeated even the relatively conservative world of typography. In some senses, the typography of Germany of the 1920s had moved on very little from the days of Gutenberg. The heavy blackletter faces based on the scriptural traditions of the medieval monastery, such as those densely blacked Gothic faces favoured by Rudolph Koch, still largely prevailed though some designers had made valiant efforts to introduce lighter roman faces. The debate is perhaps nicely summarised in the work of the designer ER Weiss whose attempt at a legible blackletter with the Fraktur face cut by Bauer in 1913, is surpassed by his elegantly useable and eponymous Weiss roman alphabet.

Within the Bauhaus, the cudgel against blackletter would be taken up first by the Hungarian designer László Moholy-Nagy and then by Herbert Bayer, who in an effort to present information clearly and in the most forcible form first proposed the use of sans serifed alphabets and then a rejection even of upper case letters as being extraneous—a vision which found its logical conclusion in Bayer's Universal face, produced in lower case only. In the catalogue to the 1938 Museum of Modern Art retrospective of the Bauhaus, Bayer makes his case, asking: "why should we write and print with two alphabets? both a large and a small sign are not necessary to indicate one single sound... we need only a single alphabet".[5]

15 An example of work from the the the De Stijl school. Bart Van Der Leck, *Composite no 1*, 1918.

16, 17 Herbert Bayer's Universal typeface, a Modernist type design that included only lower case letters.

To recall this typographic experiment, the remainder of the catalogue is printed in lower case only, but although of interest it is a typographic diversion and not one that achieved universal recognition. This is restrained by the standards of the movement, which characteristically employed enlarged letters, heavy underlining and thick black horizontal and vertical bars to give emphasis. Like Baskerville and Bodoni, lettering is used sparingly in Bauhaus composition with white space consciously involved as part of the design.

That same consciousness of page space was taken up by Jan Tschichold, who had probably come across Moholy-Nagy and Bayer at the 1923 Bauhaus exhibition in Weimar. Two years later, he had formulated his ideas into a series of guidelines, which he was able to offer as a contribution to the periodical *Typographische Mitteilungen*. That same periodical also included work by the influential Russian Constructivist El Lissitzky, best known for his graphic designs incorporating sans serif types printed in red and black and applied to the page at a variety of odd angles, much like the Futurists.

Like Moholy-Nagy and Bayer, Tschichold argued for a simplicity and clarity in typography that would promote meaning above ornament. Blackletter and roman types, with their sensuous curves and needless serifs, should be rejected in favour of the pared-back lines of the sans serif form—this, in his eyes, "is the only one in spiritual accordance with our time".[6] Unfortunately, for both Tschichold and his contemporary Paul Renner, the political if not spiritual accordance of the time in Germany embraced the doctrines of Fascism. Branded Bolshevik sympathisers they both sought sanctuary in Switzerland. Allen Lane, then the proprietor for Penguin Books, invited Tschichold to re-design some of his books, which he managed with a selfless elegance, realigning pages with an effortless sense of type and space and even tightening up the brand logo.

Back in Germany, the experience was one of contrasts. The war-ravaged country had been divided by the conquering

Allies, with the Eastern part plunged into Communist-dominated gloom. In West Germany, though, American money had made recovery possible, and a new creative era was set to emerge. The pre-eminence of blackletter had been challenged, paving the way for exciting typographic developments. It was during this period of flux that Hermann Zapf emerged onto the scene. His career had been interrupted by the war but he had weathered the storm to become art director at the Stempel Company, where he designed one of the most influential faces of the second half of the twentieth century. Palatino reflects the influence of Edward Johnston's calligraphic style in its free-flowing penned strokes, together with something of the great Renaissance types. His other notable face is Optima, which he described as a 'serifless roman'—its thicks and thins promoting a poise that is quite indefinable and yet firmly locates it as a part of the new wave of German sans serif faces. Not all achieved the recognition they might have desired. Erbar, an angular sans serif designed by Jakob Erbar for Ludwig and Mayer never managed widespread distribution. By contrast Paul Renner

18

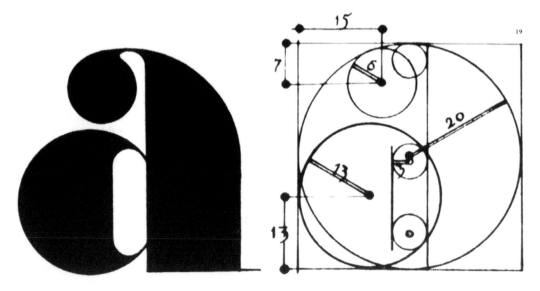

19

was to achieve a degree of commercial success with the creation of his Futura face. First issued in by the Bauer foundry in 1927, the initial letters were profoundly Constructivist with geometrically shaped and—in some cases—unconnected letters. A re-issue in 1928 saw that radicalism muted in favour of more conventional letterforms so that, along with Gill Sans, it stands as one of the classic typefaces of the twentieth century.

In America, Frederic Goudy, though a commercial type designer, managed to retain something of the Arts and Crafts Movement with its departure from the mechanistic world of the twentieth century. Peter Bielenson in *The Story of Frederic W Goudy* quotes him as saying "I really believe I am the first (in this country at least) to attempt to draw letters for types as things artistic as well as useful, rather than to construct them as a mechanic might, without regard for any aesthetic considerations."[7] Goudy set up the Village Press for which he designed the Village type, but it was not until the Monotype Corporation asked him to design a face for *Life* magazine that

he came to more universal recognition. Monotype issued the resultant font under the code 38-E, but it soon became better known as Goudy Old Style—the most enduring and most easily useable of all his faces, with its generous x height, gently sweeping characters and short descenders.

Goudy's successes, though, did not please everyone, particularly some of the more academic type designers like Stanley Morison. Morison was typographic advisor to the Monotype Corporation and was responsible for their programme of resurrecting historic typefaces. He is, though, almost certainly best known for Times New Roman, a classic roman face produced by Monotype for the redesign of *The Times* newspaper in 1932. It still performs as well today as it did then, providing an easily readable text even in the smallest sizes within densely packed columns. As its creator said "it has the merit of not looking as if it had been designed by somebody in particular".

Through Monotype, Morison was able to become associated with many of the

20

18 An example of Hermann Zapf's Zapfino, 1996.

Courtesy of Hermann Zapf, 2000.

19 A Bauhaus typeface construction design by Schmidtt.

20 Goudy Old Style in *The Type Book of Advertising Agencies' Service Company*, printed by Creative Typographers, New York.

FUTURA Figuren-Verzeichnis

ABCDEFGHIJKLMNO
PQRSTUVWXYZÄÖÜ
abcdefghijklmnopqrſst
uvwxyzäöü ch ck ff fi fl ffi ffl ß

mager 1234567890 &.,-:;·!?'(*†«»§

Auf Wunsch liefern wir Mediäval-Ziffern 1234567890

ABCDEFGHIJKLMNO
PQRSTUVWXYZÄÖÜ
abcdefghijklmnopqrſst
uvwxyzäöü ch ck ff fi fl ffi ffl ß

halbfett 1234567890 &.,-:;·!?'(*†«»§

Auf Wunsch liefern wir Mediäval-Ziffern 1234567890

ABCDEFGHIJKLMNO
PQRSTUVWXYZÄÖÜ
abcdefghijklmnopq
rſstuvwxyzäöü ch ck
ff fi fl ffi ffl ß
1234567890

fett &.,-:;·!?'(*†«»§

21

leading figures in typographic design
of the period including most notably
Eric Gill. Having seen the work being
carried out at the Ditchling Press he
asked Gill to draw out an alphabet. This
became the basis for Perpetua, which
appeared issued by Monotype in 1925.
A few years later came Gill Sans—a sans
serif alphabet in the style of Edward
Johnston's lettering for the London
Underground, but rendered with slightly
more delicacy. Although suited to being
set for books and large bodies of text, it
was often used more sparingly. In 1934,
the railway company LNER adopted Gill
Sans for their locomotive nameplates. It is
particularly effective in the shorter names
such as the futuristically designed Mallard
train model.[8]

Continental typographers, though,
all but ignored Gill Sans, preferring
instead the modernism of Futura and
Erbar. Following the close of the Second
World War, and throughout the 1950s
there would be a new generation of
sans serifs, of which one of the most
distinctive was Antique Olive designed
by the Frenchman Roger Excoffon. It is

22

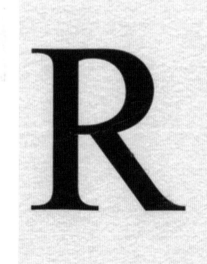

21 Paul Renner, Futura, 1927.

22 Times New Roman Letraset.

23 Eric Gill, Drawings for Gill
Sans, B P R S Overlapping, 1932.

24 A specimen book
demonstrating Roger Excoffon's
Antique Olive.

characterised by its very short ascenders and was obviously thought distinctive enough to be adopted for the Air France logo. He also designed a series of script faces that were extensively used for advertising—Diane, Banco and the quirky Mistral, one of the most successful metal types in terms of replicating the fluidity of handwriting. They are particularly redolent of this period, where the shackles of post-war austerity were being thrown off to embrace consumerist desire for household appliances, rock music and an era of unparalleled modern liberty.

The typographic synthesis of this new-found confidence in the modern world is to be found in the dominant Swiss sans serif designs of the 1950s and 60s. Two faces—Univers and Helvetica—have come to exemplify this movement. Adrian Frutiger designed Univers in 1952, for the typefounders Deberny and Peignot. The company was looking at alternatives to metal type involving photographic machines at the time, imparting this ambition as a brief to Frutiger. Univers, then, was the first face to be designed both for metal and for the

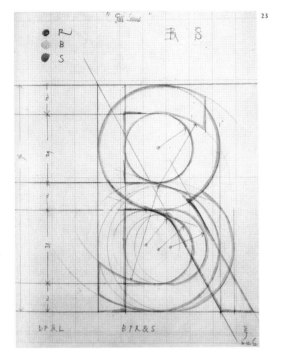

23

25

new photosetting technology. With the spirit of revolution in mind, Frutiger also threw out the old system of describing the weight and slant of a face as 'bold', 'italic' and so on, in favour of a numerical taxonomy in which the first numeral corresponds to the weight of the face and the second denotes the amount by which it is condensed.

The typographer Alan Bartram described Univers as a face "designed to avoid nineteenth century associations of strong personality".[9] Its position as the anonymous face of Swiss design was soon challenged by the arrival of Helvetica. The creator of this new face was Max Miedinger, the resident designer at the Swiss foundry, Haas. Bethold's Akzidenz Grotesk, originally dating from 1898, was then enjoying something of a revival, prompting Hass to ask for an updated version of the successful sans serif, Haas Grotesk. Miedinger's resultant design was originally known as New Haas Grotesk, but was ultimately issued by Stempel (Haas's parent company) under the name Helvetica—a corruption of Helvetia, the Latin for Switzerland. A revised version

called Neue Helvetica appeared in 1983, reinforcing the enduring appeal of this face, which together with Morison's Times New Roman has come to define twentieth century typography.

25

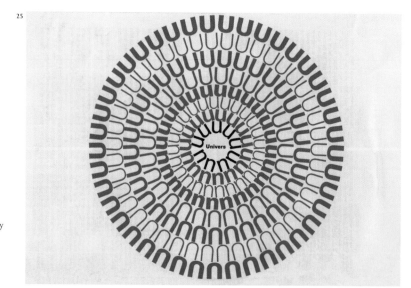

25 1964 Monotype Univers, designed by Adrian Frutiger.

26 Letterpress print using original Haas Grotesk and Helvetica lead type. Printed by Sam Mallett in Zürich during 2007, to celebrate the 50th Anniversary of Helvetica.

Image courtesy of Sam Mallett.

1957 Haas Grotesk
ABCDEFGHIJKL
mnopqrstuvwxyz
äÇçëëîöß&§/!?,....
1234567890*

1960 Helvetica
ABCDEFGHIJKL
mnopqrstuvwxyz
äÇçëëÈîöß&§/!?,....
1234567890*

afPQRS5, afPQRS5.

Letterpress Specimen
Haas Grotesk Halbfett 72pt. — Helvetica Halbfett 72pt.
Printed at Kochstrasse 18, Zürich CH-8004 in 2007

7

PETER BIL'AK

Family Planning or How Type Families Work

IT 3191973 TO DEN HAAG / AMSTERDAM
' ORLEANS' KLEZMER ALL STARS
XT ACTION PACKED SHOW
IENCE PROFESSOR
TERNATIONAL
F BASTILLE DAY
ARDEN TOOLS
OSMONAUT
VINNERS
KNIGHT
ID TEMPERATURES
ORDING ARTIST
OLUTIONARY
BSCURITY

REGULATIONS
UNIVERSAL
CLEMENT
CORNY

CODE BLUE
BANANA
PARKS
THAT
RUB

FRACTION FEV
OPERATIONA
REGULAT
DANGE
PLEAT

STRATEGIC ALLIE
FANTASY DAT
REGIMENT
TEETIME

4   Gargantua, en s
quatre vingtz quara
dra son filz Pantagr
mée Badebec, fille
en Utopie, laquelle
car il estoit si merv
lourd qu'il ne peu
ainsi suffocquer sa

Mais, pour enter
et raison de son r
en baptesme, vous n

The size and complexity of recently developed type families has reached unprecedented levels. Look, for instance, at United, a 2007 release from House Industries. The family includes 105 fonts composed of three styles (sans, serif and italic), available in seven weights and five widths. It takes a couple of minutes just to scroll through all the variants listed in the font menu. For a further example of this trend, Hoefler & Frere-Jones have just released their Chronicle type family, (2002–2007), the range of which extends through widths (from regular to compressed), weights (from extra light to black), and optical size (from text to headline). In terms of sheer size, Chronicle comprises 106 fonts and beats the rival United by a single stylistic variant.

Of course these 'superfamilies' benefit from the inventions of the past centuries; an ongoing series of typographic innovations that broke new ground for generations of designers to come.

History as a Continuous Series of Discoveries

Ever since the earliest use of movable metal type, certain typefaces have included versions cut for specific point sizes. Claude Garamond's type from the 1530s (also known as the caractères de l'Université), included 15 versions ranging in size from six to 36 points. Each size was drawn, cut and cast separately; characters were designed specifically for the optical appearance of the printed text, with optimised letter widths and contrasts between the thick and thin parts of the letterforms. When photographically scaled to the same size, it is easy to see significant differences between the different designed sizes. Earlier typographers would therefore choose various

1, 2, 3 United, type family of 105 fonts designed by Tal Leming, published by House Industries in 2007.

4 Garamond's caractères de l'Université from the 1530s includes 15 optical versions ranging from 6 to 36 points.

*La plus grande folie du monde est penser qu'il
y ayt des astres pour les Roys, Papes et gros
seigneurs, plustost que pour les pauvres et souffre-
teux, comme si nouvelles avoient esté créez depuis
le temps du deluge, ou de Romulus, ou Phara-
mond, à la nouvelle création des Roys. Ce que
Triboulet ny Cailhette ne diroient, qui ont esté
toutesfoys gens de hault sçavoir et grand renom.
Et par adventure en l'arche de Noé ledict Triboulet estoit de la lignée des Roys de Castille,
et Cailhette du sang de Priam ; mais tout cest
erreur ne procede que par deffault de vraye foy
catholicque. Tenant doncques pour certain que les
astres se soucient aussi peu des Roys comme des
gueux, et des riches comme des maraux, je lais-
seray es aultres folz Prognosticqueurs à parler
des Roys et riches, et parleray des gens de bas
estat.*

toute violence e
ne tendre, qu'o
ir et la liberté. Il

sizes, just as we might choose various weights of
a particular typeface today.

In the age of the enlightenment, there was a clear
need to organise and rationalise these differing sizes
of printing types. In 1737, Pierre Simon Fournier
published a table of graded sizes of printing types,
introducing the first-ever standardised system for
producing and using type. Fournier related type size
to the pouce (a French version of the inch), and
subdivided the pouce to 72 'points'. This new system
also became the adopted standard in the English-
speaking world, and in 1742 Fournier published his
Modèles de Caractères de L'imprimerie, in which he further
systematised the body sizes of printing types, and
suggested names for the most commonly used sizes.
The first mention of types being organised into
'families' also originates with Fournier's work.

Subsequent technological discoveries perhaps allowed
typographers to forget the great invention of optically
adjusted type sizes. Type produced by pantographic
reproduction (scaling a master drawing to many different
sizes), and the later technologies of photocomposition
and digital type, allowed working from a single master
design regardless of the size of the final application.
Typefaces made between the 1960s and 1990s almost
entirely ignored optical sizes because photocomposition
allowed unprecedented possibilities of mathematical
scaling. Optically adjusted sizes for type designs made a
minor comeback in the early 1990s, most notably in ITC
Bodoni, featuring size-specific designs similar to those
used by the types originator, Giambattista Bodoni. These
included Bodoni Six, designed for small captions, Bodoni
12 for text setting, and Bodoni 72 for display use.

However, optical size is just one parameter determining
the appearance of a typeface. It seems that typefaces
need to be linked by several other shared parameters in
order to be seen as part of a coherent group or family.
Another such parameter is the weight of the type. For
about 400 years printers and publishers did well with a
single weight of a typeface, using just the type size as the
main means of semantic differentiation. Even complex
documents, such as Samuel Johnson's *A Dictionary of the
English Language*, 1755, use only a single weight of type set
in different sizes, to show the hierarchical differences
between keywords, definitions and descriptions.

The idea of varying the weight of a single typeface
probably happened in the mid-nineteenth century.
Heavy typefaces did exist before that time, but they were
generally seen on their own and not in relationship to
the regular (text) weight. The commercial pressures
of the Industrial Revolution inspired the creation of
different weights of typefaces. The idea was simple:
to differentiate one text from another, or to highlight
a particular part of the text. There were plenty of
opportunities to use different weights of type in a
western market-driven economy in the nineteenth
century. For example, the Besley and Company foundry's
Clarendon type (1842) is widely acknowledged as one
of the first bold typefaces, but soon after its three-year
copyright protection expired it was extensively imitated
and pirated.

Clarendon and its clones, however, although they were
clearly designed to be used next to a roman (regular
weight, or text typeface), had not yet established a
systematic relationship between the various weights (or
widths) of a family-based type design.

5

ROMULUS SANS SERIF

A B C D E F G H I J K L M N O P
Q R S T U V W X Y Z

Irascimini, et nolite peccare: quæ dicitis in
cordibus vestris, in cubilibus vestris compungimini. Sacrificate sacrificium iustitiæ;
et sperate in Domino. Multi dicunt: Quis
ostendit nobis bona? Signatum est super
nos lumen vultus tui Domine: dedisti lætitiam in corde meo. A fructu frumenti, vini,
et olei sui multiplicati sunt. In pace in idip-
sum dormiam, et requiescam; Quoniam tu
Domine singulariter in spe constituisti me.

6

ROMULUS ROMAN

A B C D E F G H I J K L M N
O P Q R S T U V W X Y Z

Irascimini, et nolite peccare: quæ
dicitis in cordibus vestris, in cubilibus vestris compungimini. Sacrificate sacrificium iustitiæ, et sperate
in Domino. Multi dicunt: Quis
ostendit nobis bona? Signatum est
super nos lumen vultus tui Domine: dedisti lætitiam in corde meo. A
fructu frumenti, vini, et olei sui
multiplicati sunt. In pace in idip-
sum dormiam, et requiescam; Quoniam tu Domine singulariter in spe
constituisti me.

Not One But Many

From the early twentieth century it became standard
practice to include several weights of a typeface to
complement the release of new type designs. The best
example of this may be the work of Morris Fuller
Benton, who complemented the many typefaces he
designed for American Type Founders (ATF) with both
condensed and heavy versions. Technology and aesthetics
worked hand-in-hand for Benton, who used his fathers
recently invented pantographic engraving machine
(1886), capable not only of scaling a single typeface
design to a variety of sizes, but could also condense,
extend, and slant the design. These fundamental
geometric operations are the same basic transformations
that most digital typographic systems use today.

In the later part of the twentieth century, the work
of Adrian Frutiger uniquely shifted attention from
the design of a single typeface to the design of a
complete typeface system, seeing the design of a
type family as a continuous space defined by two
axes; width and weight. In 1957 the Deberny &
Peignot Foundry released Frutiger's masterpiece,
Univers, in an unprecedented 21 variants. Frutiger's
systematic approach and innovative naming scheme
eliminated confusion in type specification, and was
perhaps even more interesting that the actual typeface
design itself. He created a novel system of double
digit numerically-referenced styles, where the initial
number five refers to the basic (roman or text) weight,
and the subsequent number refers to the width
(five being standard or normal). Higher numbers
signified increasing weight or width, so while Univers
Regular was Univers 55, Univers Bold was referred

to as Univers 75, and Univers Regular Condensed
was Univers 57. The Univers system anticipated nine
weights and nine widths (also incorporating an
oblique, or sans serif italic variant), although some
combinations of these proved unworkable in practice,
so there is no Univers 79, or Black Condensed.
Linotype further expanded the Univers family in 1997
to 63 versions—for this the numbering system was
extended to three digits to reflect the large number of
variants in the family. Frutiger originally envisioned
this system to be used with other typeface families,
however his systematic numbering convention never
gained wider acceptance with either the foundries or
his contemporary type designers.

The incorporation of two different styles of typeface
into one family was probably first explored in 1932, by
Jan van Krimpen in his Romulus project. Van Krimpen's
intention was to create a large family of types for book
printing; these would comprise a roman, an italic, a
script type, bold and condensed types, at least four
weights of sans serif, Greek text type, and possibly
more. This was deliberately more ambitious than the
type family of Lucian Bernhard, who released his types
(Bernhard Gothic, Kingsley ATF, 1930) two years earlier.

The sans and serif forms of Romulus share the same
construction principles, but the resulting letterforms
of the two styles are quite different. Van Krimpen
quotes the type historian John Dreyfus in his book
On Designing and Devising Type, 1957: "The purpose of the
Romulus family was to provide the basic necessities
for book printing and by means of a series of related
designs to make possible consistent, flexible ... style".
Interestingly, Van Krimpen attempted to separate the

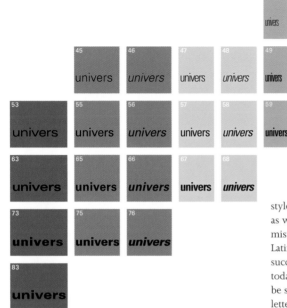

7

style of his roman type and to apply it to Greek script as well. Although Romulus Greek is a fallacy, as it misunderstands the translation of letterforms from Latin to Greek, the method Van Krimpen suggested is successfully used in localising most of non-Latin type today. When type design is understood as a system, it can be seen to consist of many shared parameters amongst letterforms from even such different origins as Greek and Latin.

Parametric Design

A radically new view to understanding type families was paradoxically not proposed by any designer but by a mathematician. In 1977, Donald Knuth conceived a programming language that he called Metafont, which defined the shapes of letterforms with powerful geometric equations. Rather than describing the outlines of glyphs (like the later PostScript and TrueType font formats), Metafont describes an imaginary 'pen' that creates the stroke paths for constructing letterforms. Because of this unique approach, one can change a single input parameter for a typeface, such as optical size, angle of slant, or size of serif, and produce a consistent change throughout the entire font. A single font file can thus be a complex type family with many different versions. Metafont can control over 70 different parameters, which theoretically can define the appearance of any typeface designed with it. Even despite the obvious advantages of the system, and Knuth's close collaboration with the celebrated type designer Herman Zapf, Metafont never became widely used. Later technologies such as Apple's GX and Adobe's MultipleMaster font formats were similarly ill-fated.

5,6 Romulus, designed by Jan van Krimpen in 1932, was one of the first type families which included Sans and Serif versions in range of weights.
The complete package included, a slanted roman, a chancery italic (Cancelleresca Bastarda), and an infamous Greek.

7 The Univers type family, designed by Adrian Frutiger in 1957, consisting of 21 typefaces. Rather than focusing on a single typeface, Frutiger developed an interrelated typeface system.

10

The Hague School

Gerrit Noordzij, who taught writing and type design
at the Royal Academy of Arts in The Hague for 30
years, outlined and developed his theory of writing
in several books. His model presents the serif style as
high-contrast type, as distinct from the sans serif style
as low-contrast type, and arranges them in a coherent
model of typographic possibilities. Therefore, instead
of ideological discussions of 'serif' vs 'sans', Noordzij
focuses on the influence of tools while making marks on
a surface. Noordzij describes three ways of producing
typefaces: translation, expansion and rotation, each
referring to different processes and the resulting stylistic
differences between various groups of typefaces.

Noordzij's pragmatic theories were highly influential
amongst a group of designers that studied at the Academy.
One of them was Lucas de Groot, who designed Thesis,
1994–99, a typeface family with three constructional
variants of the type (sans serif, serif, and mix), comprised
of eight weights and totalling 144 variants. This type
'superfamily' was later further expanded by the addition of
monospaced and condensed versions. De Groot developed
and applied his own interpolation theory to the design of
Thesis, which makes non-linear relationships between the
weights of the type design. Thesis, first released in 1994,
was the largest type family created at the time.

Part of the contemporary program at the Royal Academy
of Arts in The Hague is Type & Media, a postgraduate
program focused on type design education. It is only
natural that such a place should be at the forefront
of typographic experimentation, redefining what we
understand by the terms 'typeface' and 'type family'.

11 Kalliculator is not a
typeface but a tool that makes
typefaces based on predefined
set of parameters. User can
input a line drawing, and the
programme simulates either
broad nib or pointed pen (or
anything in between), controls
the weight and contrast, applies
the same parameters to all the
glyphs in the database, and
finally generates the font file.

10 Published in 1985 in
the book, The stroke Dutch
typographer and teacher Gerrit
Noordzij proposed a theory of
writing regardless of the used
tool. His diagram illustrates the
main argument of his theory of
writing, presenting the concept
of translation, expansion
and rotation.

11

Gustavo Ferreira, a recent graduate of Type & Media produced Elementar, 2003–2006, a comprehensive system of pixel fonts generated by a series of Python scripts. Elementar draws its inspiration from Metafont and Univers rather than existing bitmap fonts. It is a parametric system responding to selected input criteria; a basic design for a simplified pixel typeface serves as a model, on which other parameters are applied. Because of the limitations of rendering glyphs on screen in small sizes, glyphs are expressed in terms of exact fractions or multiples of the model design.

Such large typeface systems can become quite impractical to use, as the list of stylistic variations in the font menu gets larger and larger. In the case of Elementar, it is over 500 individual bitmap fonts, so an alternative solution has to be offered to the user to select the correct variant. Rather than presenting the full list of typeface possibilities this way, Elementar comes with its own online interface, whereby the user can choose the parameters, and get the right stylistic variant(s).

Kalliculator was a Type & Media graduation project of Frederik Berlaen, 2006. Instead of drawing a typeface, Berlaen made a tool that makes typefaces based on a predefined set of parameters. Similarly to Knuth's tools from the 1970s, Kalliculator simulates pens and their relationships to a drawn stroke. Berlaen's project uses Noordzij's theories as a base and the Kalliculator electronic pen ranges between pointed and broad nib styles. Users can input a line drawing, and the programme calculates the contrast around the skeleton, mixing the mathematical middle of a stroke and a path made by an imaginary pen. The idea is that the trajectory of the hand is separate from the style of the pen, so users can experiment by applying various parameters to their sketched strokes. A single drawing of an 'a', can result in hundreds of versions, with each one being directly linked to others via its source drawing. In this way, Berlaen's application challenges traditional views of type families, as a typeface generated from the same skeleton is related to its family variants in a uniform manner.

Conclusion

So what exactly defines a type family? An analogy with a real physical family is not often helpful because unlike the biological world, different generations of typefaces are usually not considered to be part of the same family.

Similarly, at the level of individual glyphs, each style of the type family must be recognisably different in order to remain functional. Yet each style must adhere to common principles governing the consistency of the type family. It is clear that individual members of the family need to share one or more attributes, and typographic history offers many examples of this; optical size, weight, width, stylistic differences (sans, serif and semi-serif), construction differences (formal and informal), are the most common parameters linking members of type families. We can also find less common relationships such as varying serif types, changing proportions of x height, ascenders and descenders, or contextually appropriate possibilities of different versions.

Work by designers like Berlaen and Ferreira build on centuries of typographic innovation and help to explore new territory for type design. They participate in a cumulative, ongoing and inspirational history of type development, requiring that we continue creating this work in progress.

8 THE DIGITAL AGE

THE DIGITAL AGE

The second half of the twentieth century saw massive shifts in technology that would ultimately lead to the end of metal type. With the close of the Second World War, the austerity of prolonged privation gave way to a renewed sense of cultural experimentation, making itself felt in all areas of life, from art to architecture to industry and technology. Offset lithography combined with photosetting opened up the realm of possibility for typographic innovation. and later, the advent of rub-down lettering systems such as Letraset, and the invention of the personal computer, meant that typeface design was becoming an increasingly democratic discipline, foregrounding a whole host of divergent principles and practices.

The Triumph of Lithography

Although lithography had been developed as a commercial printing process in the early nineteenth century, it was only when it was combined with another nineteenth century invention—photography—that it would come to triumph over type and relief printing. Indeed, the development

1

FOUR MAJOR PRINTING METHODS COMMONLY USED ARE

A OFFSET LITHOGRAPHY
B LETTERPRESS
C GRAVURE
D SCREENPRINTING

A

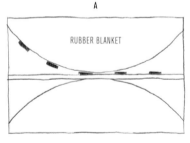

B

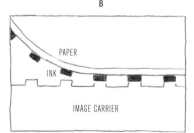

C

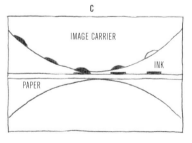

D

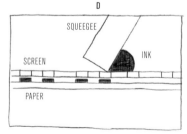

1 The four major printing methods.
Illustration by Emma Gibson.
Image courtesy of the artist.

2 Ira Rubel with the offset press he designed for indirect lithography, circa 1905.

of offset lithography at the beginning of the twentieth century marked the start of the end for metal type. Originally employed in the manufacture of printed decorations on tin novelties, it would take the innovation of another American, Ira Rubel, to adapt the process for printing on paper, setting up the first such machine in his Eastern Lithographic Company in New York during 1905. Lithography works through a process whereby images are transferred onto a composition roller from which they can be lithographically printed or offset on paper. Text reproduced by the offset lithographic process is first set into pages from which a reading proof can be pulled. Following correction, an impression of the type is photographed and the resulting negative set with other text, image or illustration. The imposed negatives are then photographically exposed onto a sensitised grained metal plate, which is itself developed and placed on the cylinder of the offset printing press. Rubel's press worked on the rotary principle, leading to welcome gains in speed and efficiency, particularly when combined with photocomposition later on in the twentieth century.

The reproduction of woodcut or engraved blocks originally required the use of a photo-litho paper onto which the image from the block could be printed in a special transfer ink, with the impression thereafter transferred from the paper to the lithographic plate. From the 1920s onward, several improvements were made to Rubel's original system, most notably with the Chromorecta process invented by H Schupp of Dresden in 1927, which still forms the basis of most modern forms of offset reproduction. In Schupp's process, the basic principle is to produce a screen transparency with a number of small dots separated by white spaces. The emulsion used is of a fine granular composition, and the light and dark parts of the plate are caused by the density (or otherwise) of this grain.[1] In later developments, bi-metallic plates were used for offset editions (rather than the usual all-zinc aluminium plates) with the image being applied to the surface in ink-attracting metal on a baseplate that is less adherent to ink. The principles of offset lithography were greatly enhanced when later combined with the advent of photocomposition. The advent of

2

Monotype's Monophoto and Linotype's Linofilm cemented this process at the heart of advanced printing methods. The photocomposition machines worked in a similar way to the Monotype or Linotype machines, but rather than casting type from a matrix case, light was passed through a negative of each character onto a film, which was then developed for proofing. One of the first books to be printed in Britain without recourse to metal type was Eric Linklater's *Private Angelo*, privately printed for Allen Lane at Penguin Books in 1957. The innovation of photocomposition really opened up typography to the possibility of unfettered creative experimentation. Metal and wooden type were constrained by the body of each character—the physical base upon which the raised letterform sits—limiting the tightness with which letters can be spaced. With photosetting, the physical base was removed, and letters could be packed as tightly as the typographer desired, even with negative spacing. The widespread use of offset lithography coupled with photocomposition ultimately engendered the end of metal type. In 1987, the

Cambridge University Press printed its last book using the old technology, melting down the remaining type to make commemorative medallions. Fittingly, this ended an era of metal type that had begun with the first University press in Cambridge some four hundred years earlier.

Letraset

The matrix cases used by photosetting machines consisted of tiny photographic negatives of each character on a plastic film, the same principle that inspired another typographic innovation, Letraset, a system of instant transfer or 'rub down' lettering. Initially designed in 1956 by Charles Davies, Letraset was not commercially announced until 1960, when the ink manufacturer Jim Reed had finally perfected a technique for printing letters in reverse onto plastic sheets and then adding a low-tacking adhesive. This was the first ever commercially-produced 'dry transfer' lettering, the product with which Letraset has become synonymous. Each sheet contained all the letters and punctuation of a particular typeface,

3

4

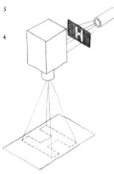

3 Projection photocompostion.

4 This illustration shows the basic principle of projection photocomposition. Light is projected through a transparent image and onto light-sensitive photopaper or film.
Illustration by Emma Gibson,
Image courtesy of the artist.

5 Monotype photosetter.
Illustration by Emma Gibson,
Image courtesy of the artist.

6 Assembling images with photosensitive type film.

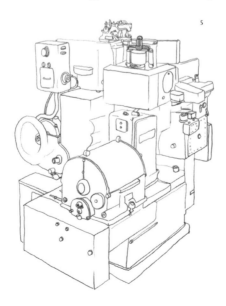

5

6

characters were provided in varying numbers and could be applied directly to camera-ready artwork by rubbing the face of the film.

The crucial element of this innovation was that it could be done by anyone, so for the first time professional-looking design could be achieved outside the typographic studio or print-works. The democratisation of typography had now begun in earnest, bolstered by the advent of desktop publishing some 25 years later.

The Letraset system was phenomenally popular, and grew to include countless typefaces and a large range of symbols and illustrations, similar in spirit to the stock illustrative blocks seen in nineteenth and early twentieth century typefounders catalogues. By 1981, the Letraset catalogue ran to some 327 pages with a 20 page appendix and—alongside a number of new designs—included many faithfully reproduced historic typefaces.

By the late twentieth century, the influence of postmodernism was making itself felt in typographic design. Where typographic modernism was characterised by Bauhaus, De Stijl and Constructivism, and best represented by the work of designers like Paul Rand, Massimo Vignelli and Erik Spiekermann, there was a new school of designers set to take typographic design to new experimental heights. The principle of form following function alive in modernism was being challenged by a newfound combination of high and low culture, where elements of the vernacular, the pastiche and the anti-aesthetic were informing typographic design.[2] The postmodern context encouraged experimentation, diversity and complexity, giving designers the critical distance to judge the results of the modernist typographic age. Designers such as Jan Tschichold and William Addison Dwiggins paved the way for younger designers such as those coming out of the Cranbrook Academy of Art in the late 1980s and 90s.

This interest in popular culture was not totally new to typography, indeed graphic designers and typographers have always had a particularly close relationship with mass literature and other cultural consumables.

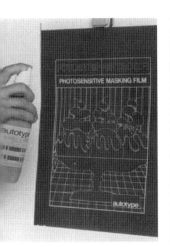 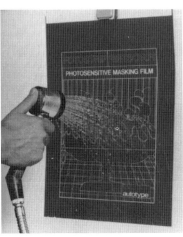 

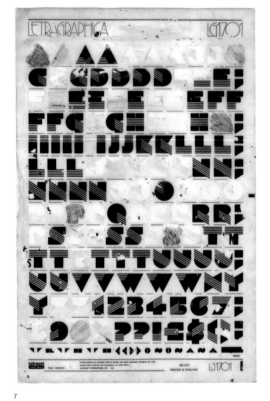

7

8

7–10 Letraset Instant Lettering,
Letraset International Ltd, 1947

Courtesy of Tony Gibson

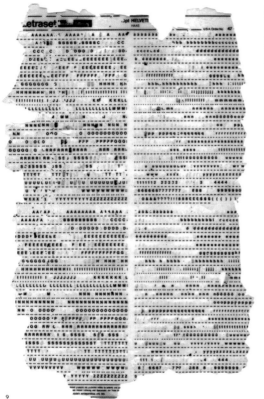

9

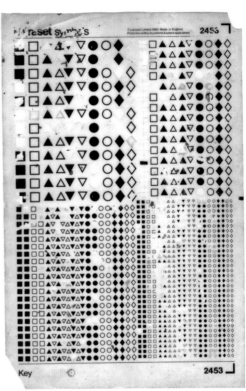

10

Album covers, for example, have long been fertile ground for typographic innovation. It was during the late 1930s that the full potential of this format was realised, when the then artistic director at Columbia Records—Alex Steinweiss—hit upon the idea of using something of the style found in poster and advertising design to promote his roster of recording artists. Jazz albums were particularly suited to graphic innovation, which in style and setting was evocative of free-style music performance, for example, display types rising in waves from the musician's instrument in ever-increasing sizes. Album covers continue to be an important experimentation ground for typographers and graphic designers, where the demands of readability are often subordinate to the creative potential of visual impact and aesthetic composition.

The multi-disciplinary approach to typographic design was at the root of some of the best work to come out of the mid-twentieth century. Robert Brownjohn emerges as one of the most influential graphic designers of the 1950s and 60s, gaining a reputation for pushing both social and aesthetic boundaries.

11

12

11 Cover of the 1981 Letraset catalogue, courtesy of the St Bride Library.
Photography by Matthew Pull.

12, 13 Interior pages of the 1981 Letraset catalogue.
Image courtesy of the St Bride Library.
Photography by Matthew Pull.

14 Jan Tschichold's poster for *Die Frau Ohne Namen*, 1927.

15 Cover design for Here Now and Sounding Good by the Dick Morrissey Quartet, Mercury Records.

16 Cover design for *Listen Up!* by the Gossip.
Designed by David Lane.

13

Brownjohn trained under László Moholy-Nagy at the Institute of Design in Chicago during the 1940s, applying the solid principles of clean design to startling effect in his later work. Known for a lavish lifestyle in the jazz culture of the 1950s and 60s, Brownjohn is remembered for his simple graphic concepts, exemplified in his opening sequences for James Bond's *Goldfinger* and *From Russia with Love*. Another graphic designer that made his influence felt in the film industry was Saul Bass, often collaborating with Alfred Hitchcock, Otto Preminger and Martin Scorsese. Bass' design for Hitchcock's 1958 *Vertigo* is typical of the daring style for which the designer became so well-known, featuring a bold use of display face against a strikingly simple composition. Bass went on to work with some of the twentieth century's most important filmmakers, becoming something of a legend in design for new media and paving the way for a new breed of inter-disciplinary practitioners.

The Digital Revolution

The renewed sense of creative potential coursing through the late twentieth century was bolstered by the invention

of the personal computer and the widespread accessibility of the tools for desktop publishing. Though the first computer—the Manchester Mark 1—was invented in 1949, it was not until the 1970s that personal computers began to filter into common usage with the PDP-11 family of mini-computers produced by the Digital Equipment Corporation. These, and other similar innovations, were to usher in the great age of digital typesetting and design, rendering the rub-down letter obsolete. Personal computers such as the Apple Macintosh used specialist software to generate letters and to place them on a page together with illustrations and other symbols. The interface used a keyboard similar to the typewriter employed throughout the nineteenth and early twentieth centuries. Type design was made increasingly accessible through various software and hardware innovations, and there seemed to be no limit to the possibilities for experimentation open to typographers across all levels of experience. Coupled with the advent of the World Wide Web in the early 1990s, the world of typography

and graphic design became increasingly accessible to an ever-wider design user. However, computerised design presented its own particular limitations, and it took a variety of experimentations and innovations to overcome the growing pains of the digital age.

Digital fonts store the image of each character in one of two ways, either the letterforms are stored as bitmap files, in a bitmap font, or by a mathematical description of lines and curves in an outline or vector font. In the case of the outline font, a 'rasterising' process is undertaken by the application software, operating system or printer, which renders the character outlines, interpreting the vector instructions to allocate black and white pixels. There were, however, drawbacks to the digital reproductions of conventional typefaces. When originally cut, faces such as Garamond or Baskerville were designed to be printed from metal type, inked and impressed into dampened paper. This would result in a slight spread of ink on paper, thus thickening the letter image. With laser, ink jet or offset lithographic printing, the image sits on the

17 Saul Bass' poster for Alred Hitchcock's *Vertigo*, 1958.

18 The first computer was the Manchester Mark I, unveiled in June 1949.

19 Apple Macintosh Computer, model M001, 1984.

surface of the paper with no consequent ink spread. Thus, in comparison to their 'historic' appearance, some typefaces can appear somewhat thin and unstructured. Much of this issue has been rectified in the new generation of PostScript typefaces, which have been optically re-aligned to give the correct weight and feel. Generally, PostScript types are rendered somewhat visually larger than in their traditional metal versions, with an increased x height in relation to the ascender height, and with lower case letters more rounded and open.

There was another issue with digital type design, again particularly prevalent in the early days of digitalisation. With comparatively low memory available on the systems in use at the beginning of the digital age, individual letters could be digitised only in a relative small number of pixels. When printed, the curves and slants of classic faces no longer appeared smooth or rounded, but could be seen as disintegrating into square and rectangular pixelated building blocks. Wim Crouwel responded to this problem with the design of his New Alphabet in the 1960s, which was composed of vertical and horizontal lines. It has a curiously futuristic look about it, with a number of odd features, most notably the absence of the letters m and w, replaced with an underscored n and v.

PostScript represented a considerable move forward in digital type design. The seeds for this program were first sown in 1976, when John Warnock was working at Evans and Sutherland, a famous computer graphics company. At the time, Warnock was developing an interpreter for a large three-dimensional graphics database of the New York Harbour, inventing the Design System language to process the graphics for the project. Meanwhile, researchers at Xerox PARC had developed the first laser printer, and had recognised the need for a standard means of defining page images. Between 1975 and 1976, a team led by Bob Sproull developed the Press format, which was eventually used in the Xerox Star system to drive laser printers. But Press, a data format rather than a software language, lacked flexibility, and PARC mounted the InterPress in an effort to create an alternative, though the endeavour wasn't altogether successful.

18

19

In 1978, Evans and Sutherland asked Warnock to move from the San Francisco Bay Area to their main headquarters in Utah, but he wasn't interested in relocating, choosing to work with Martin Newell at Xeros PARC instead. Together the two rewrote Design System to create JaM (for John and Martin), which was used for VLSI design and the investigation of type and graphics printing. This work later evolved to expand into the InterPress language devised some years before. Warnock parted company with Xerox and teamed up with Chuck Geschke to found Adobe Systems in December 1982. This new, and soon to be hugely successful, company began by creating a simpler language, similar to InterPress, called PostScript, which was commercially released in 1984. At about the same time Adobe was visited by Steve Jobs, who urged the team to adapt PostScript for use as the language driving laser printers.

In March 1985, the Apple LaserWriter was the first printer to ship with PostScript, sparking the desktop publishing (DTP) revolution that grew out of the 1980s. The combination

of technical merit and widespread availability made PostScript one of the most important innovations driving the digital age. The system benefited from on-the-fly rasterisation capabilities, which had every character and symbol specified in terms of straight lines and cubic Bezier curves, previously found only in CAD applications, which allows for arbitrary scaling, rotating and other transformations. When the PostScript program is deployed, the interpreter converts these instructions into the dots needed to form the output.

Once the de facto standard for electronic distribution of final documents meant for publication, PostScript is steadily being supplanted by one of its own descendants, the Portable Document Format, or PDF. By 2001 there were fewer printer models which came with support for PostScript, largely due to the growing competition from much cheaper non-PostScript ink jet printers, and new software-based methods to render PostScript images on the computer, making them suitable for any printer. The use of a PostScript laser printer still

20

20 Top: Image demonstrating a bitmap version of Garamond in Adobe Photoshop.
Bottom: Image demonstrating a vector version of Garamond in Adobe Illustrator.
Image courtesy of Emma Gibson.

21 Packaging design for the Trojan Phaser Gun, demonstrating the use of the Sinola typeface, circa 1980s.
Image courtesy of Tony Gibson.

22 The Xerox 9700 printer, 1977.
Image courtesy of Xerox.

23 Scanmaster D4000 drum scanner, used in prepress production.

21

can, however, significantly reduce the digital workload involved in printing documents, transferring the work of rendering PostScript images from the computer to the printer.

The way PostScript handles fonts is almost as complex as the functioning of the system itself. The rich font system used the PS graphics primitives to draw glyphs as line art, which could then be rendered at any resolution. Though this sounds like a reasonably straightforward concept, there were a number of typographic issues that had to be considered. One is that fonts do not actually scale linearly at small sizes; features of the glyphs will become proportionally too large or small as they start to degrade. PostScript avoided this problem with the inclusion of hints that could be saved along with the font outlines. Basically, there is additional information in horizontal or vertical bands that help identify the features in each letter that are important for the rasteriser to maintain. The result was significantly better-looking fonts, even at low resolution.

At the time, the technology for including these 'hints' in digital font files was carefully guarded, and the hinted fonts were compressed and encrypted into what Adobe called a Type 1 Font (also known as PostScript Type 1 Font, PS1, T1 or Adobe Type 1). Type 1 was effectively a simplification of the PostScript system to store outline information only, as opposed to being a complete language (PDF is similar in this regard). Adobe would then sell licenses for the Type 1 technology to those wanting to add hints to their own fonts. Those who did not license the technology were left with the Type 3 Font (also known as, PostScript Type 3 Font, PS3 or T3). Type 3 fonts allowed for all the sophistication of the PostScript language, but without the standardised approach to hinting. Type 2 was designed to be used with the Compact Font Format (CFF), and were implemented for a compact representation of the glyph description procedures to reduce the overall font file size. It was this CFF/Type2 format that later became the basis for Type 1 OpenType fonts.

22

23

The PostScript language has had two major upgrades. The first version, known as PostScript Level 1, was introduced in 1984. PostScript Level 2 was introduced in 1991, and included several improvements: improved speed and reliability, support for in-RIP separations, image decompression (for example, JPEG images could be rendered by a PostScript program), support for composite fonts, and the form mechanism for caching reusable content. PostScript 3 (Adobe dropped the 'level' terminology in favour of simple versioning) came at the end of 1997, and along with many new dictionary-based versions of older operators, introduced better color handling, and new filters (which allow in-program compression/decompression, program chunking, and advanced error-handling). PostScript 3 was significant in terms of replacing the existing proprietary colour electronic prepress systems, then widely used for magazine production, through the introduction of smooth shading operations with up to 4,096 shades of grey (rather than the 256 available in PostScript 2), as well as DeviceN, a color space that allowed the addition of a greater variety of ink colours (called spot colours) into composite colour pages.

CID-keyed font format was also designed, to solve the problems in the OCF/Type 0 fonts, for addressing the complex Asian-language encoding and very large character set issues. CID-keyed font format can be used with the Type 1 font format for standard CID-keyed fonts, or Type 2 for CID-keyed OpenType fonts.

Adobe's rates were widely considered to be prohibitively high, leading Apple to design their own system around 1991, which they named TrueType. Immediately following the announcement of TrueType, Adobe published the specification for the Type 1 font format. Retail tools such as Altsys Fontographer (acquired by Macromedia in January 1995, owned by FontLab since May 2005) added the ability to create Type 1 fonts. Since then, many free Type 1 fonts have been released; for instance, the fonts used with the TeX typesetting system are available in this format.

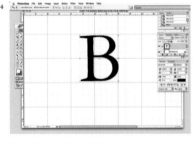

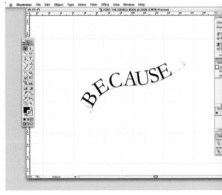

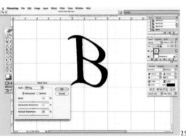

24 Demonstration of font (Garamond) in software program Adobe Photoshop.

25 Demonstration of font manipulation (Garamond) in software program Adobe Photoshop using Warp Text.

26 Demonstration of font manipulation (Garamond) in software program Adobe Illustrator using the Type on a Path tool.

Throughout the early 1990s, there were several other systems for storing outline-based fonts, developed by Bitstream and Metafont for instance, but none included a general-purpose printing solution and they were not widely used as a result. In the late 1990s, Adobe joined Microsoft in developing OpenType, essentially a functional superset of the Type 1 and TrueType formats. When printed to a PostScript output device, the unnecessary parts of the OpenType font are omitted, and what is sent to the device by the driver is the same as it would be for a TrueType or Type 1 font, depending on which kind of outlines were present in the OpenType font. As with TrueType fonts, OpenType fonts allow the handling of large glyph sets using Unicode encoding. Such encoding allows broad international support for the entire file set, including typographic glyph variants. Additionally, OpenType fonts may contain digital signatures, allowing operating systems and browsers to identify the source and integrity of font files, including embedded font files obtained in online documents. Also, font developers can encode embedding

restrictions in OpenType fonts, and these restrictions cannot be altered in a font signed by the developer.

Today, The digital creation of type is dominated by two software programs, the foremost being Fontographer (or FOG), originally developed by Altsys for Applie Macintosh, but available for both Mac and PC platforms. Released in the fall of 1986 (before Adobe Illustrator) it was the first commercially available Bézier curve-editing software designed for a personal computer. In January 1995, Altsys was acquired by Macromedia and a new version of Fontographer was included in the Macromedia Graphics Suite, helping to raise the profile of the software.

The other major software now associated with digital type design is Adobe Illustrator, perhaps the first software to make the work of typography synonymous with that of graphic design. Adobe Illustrator was first developed for Apple Macintosh in 1986 (shipping in January 1987) as a commercialisation of Adobe's in-house font development software and PostScript file format.

27

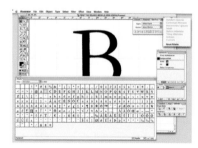

27 Demonstration of font manipulation (Garamond) in software program Adobe Illustrator, layering regular, bold and italic versions with stroke only.

28 Demonstration of font manipulation (Garamond) in software program Adobe Illustrator, layering regular, bold and italic versions with fill only at varying transparencies. Here the outlines have been selected.

29 Demonstration of font options (Garamond) using the Glyphs palette in software program Adobe Illustrator.

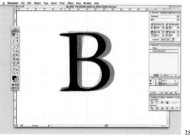

29

28

Adobe Illustrator is the companion product of Adobe Photoshop, a product geared toward digital photo manipulation and photorealistic styles of computer illustration, where Illustrator is more suited to typesetting and the logo graphic areas of design.

The Adobe developers built upon the first version of Illustrator, with Illustrator CS, the first version to include three-dimensional capabilities, allowing users to extrude or revolve shapes to create simple forms or objects. Illustrator CS2 included new features such as Live Trace, Live Paint, a control palette and custom workspaces. Live Trace gave designers the ability to convert bitmap imagery into vector art, and improves upon previous tracing capabilities, where Live Paint allows users more flexibility in applying colour to objects, particularly those that overlap. From these and other technological developments sprang up a new working method and a cast of new practitioners to map the shifting terrain of modern type design.

Matthew Carter is noteworthy, not only for his elegant designs, but also because

he was one of the last type designers to be classically trained in elements of traditional type design. Born in 1937, Carter was taught the art of punch cutting by Jan van Krimpen's assistant at the Joh Enschede type foundry. Carter went onto design some of the most famous typefaces of the past 50 years, including Georgia and Verdana, both of which were created primarily for viewing on a computer monitor.

Sumner Stone bears some similarity to Matthew Carter in that his education also included something of the classical. Stone studied calligraphy with Lloyd Reynolds at Reed College in Portland, Oregon, and has gone on to work in the fields of typography, graphic design and education. He has taught lettering and typography at several institutions, lecturing and writing widely on various elements of type design. From 1984 to 1989, Stone was director of typography for Adobe Systems in Mountain View, California, where he innovated and implemented Adobe's typographic program, including the Adobe Originals. In 1990, he founded the Stone Type Foundry in Guinda, California, which

30 Left to right Lower case Garamond b in Adobe Illustrator.; Lower case Garamond b outlines created with Adobe Illustrator; Lower case Garamond b outlines selected, Adobe Illustrator; Lower case Garamond b demonstrating the 3D effect, Extrude and Bevel functions in Adobe Illustrator.

Images courtesy of Emma Gibson.

31, 32 Neville Brody cover designs for *The Face*

30

designs and produces new typefaces and creates custom designs for a diverse range of clients. Stone has designed various influential faces, including ITC Stone, Stone Print, Silica, Arepo, Cycles and Basalt typeface families, and was the art director of the prize-winning ITC Bodoni.

During the 1980s, several advancements in letterform served to cement a new generation of type designers. Neville Brody has become one of the key graphic designers of the last two decades. Rising to notoriety with his revolutionary work as art director of *The Face*, Brody is now famous for exploring new layout techniques and pushing the boundaries of typographic design, producing such notable fonts as Blur and Harlem.

In 1982, Robin Nicholas and Patricia Saunders designed the Arial typeface for Monotype Typography. Arial was originally known as Sonoran Sans Serif [1], acquiring its current name when Microsoft decided to include it within its Windows package. Though nearly identical to Linotype Helvetica in both proportion and weight, the design of Arial is in fact

a variation of Monotype Grotesque, and was designed specifically for IBM's laser xerographic printer. Subtle variations were made to both the letterforms and the spacing between characters, in order to make it a more readable face across a variety of resolutions.

Emigre magazine also came onto the scene in the early 1980s, which showcased Zuzana Licko's ground-breaking designs cut on the first generation of Macintosh computers. Emperor, Oakland, and Emigre were designed to accommodate low-resolution printer output. Licko founded Emigre Fonts with her partner and husband Rudy VanderLans in order to distribute their own typefaces, and those of other young practitioners. Zuzana Licko designed a series of coarse bitmap fonts, created on the newly introduced Macintosh computer with crude public domain software.

In 1989, Erik Spiekermann—together with his wife Joan—started FontShop, the first mail-order distributor for digital fonts. On the back of the success of FontShop,

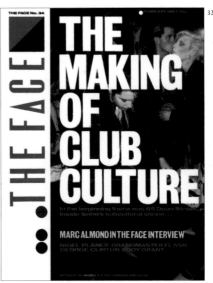

33

34

35

36

the Spiekermanns launched FontShop International, complete with its own range of FontFont typefaces. Spiekermann has been responsible for the design of many influential faces, none the least of which being Meta, a humanist sans serif that is at once basic, sturdy and unique, widely recognisable as the corporate typeface for the Deutsche Bundespost.

Stefan Sagmeister is another member of graphic design's new order. Known for maintaining a small studio (just himself, another designer and an intern), Sagmeister's has created album cover designs for Lou Reed, David Byrne and Talking Heads, for which he won a Grammy Award in 1995. Sagmeister is widely known for maintaining a hand-made aesthetic, and expressing a variety of visual methods that he does not try to discipline into any one characteristic style.

Jonathan Barnbrook is known for creating typographical work with a conscience, using his success as a graphic designer to platform issues of social or political importance. Epitomising the new breed of graphic designer cum fine artist,

37

38

33–38 *Having Guts Always Works
Out For Me*, art direction by
Stefan Sagmeister.

Images courtesy of the artist.

39

Barnbrook has recently exhibited at London's Design Museum, with work responding to the first and second Iraqi conflicts, entitled *Friendly Fire*. Apart from Barnbrook's fine art accomplishments, he has designed a number of serviceable typefaces such as Priori, which debuted on the cover of David Bowie's *Heathen* album.

Peter Bil'ak is another designer who is pushing the boundaries of type design to remarkable effect, Bil'ak's 2001 Fedra Sans design was devised to work equally well on paper and digital formats, and this multi-lingual sans serif works exceptionally well in small point sizes, while remaining elegant and distinctive in larger ones. Bil'ak continues to lead the pack when it comes to intelligent type design, heading up the now-famous Typotheque foundry and co-founding *Dot Dot Dot* design magazine. The new generation of software program has cleaved open the realm of possibility for today's typographer, encouraging a multi-disciplinary approach to type design, one that expresses as many influences as it does potential applications.

40

Fedra Sans
by Peter Bil'ak

A new sans serif, originally designed as a corporate font for one of those huge companies; now completed, updated, and ready to use in all formats. Available in five weights, with three different numeral systems, real italics, small capitals, and expert sets full of ligatures, fractions, arrows, symbols and other useful little things.

Aa Aa

Fedra Sans Light
Fedra Sans *Book*
Fedra Sans **Normal**
Fedra Sans *Medium*
Fedra Sans Bold

41

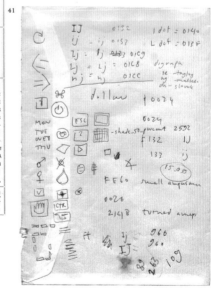

39 Album design for David Bowie's *Heathen* album, 2002, designed by Jonathan Barnbrook, and debuting his Priori typeface.

40 Fedra Sans by Peter Bil'ak. Published in *Dot Dot Dot* Issue no 3, 2001.

41 Process drawings for Fedra Sans by Peter Bil'ak.

Image courtesy of the artist.

8

EXPERIMENTAL JETSET

A Conversation with Danny, Marieke and Erwin

1 Badges from *We Are the World*, group exhibition, Bennale di Venezia, 2003.

2 Poster from *We Are the World* 2, group exhibition, Rotterdam Edition: Museum van Beuningen, 2004.

EXPERIMENTAL JETSET
A Conversation with Danny, Marieke and Erwin

What makes a good font? What makes a bad font?

We know this is an absolute cliche, but there's still truth in it: there is no such thing as a good or bad typeface, only good or bad ways to use that typeface. There are designers out there that can take a really unpopular typeface, and turn it into something truly interesting. An example that springs to mind is the cover of the first issue of art magazine *Tourette's*, designed in 2003 by Goodwill (Will Holder), featuring hand-drawn renderings of the typeface Comic Sans.
See: http://www.dextersinister.org/index.html?id=17

Are fonts a matter of fashion, or progression?

If, by the word 'fashion', you mean a succession of trends without any development, then we would certainly say that typefaces are a matter of progression. Everything evolves. It might not be a clearly visible linear progression, but we think there's certainly a dialectical progression, where opposing, already existing movements are synthesised into new ones. Progress can only exist in continuous dialogue with the past. We see even type revivals as clear signs of progress, because they hint at new interpretations, and a growing awareness, of existing typefaces. However, we have to say that it's a bit unfair to use the word 'fashion' as a sort of opposite of 'progression', because fashion, in the sense of clothing design, is actually quite an astonishing platform of technological, aesthetical and conceptual progress.

How do you go about choosing a typeface for a new project?

Sometimes there are clear conceptual reasons to choose a certain typeface. For example, in the graphic identity and sign system we designed in 2004 for Stedelijk Museum CS (SMCS), we used Univers explicitly to refer to the old graphic identity of Stedelijk Museum, and thus to the history of the institute. Sometimes there are no clear conceptual reasons to choose a certain typeface. In that case, we use the typefaces we were brought up with, typefaces that feel like our mother tongue, our natural language. Typefaces such as Helvetica.

What is the perfect font, if there is such a thing?

There is no such thing as a perfect typeface. There might be a perfect typeface for a specific assignment, but even that is doubtful. It's all completely dependent on context.

Is there a type revival you would like to see developed?

3 Modernism Backdrop, exhibited at The Free Library, 2004. Originally designed in 1998 as part of the installation *Black Metal Machine.*

Awkward grotesk type (grotesk as in sans serif). Letters that look overtly conscious of themselves, a bit 'off', a bit uncomfortable, too geometric for their own good. Type revivals such as Ian Brown's Number Nine:
http://www.ianswork.net/number9/number901.html
http://www.ianswork.net/number9/number9info.html

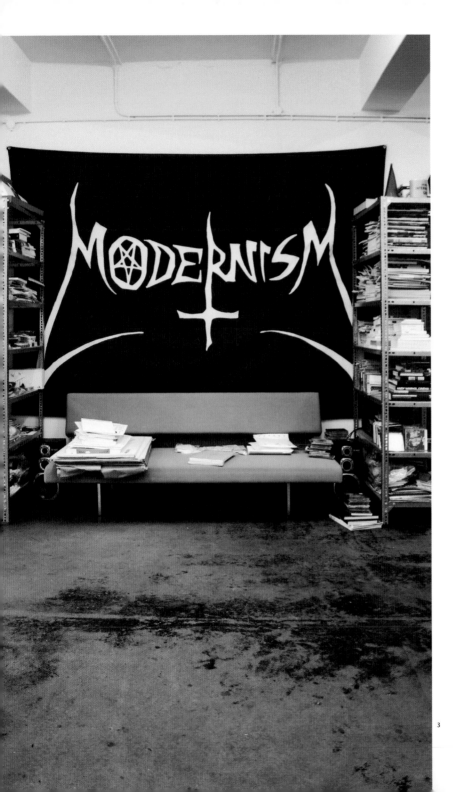

3

How many different fonts should one use on a page?

There's no general rule. Whatever the concept asks for. As for our own, our challenge has always been to solve everything with as little different typefaces and weights as possible, but that's a purely personal principle. There are many examples of excellent pieces featuring several different typefaces used together; look for instance at Jamie Reid's iconic sleeve design for *Nevermind the Bollocks*.

How would you approach the design of a typeface based on typography and graphic design of the recent past?

Well, first of all, we want to make clear that we aren't type designers; we are answering these questions as graphic designers, as users of type, not as producers of type. But if we were type designers (and that's a big 'if'), we would probably be really influenced by Neville Brody's early 1990s Fuse label/foundry/zine, because it really redefined type. It showed that a digital typeface, a 'font', could be a medium in its own right; that basically every sort of information that you can put under the keys of your computer keyboard can be seen as a typeface of some sort. That's a marvellous concept. You can see this influence in foundries such as Richard Rhys' Pattern Foundry: http://www.patternfoundry.com/mapper.html

Is typography culturally-specific? Can you determine the country of origin of a particular typeface just by looking at it?

Typography is absolutely culturally-specific, although, to us, the way a certain typeface is used is often more culturally-specific than the design of the typeface itself typeface itself. For example, the way Crouwel uses Helvetica is typically Dutch, while the way Vignelli uses Helvetica is Italian, with a New York edge. The typeface itself is Swiss. That's the beauty of it. Typefaces such as Helvetica can be platforms of national identity and international diversity at the same time.

In your opinion, what is the most critical aspect of type design today?

We have no idea. We are graphic designers, not type designers. We can only assume that what keeps type designers occupied right now are matters of copyright, piracy, open source, software licenses... stuff like that. In many ways, they are facing the same difficulties (or challenges) as the music industry. Or at least, that's what we assume.

What is the future of type?

We always dislike questions like this (sorry!). 'The Future of Print', 'The Future of Books', 'The Future of Type', etc. etc. As if there is some unchangeable *zeitgeist* that everybody just has to adjust to. In our view, the good thing about being a designer is this heightened awareness of the fact that everything around us is constructed by humans, and that goes especially for the future. Everybody has their own future to shape. If three people decide that they want to use some obscure version of blackletter for the rest of their lives, then this is just as much the future as millions of people using Helvetica. The future is in our own hands.

4 Stedelijk Museum CS (SMCS), Part of a series of Stairwell installation, 2004

5 Catalogue for Kelly 1:1: An Interpretation of Ellsworth Kelly's Blue, Green, Yellow, Orange, Red, 1966. A Cover Version by Experimental Jet Set.

6 Program poster for Stedelijk Museum CS, 2004

7 Poster for Pillowman, De Theater Compagnie, 2004

9
SAM WINSTON
Visual Essay

Introduction

When it comes to typography, language always comes first. This might seem like a fairly obvious statement to make, but to find this harmony between content and form is incredibly hard.

It was the first problem I came across when I started making books, and it stemmed from being both author and designer. There is a need to achieve legibility but also have a strong visual aesthetic. I don't think they are exclusive but at times they can be at odds.

A dictionary entry; William Winston, 2002. Second edition of 197.
Best Purist Prize. www.dictionaryposters.com

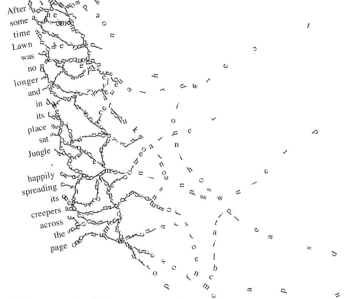

a dictionary story description

An example of exploring this balance came about in a project called *a dictionary story*. Initially the project started as a short narrative in which certain words from the dictionary became living characters that met each other.

"Spring's next victim was Lawless who was rejoicing in being knocked away from such a boring neighbour as Lawful. Lawless landed straight on top of Lawn which suddenly became very unruly. After some time Lawn was no longer and in its place sat Jungle, happily spreading its creepers across the page."

From exploring the meaning in writing it was then applied to its design. As I came to set the type I realised, by creating two columns, you could have the story running in one, whilst the definitions of the words ran in the other.

The final element to *a dictionary story* was the typographic illustrations. Here I used the definitions to illustrate what was happening in the narrative.

This project hopefully goes some way to explaining some of my thoughts around language and design.

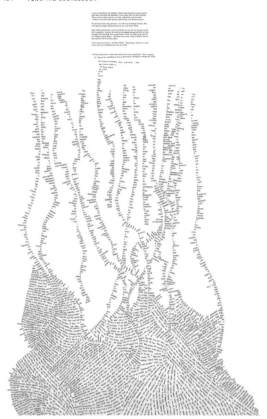

a made up true story

"Winston's experiments came from looking at the structures of different types of literature: from storybooks to bus timetables: 'The way you navigate a timetable is very different to the way you read a short story' he comments. 'I wanted to take these different types of visual navigation and introduce them to each other: a timetable re-ordering all the words from beauty and the beast, or a newspaper report on Snow White'. By imposing the visual rules of one style of writing to a different system of organising language, Winston has created a visually arresting and verbally intriguing piece."

Paula Carson, *Graphic Poetry*, June 2005.

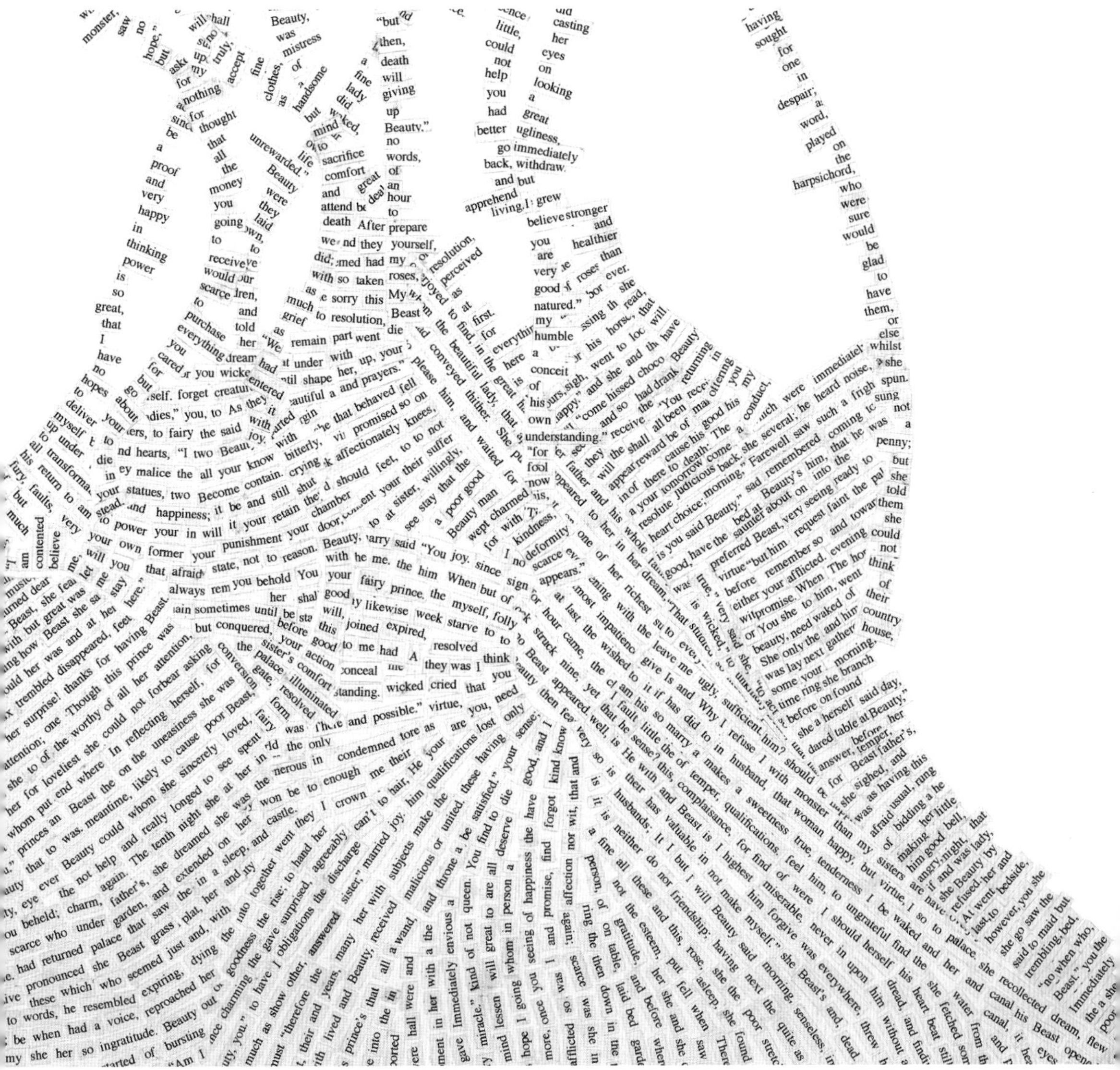

The encyclopedia was viewing the events on the other pages with immense satisfaction and decided to introduce some facts to Jack from Jack and the Beanstalk. Almost immediately the golden goose keeled over. Next to the bird's lifeless body was a group of words claiming 'no animal is able to sustain metal ore in its digestive tract'. Jack spun round to see more words declare, 'a garden beanstalk is unable to grow beyond 13 feet'. Suddenly all his words were swamped with explanations.

And so, like the beast's enforced timeline, Jack's tale was now inhabited with the encyclopedia's 'facts'.

Jack's Bean was looking considerably less Magic

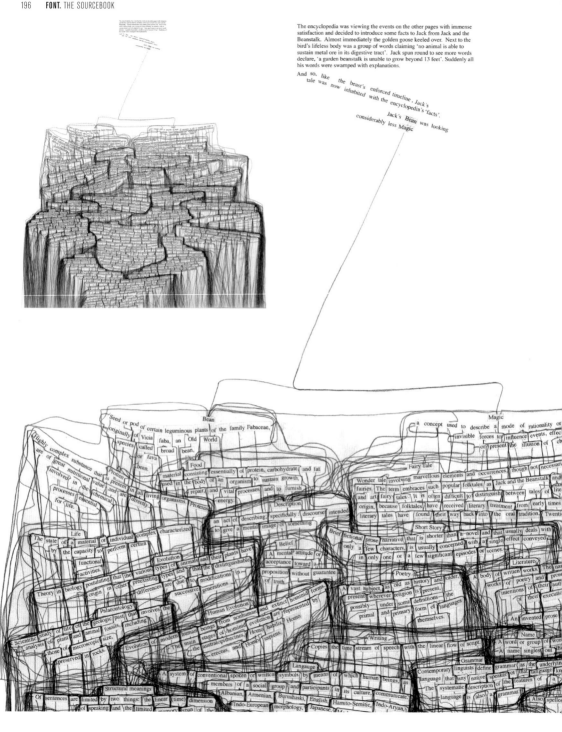

If you were to place an adult and child's world alongside each other you
would see two extremely different landscapes. One is populated with facts
and structure where as the other one is wild with make believe.

The bridge between these two happens in the grey place we call growing up.
A place where facts aren't fully understood and fantasy completely tamed.

a made-up | true story

Even though books aren't human they still manage to have personalities
beyond their authors. This starts when they leave the writer's desk and
enter the world at large.

Take fairytales and rule books, they couldn't be more different from each
other - fairytales have the agility to get away with whatever myth they see
fit and are loved by children, while rule books bear the duty of getting things
done precisely and correctly.

So what happens when a timetable, an encyclopedia and a newspaper
approach some fairytales and hold them to account?

The beast, from Beauty and the Beast, felt a bump on the page and turned
round to see his story change. The timetable had arrived.

The tree's bark was awaiting delivery, the stream had unforeseen delays and
everyone was a little more confused because the 'who' 'why' and
'what' had been stuck together. The timetable had
re-ordered his fantasy world so that
every thing fitted into a time line;
here was a
story in
which
the
words
had
been
arranged
by
their
order
of
arrival.
Starting
with
a
and
ending
on
z

space between words **description**

After spending such a considerable time working with
narratives and type, I came across this process of cutting
out type to create an image. The columns of a newspaper
were its original inspiration.

Obviously, this piece is no longer about the actual words.
Instead, I was implying that the 'space between the
words' is where our thoughts take shape.

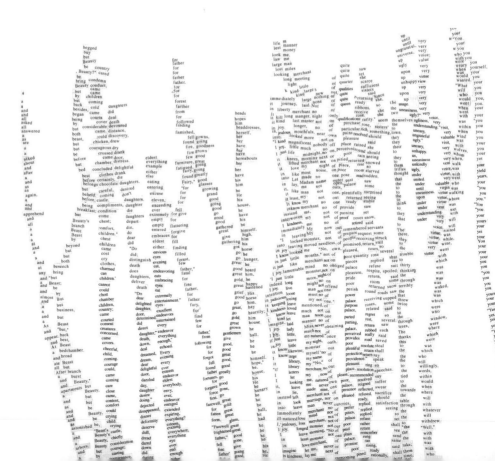

CONCLUSION

With the creation of the World Wide Web came a whole new dimension of visual communication. The Web, as we now know it, was the first programme that used both common File Transfer Protocol and Hypertext Transfer Protocol. The source code was released into the public domain in 1993, licensing the software for free public use. With the increasing prevalence of modern technology, the presentation of text and image on the computer screen became the focus of visual communication. Recent research in the field of typography has focused on web design and digitally-oriented usability.

The 1980s and 90s saw an exploration of new computerised forms of design, typography, and photography. For example, music marketing, record sleeves, clothing, logos, magazines and music videos all continued to be stages upon which the drama of digital graphic design was playing out in the public eye. Legibility and readability advanced in equal measure to creative innovation, and the adaptation of the onscreen page paved the way to this new widespread mass communication. Visual language thrives at the crossroads of technology and culture and new systems of recording, editing, transmitting and receiving information feed into the evolving role of type in the new complexion of public communication, influencing the look and feel of letterforms and diversifying their relationship to the wider visual world.

Widespread computerisation was once thought to be driven by time and economic efficiency, but there is now a new generation, a mass movement of designers eager to grapple with the challenges and particular opportunities alive in digital design.

Desktop publishing and word processing has made unwitting typographers of the unlikely and everyday office workers, but in the same vein corporate identity programmes have been written to ensure only house styles and fonts can be used within documents, which traditionalists would argue have muffled attempts to build better typographic systems or educate users of typography. The democratisation of typography has allowed amateurs the ability to experiment with typesetting and layout, and armed experts with increasingly sophisticated tools to map out new typographic terrain.

Information has grown more complex with the current cultural climate of immediacy, fuelled by the introduction of updatable type involved in Hypertext and Hypermedia. The traditional book format encourages a linear reading from beginning to end, but new digital formats are not limited to serial modalities, rather enabling the user to jump from topic to topic at a moment's notice. Now totally separate from its printing traditions, writing in its current form is wholly flexible and interactive, words are freely circulated around the Internet as the first totally user-driven medium for finding, reproducing and redistributing information. Typographers designing for Hypertext and new media are lead to create ever more innovative forms of presentation, as these formats allow for documents to be linked to and from any number of other locations within the Internet. The emergence of new media has thrown up issues of authorship, originality and permanence, where the physical aspects of printed type take up a stable place in the world, hypertext does not, allowing equal parts creative freedom and intellectual unreliability.

Just as in the fifteenth century when it was first possible for every household to own a book, printing was dubbed the great liberator of the human condition, could the same be said for Hypermedia?

There are many specialist challenges for the typographer associated with new media. For example, screen display faces must cater for legibility over several screen sizes and formats, such as in the case of downloading a film you watched at the cinema from the Internet and thereafter watching it on a hand-held mobile device. The typeface designed must work equally well across the widest range of point size in typographical history, and over the widest range of formats in the history of communication technology as a whole.

The tools of type design are constantly evolving, most computer interfaces—mice and Wacom pads to name a few—are input devices only, meaning that they track the user's physical manipulations, but provide no manual feedback. The increased availability of haptic devices (or haptic interfaces) provide mechanical tools that mediate communication between user and computer that allow users to manipulate three dimensional objects in virtual environments on a two-way feed. This new generation of interface are input-output devices, meaning that they can provide realistic touch sensations coordinated with on-screen events. The study of the interaction between people (users) and computers—Human Computer Interaction (HCI)—is often described as the intersection of computer science, behavioural science and design. Its overarching goal is to improve interactions between users and computers by making technology more usable and receptive to human needs. HCI informs the new generation of type designer, encouraging an approach

to typography that responds to the different conditions under which that type will be used. For example, designing type for multi-lingual platforms that create the possibility for digital hybrid libraries developed for users across various language formats.

With the advent of new technologies like the super-fast grid system Internet and Artificial Intelligence, type design is continually butting up against new challenges, and the age-old typographic demands of readability, elegance and proportion are finding new expressions through digital media. While parchments replaced papyrus, books replaced scrolls, printing replaced hand-written books and digital replaced metal, the deployment of traditional values of typography will always reinforce a sense of beauty and authority in whatever media it finds itself expressed.

First Things First

A Manifesto
1964

We, the undersigned, are graphic designers, photographers and students who have
been brought up in a world in which the techniques and apparatus of advertising have
persistently been presented to us as the most lucrative, effective and desirable means
of using our talents. We have been bombarded with publications devoted to this belief,
applauding the work of those who have flogged their skill and imagination to sell
such things as: cat food, stomach powders, detergent, hair restorer, striped toothpaste,
aftershave lotion, beforeshave lotion, slimming diets, fattening diets, deodorants, fizzy
water, cigarettes, roll-ons, pull-ons and slip-ons.

By far the greatest effort of those working in the advertising industry are wasted on
these trivial purposes, which contribute little or nothing to our national prosperity.

In common with an increasing numer of the general public, we have reached a
saturation point at which the high pitched scream of consumer selling is no more
than sheer noise. We think that there are other things more worth using our skill
and experience on. There are signs for streets and buildings, books and periodicals,
catalogues, instructional manuals, industrial photography, educational aids, films,
television features, scientific and industrial publications and all the other media
through which we promote our trade, our education, our culture and our greater
awareness of the world.

We do not advocate the abolition of high pressure consumer advertising: this is not
feasible. Nor do we want to take any of the fun out of life. But we are proposing
a reversal of priorities in favour of the more useful and more lasting forms of
communication. We hope that our society will tire of gimmick merchants, status
salesmen and hidden persuaders, and that the prior call on our skills will be for
worthwhile purposes. With this in mind we propose to share our experience and
opinions, and to make them available to colleagues, students and others who may
be interested.

Signed:Edward Wright, Geoffrey White, William Slack,
Caroline Rawlence, Ian McLaren, Sam Lambert, Ivor Kamlish,
Gerald Jones, Bernard Higton, Brian Grimbly, John Garner,
Ken Garland, Anthony Froshaug, Robin Fior, Germano Facetti,
Ivan Dodd, Harriet Crowder, Anthony Clift, Gerry Cinamon,
Robert Chapman, Ray Carpenter and Ken Briggs.

First Things First

A Manifesto
2000

We, the undersigned, are graphic designers, art directors and visual communicators who have been raised in a world in which the techniques and apparatus of advertising have persistently been presented to us as the most lucrative, effective and desirable use of our talents. Many design teachers and mentors promote this belief; the market rewards it; a tide of books and publications reinforces it.

Encouraged in this direction, designers then apply their skill and imagination to sell dog biscuits, designer coffee, diamonds, detergents, hair gel, cigarettes, credit cards, sneakers, butt toners, light beer and heavy-duty recreational vehicles. Commercial work has always paid the bills, but many graphic designers have now let it become, in large measure, what graphic designers do. This, in turn, is how the world perceives design. The profession's time and energy is used up manufacturing demand for things that are inessential at best.

Many of us have grown increasingly uncomfortable with this view of design. Designers who devote their efforts primarily to advertising, marketing and brand development are supporting, and implicitly endorsing, a mental environment so saturated with commercial messages that it is changing the very way citizen-consumers speak, think, feel, respond and interact. To some extent we are all helping draft a reductive and immeasurably harmful code of public discourse.

There are pursuits more worthy of our problem-solving skills. Unprecedented environmental, social and cultural crises demand our attention. Many cultural interventions, social marketing campaigns, books, magazines, exhibitions, educational tools, television programs, films, charitable causes and other information design projects urgently require our expertise and help.

We propose a reversal of priorities in favor of more useful, lasting and democratic forms of communication—a mindshift away from product marketing and toward the exploration and production of a new kind of meaning. The scope of debate is shrinking; it must expand. Consumerism is running uncontested; it must be challenged by other perspectives expressed, in part, through the visual languages and resources of design.

In 1964, 22 visual communicators signed the original call for our skills to be put to worthwhile use. With the explosive growth of global commercial culture, their message has only grown more urgent. Today, we renew their manifesto in expectation that no more decades will pass before it is taken to heart.

Signed: Jonathan Barnbrook, Nick Bell, Andrew Blauvelt, Hans Bockting, Irma Boom, Sheila Levrant de Bretteville, Max Bruinsma, Siân Cook, Linda van Deursen, Chris Dixon, William Drenttel, Gert Dumbar, Simon Esterson, Vince Frost, Ken Garland, Milton Glaser, Jessica Helfand, Steven Heller, Andrew Howard, Tibor Kalman, Jeffery Keedy, Zuzana Licko, Ellen Lupton, Katherine McCoy, Armand Mevis, J. Abbott Miller, Rick Poynor, Lucienne Roberts, Erik Spiekermann, Jan van Toorn, Teal Triggs, Rudy VanderLans, Bob Wilkinson, and many more.

1 THE MECHANICS OF TYPE

THE ANATOMY OF TYPE

Ascent line

Apex

Cap line

Cap height

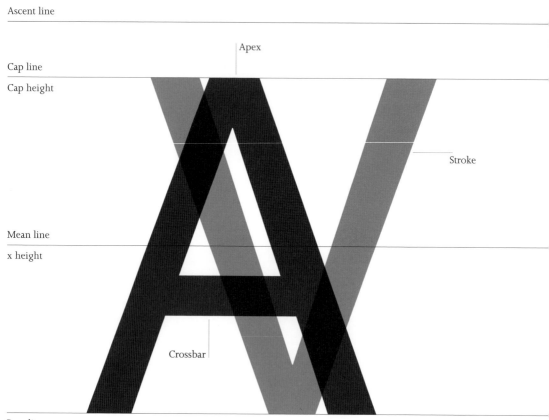

Stroke

Mean line

x height

Crossbar

Base line

Descent line

HELVETICA MEDIUM

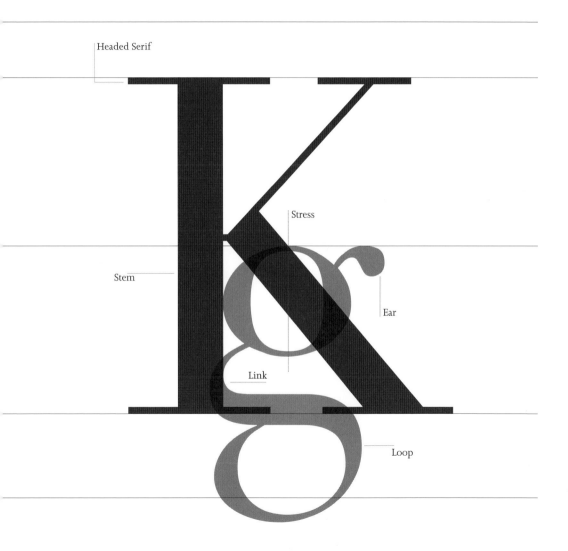

Headed Serif

Stress

Stem

Ear

Link

Loop

DIDOT REGULAR

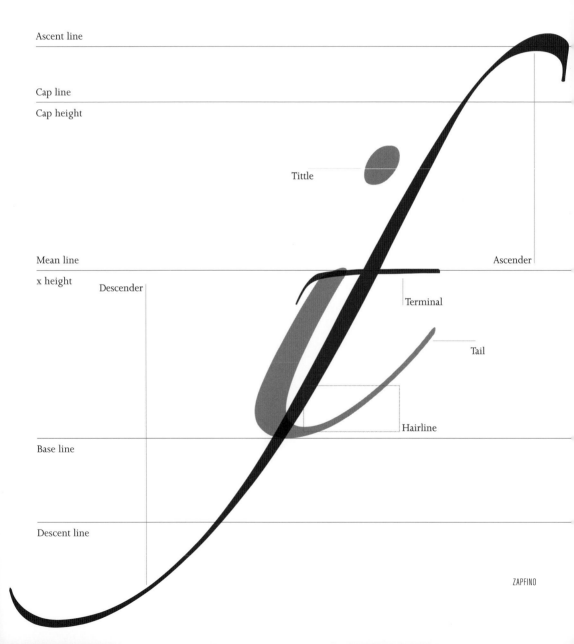

Ascent line

Cap line

Cap height

Tittle

Mean line

x height

Descender

Ascender

Terminal

Tail

Hairline

Base line

Descent line

ZAPFINO

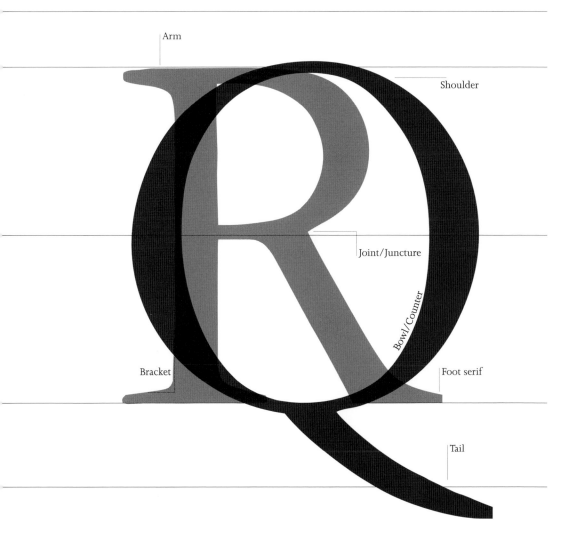

Arm

Shoulder

Joint/Juncture

Bowl/Counter

Bracket

Foot serif

Tail

GARAMOND REGULAR

2 FONT RESOURCE

akzidenz grotesk

Released by the H Berthold AG type foundry, Berlin, in 1896, the realist typeface Akzidenz-Grotesk (originally Accidenz-Grotesk) was the first sans serif typeface to be broadly used. It influenced many later neo-grotesque typefaces, including Morris Benton's Franklin Gothic,1903, and Adrian Frutiger's Univers released in 1957. Akzidenz might be, at first glance, mistaken for the apparently similar Helvetica typeface, released by the Haas Foundry in 1957 as Neue Haas Grotesk and which drew heavily upon Akzidenz as an original model.

Contemporary versions of Akzidenz-Grotesk come from a project directed by Günter Gerhard Lange at Berthold.

Since the late 1950s, he has been responsible for the many variant styles of the Akzidenz family, adding a larger character set to the typeface group while retaining the subtle characteristics of the 1896 version.

The Akzidenz Grotesk family of typefaces has expanded since 1896 to include both medium and bold weights as well as italic and condensed styles. The italic can be used to create dramatic display titles, by exploiting the rational nature of the font to align letters in an illustrative manner.

QUICK ZEPHYRS BLOW

LIGHT

Aa Bb Cc Dd Ee Ff Gg Hh Ii Jj Kk Ll Mm
Nn Oo Pp Qq Rr Ss Tt Uu Vv Ww Xx Yy Zz
0123456789 , . : ; / & ! ? £ $ *

REGULAR

Aa Bb Cc Dd Ee Ff Gg Hh Ii Jj Kk Ll Mm
Nn Oo Pp Qq Rr Ss Tt Uu Vv Ww Xx Yy Zz
0123456789 , . : ; / & ! ? £ $ *

ITALIC

Aa Bb Cc Dd Ee Ff Gg Hh Ii Jj Kk Ll Mm
Nn Oo Pp Qq Rr Ss Tt Uu Vv Ww Xx Yy Zz
*0123456789 , . : ; / & ! ? £ $ **

MEDIUM

Aa Bb Cc Dd Ee Ff Gg Hh Ii Jj Kk Ll Mm
Nn Oo Pp Qq Rr Ss Tt Uu Vv Ww Xx Yy Zz
0123456789 , . : ; / & ! ? £ $ *

BOLD

Aa Bb Cc Dd Ee Ff Gg Hh Ii Jj Kk Ll Mm
Nn Oo Pp Qq Rr Ss Tt Uu Vv Ww Xx Yy Zz
0123456789 , . : ; / & ! ? £ $ *

CONDENSED

Aa Bb Cc Dd Ee Ff Gg Hh Ii Jj Kk Ll Mm Nn Oo Pp Qq Rr Ss
Tt Uu Vv Ww Xx Yy Zz
0123456789 , . : ; / & ! ? £ $ *

EXTENDED

Aa Bb Cc Dd Ee Ff Gg Hh Ii Jj Kk
Ll Mm Nn Oo Pp Qq Rr Ss Tt Uu
Vv Ww Xx Yy Zz
0123456789 , . : ; / & ! ? £ $ *

aldus

Aldus was designed in 1954 by Hermann Zapf, for the D Stempel AG foundry. An old style serif typeface, Zapf's inspiration came from the Reinaissance Venetian printer Aldus Manutius, whose work is considered to be among the best of the period. Designed to be a lighter bookweight text face than Zapf's previous font, Palatino, the new design's counters were more open for increased legibility, again emphasised by its lack of ligatures. Aiming to create a contemporary variant of old face typefaces, Zapf's new design was clearer at small point sizes and low resolutions, and had a greater elegance than the heavier Palatino. Aldus is still regarded as a classic 1950s Zapf design.

Bright vixens jump, dozy fowl quack.

Aldus is an elegant old style serif face influenced by Renaissance type, as shown by its venetian lower case e. Aldus works particularly well when paired with Palatino bold, also designed by Hermann Zapf, as shown on the opposite page.

ROMAN

Aa Bb Cc Dd Ee Ff Gg Hh Ii Jj Kk Ll Mm
Nn Oo Pp Qq Rr Ss Tt Uu Vv Ww Xx Yy Zz
0123456789 , . : ; / & ! ? £ $ *

ITALIC

*Aa Bb Cc Dd Ee Ff Gg Hh Ii Jj Kk Ll Mm
Nn Oo Pp Qq Rr Ss Tt Uu Vv Ww Xx Yy Zz
0123456789 , . : ; / & ! ? £ $ **

SMALL CAPS & OLDSTYLE FIGURES

Aa Bb Cc Dd Ee Ff Gg Hh Ii Jj Kk Ll Mm
Nn Oo Pp Qq Rr Ss Tt Uu Vv Ww Xx Yy Zz
0123456789 , . : ; / & ! ? £ $ *

ab bb cc dd ee ff
gg hh ii jj kk ll
mm nn oo pp qq
rr ss tt uu vv ww
xx yy zz

avant garde

Avant Garde was designed by Herb Lubalin and Tom Carnase as the logotype for *Avant Garde* magazine, published in New York between 1968 and July 1971. The typeface evolved by tightly placing the hand-drawn letterforms together to create unusual ligatures, combinations of letters and alternate characters. Distinctive and instantly recognisable, Avant Garde's letterform became extremely popular amongst the design community of the time. Resultingly, Lubalin released ITC Avant Garde in 1970, but the idiosyncrasies of the letterform led not only to its wide misuse but to its overuse, eventually becoming a cliched font of the 1970s. Avant Garde works best as a display face when all of its unique ligatures and letter combinations can be explored and expressed, as shown by its expert use in the original magazine logo.

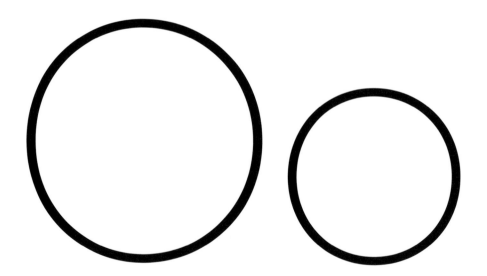

Avant Garde's perfect circles as demonstrated in the upper and lower case Os.

EXTRA LIGHT

Aa Bb Cc Dd Ee Ff Gg Hh Ii Jj Kk Ll Mm
Nn Oo Pp Qq Rr Ss Tt Uu Vv Ww Xx Yy Zz
0123456789 , . : ; / & ! ? £ $ *

BOOK

Aa Bb Cc Dd Ee Ff Gg Hh Ii Jj Kk Ll Mm
Nn Oo Pp Qq Rr Ss Tt Uu Vv Ww Xx Yy Zz
0123456789 , . : ; / & ! ? £ $*

BOOK OBLIQUE

*Aa Bb Cc Dd Ee Ff Gg Hh Ii Jj Kk Ll Mm
Nn Oo Pp Qq Rr Ss Tt Uu Vv Ww Xx Yy Zz
0123456789 , . : ; / & ! ? £ $ ** *

MEDIUM

Aa Bb Cc Dd Ee Ff Gg Hh Ii Jj Kk Ll Mm
Nn Oo Pp Qq Rr Ss Tt Uu Vv Ww Xx Yy Zz
0123456789 , . : ; / & ! ? £ $ *

MEDIUM OBLIQUE

*Aa Bb Cc Dd Ee Ff Gg Hh Ii Jj Kk Ll Mm
Nn Oo Pp Qq Rr Ss Tt Uu Vv Ww Xx Yy Zz
0123456789 , . : ; / & ! ? £ $ ** *

BOLD

**Aa Bb Cc Dd Ee Ff Gg Hh Ii Jj Kk Ll Mm
Nn Oo Pp Qq Rr Ss Tt Uu Vv Ww Xx Yy Zz
0123456789 , . : ; / & ! ? £ $ ***

BOLD OBLIQUE

***Aa Bb Cc Dd Ee Ff Gg Hh Ii Jj Kk Ll Mm
Nn Oo Pp Qq Rr Ss Tt Uu Vv Ww Xx Yy Zz
0123456789 , . : ; / & ! ? £ $ ****

baskerville

Baskerville was originally designed by John Baskerville in Britain during 1757 and has been widely used for books and other long texts. It is considered a transitional or mediator type, having elements of both traditional and contemporary designs.

Taking William Caslon's work as inspiration and reworking it, Baskerville developed a more legible face with a greater level of consistency, which itself reflects his own principles of refinement and simplicity.

Although respected by younger designers of the time such as Giambattista Bodoni and Benjamin Franklin, Baskerville fell out of use for a time, and it was only in 1917 that it experienced a revival, being redrawn by Bruce Rogers at the Harvard University Press. More recently, Zuzana Licko modelled her Mrs Eaves typeface, 1996, on Baskerville's design.

JJ𝒥NN
TT𝒯YY

A comparison of Baskerville's regular and italic capitals; the latter showcase the typeface's refinement at its strongest.

REGULAR

Aa Bb Cc Dd Ee Ff Gg Hh Ii Jj Kk Ll Mm
Nn Oo Pp Qq Rr Ss Tt Uu Vv Ww Xx Yy Zz
0123456789 , . : ; / & ! ? £ $ *

ITALIC

Aa Bb Cc Dd Ee Ff Gg Hh Ii Jj Kk Ll Mm
Nn Oo Pp Qq Rr Ss Tt Uu Vv Ww Xx Yy Zz
*0123456789 , . : ; / & ! ? £ $ **

SEMIBOLD

Aa Bb Cc Dd Ee Ff Gg Hh Ii Jj Kk Ll Mm
Nn Oo Pp Qq Rr Ss Tt Uu Vv Ww Xx Yy Zz
0123456789 , . : ; / & ! ? £ $ *

SEMIBOLD ITALIC

Aa Bb Cc Dd Ee Ff Gg Hh Ii Jj Kk Ll Mm
Nn Oo Pp Qq Rr Ss Tt Uu Vv Ww Xx Yy Zz
***0123456789 , . : ; / & ! ? £ $ ***

BOLD

Aa Bb Cc Dd Ee Ff Gg Hh Ii Jj Kk Ll Mm
Nn Oo Pp Qq Rr Ss Tt Uu Vv Ww Xx Yy Zz
0123456789 , . : ; / & ! ? £ $ *

BOLD ITALIC

Aa Bb Cc Dd Ee Ff Gg Hh Ii Jj Kk Ll Mm
Nn Oo Pp Qq Rr Ss Tt Uu Vv Ww Xx Yy Zz
***0123456789 , . : ; / & ! ? £ $ ***

bell centennial

Bell Centennial was designed by Matthew Carter and released in 1978 for the hundredth anniversary of the AT&T telephone directory. Created to replace the document's previous typeface, Bell Gothic, Carter was given a tight brief in order that the design be appropriate for its application— particularly in telephone directories. The text would need to be legible at very small sizes and be economical with space, and the high speed printing process for telephone directory newsprint meant that the typeface should also take into consideration any ink spread or 'dot gain'. An increase in counter spaces therefore increased its legibility, curved terminals helped define the stroke and ink traps or 'notches' were exaggerated on letters x, w and k in order to preserve the shape of the letter in adverse printing conditions.

123
456

Designed for telephone books, Bell Centennial has forms that are optimised for small print under difficult circumstances. The giant ink traps were introduced to avoid cluttering of ink on high-speed presses. More recently, Bell Centennial has been used at large display sizes in order to exaggerate the ink traps for an usual design.

ADDRESS

Aa Bb Cc Dd Ee Ff Gg Hh Ii Jj Kk Ll Mm
Nn Oo Pp Qq Rr Ss Tt Uu Vv Ww Xx Yy Zz
0123456789 , . : ; / & ! ? £ $ *

NAME AND NUMBER

Aa Bb Cc Dd Ee Ff Gg Hh Ii Jj Kk Ll Mm
Nn Oo Pp Qq Rr Ss Tt Uu Vv Ww Xx Yy Zz
0123456789 , . : ; / & ! ? £ $ *

SUB CAPTION

Aa Bb Cc Dd Ee Ff Gg Hh Ii Jj Kk Ll Mm
Nn Oo Pp Qq Rr Ss Tt Uu Vv Ww Xx Yy Zz
0123456789 , . : ; / & ! ? £ $ *

BOLD LISTING

Aa Bb Cc Dd Ee Ff Gg Hh Ii Jj Kk
Ll Mm Nn Oo Pp Qq Rr Ss Tt Uu Vv
Ww Xx Yy Zz
0123456789 , . : ; / & ! ? £ $ *

BOLD LISTING ALTERNATE

Aa Bb Cc Dd Ee Ff Gg Hh Ii Jj Kk
Ll Mm Nn Oo Pp Qq Rr Ss Tt Uu Vv
Ww Xx Yy Zz
0123456789 , . : ; / & ! ? £ $ *

bell gothic

Bell Gothic is a condensed sans serif originally designed for the AT&T telephone directory. In 1938, typographic developer Chauncey H Griffiths was commissioned at Mergenthaler Linotype to design a typeface that would permit high legibility and economy of page space. Bell Gothic was used in the directory for over 40 years, until changes in technology forced AT&T to develop a new typeface to meet the demands of high–speed printing: Bell Gothic performed well with the hot metal Linotype printing machine, but difficulties emerged with the new phototypesetting technologies. In 1975, Matthew Carter began developing Bell Centennial in order to meet the new demands of phototypesetting, while Bell Gothic was licensed for general use. It is now sometimes used as a headline font, exaggerating its ink traps for dramatic effect.

Bell Gothic is unusual in its design because it was devised to be printed at very small sizes in the AT&T telephone directory, therefore the bowls and counter spaces are more exaggerated than other roman letterforms. The illustration, right, shows a comparison between the roman and italic faces, exaggerating the unusual shape of the bowl.

bd

bd pq

pq

ROMAN

Aa Bb Cc Dd Ee Ff Gg Hh Ii Jj Kk Ll Mm
Nn Oo Pp Qq Rr Ss Tt Uu Vv Ww Xx Yy Zz
0123456789 , . : ; / & ! ? £ $ *

OBLIQUE

Aa Bb Cc Dd Ee Ff Gg Hh Ii Jj Kk Ll Mm
Nn Oo Pp Qq Rr Ss Tt Uu Vv Ww Xx Yy Zz
0123456789 , . : ; / & ! ? £ $ *

BOLD

Aa Bb Cc Dd Ee Ff Gg Hh Ii Jj Kk Ll Mm
Nn Oo Pp Qq Rr Ss Tt Uu Vv Ww Xx Yy Zz
0123456789 , . : ; / & ! ? £ $ *

BOLD OBLIQUE

Aa Bb Cc Dd Ee Ff Gg Hh Ii Jj Kk Ll Mm
Nn Oo Pp Qq Rr Ss Tt Uu Vv Ww Xx Yy Zz
0123456789 , . : ; / & ! ? £ $ *

BLACK

Aa Bb Cc Dd Ee Ff Gg Hh Ii Jj Kk Ll Mm
Nn Oo Pp Qq Rr Ss Tt Uu Vv Ww Xx Yy Zz
0123456789 , . : ; / & ! ? £ $ *

BLACK OBLIQUE

Aa Bb Cc Dd Ee Ff Gg Hh Ii Jj Kk Ll Mm
Nn Oo Pp Qq Rr Ss Tt Uu Vv Ww Xx Yy Zz
0123456789 , . : ; / & ! ? £ $ *

bembo

Bembo is a venetian roman typeface, first cut by Francesco Griffo as Aldine Roman in 1495 and revived by Stanley Morison at Monotype in 1929. Bembo was originally designed to be used in a book by Pietro Bembo and was inspired by the handwriting style of the scholarly scribes in northern Italy. With its modulated stroke and crisp serifs, Bembo echoed the lightness, legibility and consistent appearance of the scribes' handwriting. It became an instant success making its way through the printing houses of Europe and forerunning all subsequent old style type designs. Bembo is a classic piece of typography, exemplified perfectly by its ongoing popularity in the digital age, particularly for use in extended text.

As an Aldin roman typeface, Bembo has a strong calligraphic basis. The stroke is based on a broadnibbed pen, which is particularly apparent in the bowl and loop of the lower case g. The serifs are triangular with a moderated stroke throughout based around a humanist axis.

A very *bright* paint

REGULAR

Aa Bb Cc Dd Ee Ff Gg Hh Ii Jj Kk Ll Mm
Nn Oo Pp Qq Rr Ss Tt Uu Vv Ww Xx Yy Zz
0123456789 , . : ; / & ! ? £ $ ★

ITALIC

Aa Bb Cc Dd Ee Ff Gg Hh Ii Jj Kk Ll Mm
Nn Oo Pp Qq Rr Ss Tt Uu Vv Ww Xx Yy Zz
0123456789 , . : ; / & ! ? £ $ ★

SEMIBOLD

Aa Bb Cc Dd Ee Ff Gg Hh Ii Jj Kk Ll Mm
Nn Oo Pp Qq Rr Ss Tt Uu Vv Ww Xx Yy Zz
0123456789 , . : ; / & ! ? £ $ ★

SEMIBOLD ITALIC

Aa Bb Cc Dd Ee Ff Gg Hh Ii Jj Kk Ll Mm
Nn Oo Pp Qq Rr Ss Tt Uu Vv Ww Xx Yy Zz
0123456789 , . : ; / & ! ? £ $ ★

BOLD

Aa Bb Cc Dd Ee Ff Gg Hh Ii Jj Kk Ll Mm
Nn Oo Pp Qq Rr Ss Tt Uu Vv Ww Xx Yy Zz
0123456789 , . : ; / & ! ? £ $ ★

EXTRA BOLD

Aa Bb Cc Dd Ee Ff Gg Hh Ii Jj Kk Ll Mm
Nn Oo Pp Qq Rr Ss Tt Uu Vv Ww Xx Yy
Zz 0123456789 , . : ; / & ! ? £ $ ★

SMALL CAPS
& OLDSTYLE FIGURES

Aa Bb Cc Dd Ee Ff Gg Hh Ii Jj Kk Ll Mm
Nn Oo Pp Qq Rr Ss Tt Uu Vv Ww Xx Yy Zz
0123456789 , . : ; / & ! ? £ $ ★

blur

Neville Brody's Blur defies all rules of type classification. Designed in 1991, Brody sought to evoke the experience of living in an 'information society' with his design. Blur is a process font, meaning that it isn't written or drawn, but produced through mechanical (or in this case digital) means. Going against the traditional aims of type design—which prioritises legibility over creativity—Brody used photographic processes to extort and extrude his letterforms into contorted illegible shapes. After attending the London College of Printing, which promoted a traditional approach to typography, Brody designed the lifestyle magazine *The Face* and was art director of Fetish Records and *Arena* magazine, platforming his experimental type designs. Brody is involved with FontFont digital type foundry and *Fuse* magazine and is widely regarded as one of the first great type designers of the digital age.

Aa Bb Cc Dd
Aa Bb Cc Dd
Aa Bb Cc Dd

This experimental typeface by Brody is widely regarded as one of the first truly original digital typefaces. Blur was widely used as a display face in the 1990s and has become a byword for that era. The design stems from the extruded bowls and counter spaces of a sans serif font, reminiscent of over and under photographic exposure.

LIGHT

Aa Bb Cc Dd Ee Ff Gg Hh Ii Jj Kk Ll Mm
Nn Oo Pp Qq Rr Ss Tt Uu Vv Ww Xx Yy Zz
0123456789 , . : ; / & ! ? £ $ *

MEDIUM

Aa Bb Cc Dd Ee Ff Gg Hh Ii Jj Kk Ll Mm
Nn Oo Pp Qq Rr Ss Tt Uu Vv Ww Xx Yy Zz
0123456789 , . : ; / & ! ? £ $ *

BOLD

Aa Bb Cc Dd Ee Ff Gg Hh Ii Jj Kk Ll
Mm Nn Oo Pp Qq Rr Ss Tt Uu Vv Ww
Xx Yy Zz
0123456789 , . : ; / & ! ? £ $ *

Ee Ff Gg Hh Ii Jj

Ee Ff Gg Hh Ii Jj

Ee Ff Gg Hh Ii Jj

bodoni

The Italian Giambattista Bodoni created Bodoni in 1795. Truly passionate about type, Bodoni's designs were to revolutionise the shape of letterforms, creating the most important typeface of the Romantic period. Unlike previous typefaces, Bodoni has a high contrast between the thick and thin strokes, with flat, abrupt serifs.

It is based on a rational axis: the stroke is straight and goes against the natural handwriting curve. The venetian typefaces of the fifteenth century such as Bembo were based on the handwriting of scribes, who used a broadnib pen. In the eighteenth century Bodoni would have been using a pointed quill that enabled writing

to change quickly between thick and thin strokes, unlike before. This structural shift broke with tradition and reflected the changing tools of the time, creating a much more geometric form with a pure, unembellished style.

The highly exaggerated contrast between Bodoni's thicks and thins is particularly noticeable in the capital letters. It is drawn according to a rationalist axis and with a pointed quill to give the distinctive straight sharp serifs. A demonstration of Bodoni's distinguishing hairlines through the different weights is illustrated opposite, showing that the serifs do not change in width in the heavier weights.

AEHW
AEHW
AEHW
AEHW

BOOK

Aa Bb Cc Dd Ee Ff Gg Hh Ii Jj Kk Ll Mm
Nn Oo Pp Qq Rr Ss Tt Uu Vv Ww Xx Yy Zz
0123456789 , . : ; / & ! ? £ $ *

BOOK ITALIC

Aa Bb Cc Dd Ee Ff Gg Hh Ii Jj Kk Ll Mm
Nn Oo Pp Qq Rr Ss Tt Uu Vv Ww Xx Yy Zz
*0123456789 , . : ; / & ! ? £ $ **

ROMAN

Aa Bb Cc Dd Ee Ff Gg Hh Ii Jj Kk Ll Mm
Nn Oo Pp Qq Rr Ss Tt Uu Vv Ww Xx Yy Zz
0123456789 , . : ; / & ! ? £ $ *

BOLD

Aa Bb Cc Dd Ee Ff Gg Hh Ii Jj Kk Ll Mm
Nn Oo Pp Qq Rr Ss Tt Uu Vv Ww Xx Yy Zz
0123456789 , . : ; / & ! ? £ $ *

BOLD ITALIC

Aa Bb Cc Dd Ee Ff Gg Hh Ii Jj Kk Ll Mm
Nn Oo Pp Qq Rr Ss Tt Uu Vv Ww Xx Yy Zz
0123456789 , . : ; / & ! ? £ $ *

POSTER

Aa Bb Cc Dd Ee Ff Gg Hh Ii Jj Kk
Ll Mm Nn Oo Pp Qq Rr Ss Tt Uu Vv
Ww Xx Yy Zz
0123456789 , . : ; / & ! ? £ $ *

POSTER COMPRESSED

Aa Bb Cc Dd Ee Ff Gg Hh Ii Jj Kk Ll Mm Nn Oo Pp Qq Rr Ss Tt Uu
Vv Ww Xx Yy Zz
0123456789 , . : ; / & ! ? £ $ *

caslon

Caslon is a typeface derived from the work of William Caslon, widely credited as the first British type designer. Caslon's main features are its short descenders and bracketed serifs, and a moderately high contrast between stroke widths. The ligatures in the face are expressive and full of character, particularly 'ct' and 'st'—expressing its historical charm—and its italic is calligraphic with old style swashes. First designed in 1734, Caslon rose to immediate popularity, even finding its way into the layout of the United States Declaration of Independence in 1776. George Bernard Shaw reportedly insisted that all his work should be set in Caslon; its warm, solid and straightforward qualities led to it becoming a reliable 'rule of thumb' typeface for many printers. Its influence can be seen in type designers of all subsequent eras including John Baskerville and Monotype's 1913 Imprint typeface.

A distinguishing feature of William Caslon's work is his swash capital letters, shown here alongside the regular roman capital. The swash capitals, ornaments and ligatures bring Caslon's type to life, showcasing his famed dexterity as a type cutter.

AE NT AE NT

REGULAR

Aa Bb Cc Dd Ee Ff Gg Hh Ii Jj Kk Ll Mm
Nn Oo Pp Qq Rr Ss Tt Uu Vv Ww Xx Yy Zz
0123456789 , . : ; / & ! ? £ $ *

ITALIC

Aa Bb Cc Dd Ee Ff Gg Hh Ii Jj Kk Ll Mm
Nn Oo Pp Qq Rr Ss Tt Uu Vv Ww Xx Yy Zz
*0123456789 , . : ; / & ! ? £ $ **

SEMIBOLD

Aa Bb Cc Dd Ee Ff Gg Hh Ii Jj Kk Ll Mm
Nn Oo Pp Qq Rr Ss Tt Uu Vv Ww Xx Yy Zz
0123456789 , . : ; / & ! ? £ $ *

BOLD

Aa Bb Cc Dd Ee Ff Gg Hh Ii Jj Kk Ll Mm
Nn Oo Pp Qq Rr Ss Tt Uu Vv Ww Xx Yy Zz
0123456789 , . : ; / & ! ? £ $ *

SMALL CAPS
& OLDSTYLE FIGURES

Aa Bb Cc Dd Ee Ff Gg Hh Ii Jj Kk Ll Mm
Nn Oo Pp Qq Rr Ss Tt Uu Vv Ww Xx Yy Zz
0123456789 , . : ; / & ! ? £ $ *

ITALIC SWASH

A B C D E F G H I J K L M
N O P Q R S T U V W X Y Z

ORNAMENTS

clarendon

The name Clarendon is used to describe many different cuts of type. Its main defining features are truncated and bracketed serifs and an amalgamation of slab serifs with classic roman letterforms. The first Clarendon typeface was cut by Robert Besley at the Fann Street Foundry, London, in 1845. It was influenced by Caslon's Double Pica Ionic, issued the year before, and was a great success upon its release as a display face, with the booming advertising and printing industries of the nineteenth century. In 1879, William Page cut French Clarendon (also known as Circus Letter), a thin condensed version with exaggerated serifs famously used on reward posters of the period. Clarendon witnessed a revival in America during the 1920s as it proved to be robust under the new strains of high-speed newspaper printing.

Clarendon is an ionic typeface with truncated and bracketed serifs, a result of the combination of roman and slab serif letterforms. One of the most recognisable aspects of Clarendon is the 'smiling' lower case a, with its upward turning tail.

LIGHT

Aa Bb Cc Dd Ee Ff Gg Hh Ii Jj Kk
Ll Mm Nn Oo Pp Qq Rr Ss Tt Uu
Vv Ww Xx Yy Zz
0123456789 , . : ; / & ! ? £ $ *

ROMAN

Aa Bb Cc Dd Ee Ff Gg Hh Ii Jj Kk
Ll Mm Nn Oo Pp Qq Rr Ss Tt Uu
Vv Ww Xx Yy Zz
0123456789 , . : ; / & ! ? £ $ *

BOLD

Aa Bb Cc Dd Ee Ff Gg Hh Ii Jj Kk
Ll Mm Nn Oo Pp Qq Rr Ss Tt Uu
Vv Ww Xx Yy Zz
0123456789 , . : ; / & ! ? £ $ *

BLACK

Aa Bb Cc Dd Ee Ff Gg Hh Ii Jj Kk
Ll Mm Nn Oo Pp Qq Rr Ss Tt Uu
Vv Ww Xx Yy Zz
0123456789 , . : ; / & ! ? £ $ *

CONDENSED

Aa Bb Cc Dd Ee Ff Gg Hh Ii Jj Kk Ll Mm Nn Oo Pp
Qq Rr Ss Tt Uu Vv Ww Xx Yy Zz
0123456789 , . : ; / & ! ? £ $ *

cooper black

Cooper Black is an extra bold roman typeface with rounded serifs designed by Oswald Bruce Cooper in 1921. Cooper was a designer working in advertising and typesetting and had studied lettering under Frederic Goudy at the Frank Home School of Illustration in Chicago. Cooper Black is a heavy bold version of Cooper's previous typeface, Cooper Old Style, and was created as a display face for advertising. Reminiscent of Art Deco styles, the typeface was popular during the 1920s and 30s, and Goudy's influence on the design can be seen in its organic calligraphic shapes. One iconic and influential use of Cooper Black was on the cover of the Beach Boys album *Pet Sounds* in 1966. Revived during the 1970s, it is emblematic of graphic design of that decade and has enjoyed periodic spurts of good favour since its creation in the early twentieth century.

As an extra bold roman face, Cooper Black is best suited as a display face, as every part of the typeface is exaggerated to create a heavy outline. The stroke is calligraphic and the serifs are enlarged and curved, evidencing an Art Deco influence.

The qui goblin j the lazy

Aa Bb Cc Dd Ee Ff Gg Hh Ii Jj Kk Ll Mm
Nn Oo Pp Qq Rr Ss Tt Uu Vv Ww Xx
Yy Zz
0123456789 , . : ; / & ! ? £ $ *

k onyx

mps over

dwarf

courier

Howard 'Bud' Kettler designed Courier in 1955 to be used in IBM's typewriters. It is a monospaced slab serif that is monotone in weight with geometric features, making it very easy to read. Although it was designed to be used with only IBM typewriters, copyright difficulties meant that Courier became the default typeface for all typewriters, and the accepted typeface for all bureaucratic correspondences for many years. Courier fonts are still widely used despite the demise of the typewriter: computer coding, such as ASCII and HTML, is written in Courier because it is monospaced and available on most machines.

Some designers use Courier for its nostalgic analogue qualities, inspiring typefaces such as Courier Sans by James Goggin, a geometric sans serif, and Erik van Blokland's Trixie, which gives the impression of a dirty typewriter.

Aa Bb Cc Dd Ee Ff

Gg Hh Ii Jj Kk Ll

Mm Nn Oo Pp Qq Rr

Courier is a monospaced font: each letter takes up exactly the same space as the next so that corrections on the typewriter could be done as easily as possible. It is drawn geometrically with no contrast in stroke weight, with strong slab serifs and became the default font for typewriters. The monospaced effect can be used to creat ASCII art, where letters are placed to create illustrative forms.

Ss Tt Uu Vv Ww Xx

Yy Zz

REGULAR

Aa Bb Cc Dd Ee Ff Gg Hh Ii Jj Kk
Ll Mm Nn Oo Pp Qq Rr Ss Tt Uu Vv
Ww Xx Yy Zz
0123456789 , . : ; / & ! ? £ $ *

OBLIQUE

Aa Bb Cc Dd Ee Ff Gg Hh Ii Jj Kk
Ll Mm Nn Oo Pp Qq Rr Ss Tt Uu Vv
Ww Xx Yy Zz
*0123456789 , . : ; / & ! ? £ $ **

BOLD

Aa Bb Cc Dd Ee Ff Gg Hh Ii Jj Kk
Ll Mm Nn Oo Pp Qq Rr Ss Tt Uu Vv
Ww Xx Yy Zz
0123456789 , . : ; / & ! ? £ $ *

BOLD OBLIQUE

Aa Bb Cc Dd Ee Ff Gg Hh Ii Jj Kk
Ll Mm Nn Oo Pp Qq Rr Ss Tt Uu Vv
Ww Xx Yy Zz
0123456789 , . : ; / & ! ? £ $ *

DIN

DIN is a large realist sans serif typeface family, the earliest version of which was issued by the D Stempel AG foundry in 1923. DIN itself was modelled upon a 1905 typeface for the Royal Prussian Railway Company. The early DIN typefaces were used initially in italic form and made into stencils, used to label technical architectural and engineering drawings. In 1936, one of its variants was chosen for its legibility and reproducibility by the German Standards Committee, to be used as a standard typeface in areas including engineering, technology, and administration. DIN variants were popular in large metal stencil format, particularly for public signage. It was not until the 1960s that DIN became popular for its application on print material—despite its use by the Bauhaus during the 1930s—when it was licensed in Letraset transfer.

Many of the letterforms for DIN are based around the shape of the capital o. The capitals g, q and c are all based around this form. As it was originally designed as a technical typeface, DIN has many geometric characteristics to give the impression of efficiency and technological advancement. It is now widely used for its legibility at small sizes and as an interesting alternative to Helvetica or Univers.

LIGHT

Aa Bb Cc Dd Ee Ff Gg Hh Ii Jj Kk Ll Mm
Nn Oo Pp Qq Rr Ss Tt Uu Vv Ww Xx Yy Zz
0123456789 , . : ; / & ! ? £ $ *

REGULAR

Aa Bb Cc Dd Ee Ff Gg Hh Ii Jj Kk Ll Mm
Nn Oo Pp Qq Rr Ss Tt Uu Vv Ww Xx Yy Zz
0123456789 , . : ; / & ! ? £ $ *

MEDIUM

**Aa Bb Cc Dd Ee Ff Gg Hh Ii Jj Kk Ll Mm
Nn Oo Pp Qq Rr Ss Tt Uu Vv Ww Xx Yy Zz
0123456789 , . : ; / & ! ? £ $ ***

BOLD

**Aa Bb Cc Dd Ee Ff Gg Hh Ii Jj Kk Ll Mm
Nn Oo Pp Qq Rr Ss Tt Uu Vv Ww Xx Yy Zz
0123456789 , . : ; / & ! ? £ $ ***

BLACK

**Aa Bb Cc Dd Ee Ff Gg Hh Ii Jj Kk Ll Mm
Nn Oo Pp Qq Rr Ss Tt Uu Vv Ww Xx Yy Zz
0123456789 , . : ; / & ! ? £ $ ***

fedra

Fedra is an extensive type family designed by Peter Bil'ak, first issued as Fedra Sans in 2001 by the Typotheque type foundry in the Netherlands. It is a constantly evolving type system, designed to meet the current demands of visual communication both on the page and on screen. It was originally commissioned by Ruedi Baur Integral Design as a corporate font for German insurance company, Bayerische Ruck, and while the commission fell through, Bil'ak continued working on Fedra for his own type foundry, Typotheque. As it was not based on a historical pre-existing model, it has been able to meet the demands of typographers in the twenty-first century by being functional and flexible enough to work on screen as well as it does on paper.

a *quart* jug *of bad* milk *might* jinx *zippy* fowls

The Fedra type family is made up of different faces, all with their own individual characteristics and voice, but when they are used in combination with each other they become dynamic sets. Each face has the same fundamental attributes yet they fit together harmoniously.

BOOK

Aa Bb Cc Dd Ee Ff Gg Hh Ii Jj Kk Ll Mm
Nn Oo Pp Qq Rr Ss Tt Uu Vv Ww Xx Yy Zz
0123456789 , . : ; / & ! ? £ $ *

BOOK ITALIC

Aa Bb Cc Dd Ee Ff Gg Hh Ii Jj Kk Ll Mm
Nn Oo Pp Qq Rr Ss Tt Uu Vv Ww Xx Yy Zz
0123456789 , . : ; / & ! ? £ $ *

BOLD

**Aa Bb Cc Dd Ee Ff Gg Hh Ii Jj Kk Ll Mm
Nn Oo Pp Qq Rr Ss Tt Uu Vv Ww Xx Yy Zz
0123456789 , . : ; / & ! ? £ $ ***

SERIF BOOK

Aa Bb Cc Dd Ee Ff Gg Hh Ii Jj Kk Ll Mm
Nn Oo Pp Qq Rr Ss Tt Uu Vv Ww Xx Yy Zz
0123456789 , . : ; / & ! ? £ $ *

SERIF BOOK ITALIC

Aa Bb Cc Dd Ee Ff Gg Hh Ii Jj Kk Ll Mm
Nn Oo Pp Qq Rr Ss Tt Uu Vv Ww Xx Yy Zz
0123456789 , . : ; / & ! ? £ $ *

SERIF BOLD

**Aa Bb Cc Dd Ee Ff Gg Hh Ii Jj Kk Ll
Mm Nn Oo Pp Qq Rr Ss Tt Uu Vv Ww
Xx Yy Zz
0123456789 , . : ; / & ! ? £ $ ***

fette fraktur

Fette Fraktur is a blackletter typeface based on the Fraktur type of Gothic script and was first designed in 1850 by Johann Christian Bauer, a German punchcutter. While intended more as an advertising typeface, Fette Fraktur was widely used as a text face in German-speaking Europe and parts of Scandinavia. The Nazi regime encouraged the use of Fette Fraktur font until January 1941 when Martin Bormann, director of the Party Chancellery commanded the end of use of blackletter faces because of suspected Jewish contribution to the development of designs for this type. At the conclusion of Second World War, it was also briefly banned by the Allied Forces due to illegibility. Now largely replaced by the antiqua (roman) alphabet, it is still used in advertising and packaging to represent rustic or traditional Germanic sensibilities.

Fette Fraktur's heavily ornamental Gothic script roots it heavily in the European historic blackletter tradition. The lower case letterforms of Fette Fraktur are somewhat distinguished from other broken-letter typefaces except by its ornamental flourishes, seen more prominently in the upper case forms.

BLACK

Aa Bb Cc Dd Ee Ff Gg Hh Ii Jj Kk Ll Mm
Nn Oo Pp Qq Rr Ss Tt Uu Vv Ww Xx Yy Zz
0123456789 , . : ; / & ! ? £ $ *

franklin gothic

Franklin Gothic was the first typeface designed by Morris Fuller Benton as chief type designer at the newly formed American Type Founders Company. The typeface was intended to be the standard font for newspapers and advertising and was greatly influenced by humanist woodcut gothic faces, and geometric sans serif type from Germany including Akzidenz-Grotesk, 1898, and Basic Commercial, 1900. This influence is evidenced by the curving taper as they flow into the stem. The calligraphic tail on the double story lower case g is unlike the German faces, which maintain a consistent moderate stroke. Franklin Gothic was released in 1902 in one weight with two widths and was an immediate success, and it continues to be popular today various printed media such as newspapers.

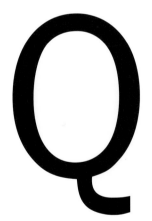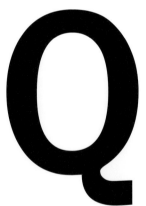

Franklin Gothic combines consistent, geometric strokes with humanist flourishes, such as the ear of the lower case g, and the tapering curves of its round letterforms. The tail of the letter q moves further along the character as it increases in weight, as shown here.

BOOK

Aa Bb Cc Dd Ee Ff Gg Hh Ii Jj Kk Ll Mm
Nn Oo Pp Qq Rr Ss Tt Uu Vv Ww Xx Yy Zz
0123456789 , . : ; / & ! ? £ $ *

BOOK ITALIC

Aa Bb Cc Dd Ee Ff Gg Hh Ii Jj Kk Ll Mm
Nn Oo Pp Qq Rr Ss Tt Uu Vv Ww Xx Yy Zz
*0123456789 , . : ; / & ! ? £ $ **

MEDIUM

Aa Bb Cc Dd Ee Ff Gg Hh Ii Jj Kk Ll Mm
Nn Oo Pp Qq Rr Ss Tt Uu Vv Ww Xx Yy Zz
0123456789 , . : ; / & ! ? £ $ *

MEDIUM ITALIC

Aa Bb Cc Dd Ee Ff Gg Hh Ii Jj Kk Ll Mm
Nn Oo Pp Qq Rr Ss Tt Uu Vv Ww Xx Yy Zz
*0123456789 , . : ; / & ! ? £ $ **

HEAVY

Aa Bb Cc Dd Ee Ff Gg Hh Ii Jj Kk Ll Mm
Nn Oo Pp Qq Rr Ss Tt Uu Vv Ww Xx Yy Zz
0123456789 , . : ; / & ! ? £ $ *

BOOK CONDENSED

Aa Bb Cc Dd Ee Ff Gg Hh Ii Jj Kk Ll Mm
Nn Oo Pp Qq Rr Ss Tt Uu Vv Ww Xx Yy Zz
0123456789 , . : ; / & ! ? £ $ *

DEMI CONDENSED

Aa Bb Cc Dd Ee Ff Gg Hh Ii Jj Kk Ll Mm
Nn Oo Pp Qq Rr Ss Tt Uu Vv Ww Xx Yy Zz
0123456789 , . : ; / & ! ? £ $ *

frutiger

Frutiger is a clean, crisp sans serif designed by Adrian Frutiger and released in 1976 by Linotype. It was originally developed for the Paris Charles de Gaulle International Airport at Roissy and each letter was designed to be quickly and easily recognisable at large sizes, from any angle or distance, whether on foot or from a car.

Frutiger wanted to create a typeface that combined the clarity and rationality of his previous font, Univers, and the humanist semsibility of Gill. Frutiger has not only been used for road signs in Switzerland and Norway, but also for the identities of the British National Health Service and Royal Navy. Frutiger's success continues with more recent adapted versions, ensuring that the typeface evolves and maintains its status as one of the most popular and applicable designs of the twentieth century.

Frutiger's ascenders and descenders stand prominently in relation to the form of the bowls. It is this clarity and definition that allows Frutiger to perform so well from obscure angles or long distances, whether in light, bold or ultra black.

bfhgqt**bfhgqt****bf**

bfhgqtbfhgqtbf

45 LIGHT

Aa Bb Cc Dd Ee Ff Gg Hh Ii Jj Kk Ll Mm
Nn Oo Pp Qq Rr Ss Tt Uu Vv Ww Xx Yy Zz
0123456789 , . : ; / & ! ? £ $ *

55 ROMAN

Aa Bb Cc Dd Ee Ff Gg Hh Ii Jj Kk Ll Mm
Nn Oo Pp Qq Rr Ss Tt Uu Vv Ww Xx Yy Zz
0123456789 , . : ; / & ! ? £ $ *

56 ITALIC

Aa Bb Cc Dd Ee Ff Gg Hh Ii Jj Kk Ll Mm
Nn Oo Pp Qq Rr Ss Tt Uu Vv Ww Xx Yy Zz
*0123456789 , . : ; / & ! ? £ $ **

65 BOLD

Aa Bb Cc Dd Ee Ff Gg Hh Ii Jj Kk Ll Mm
Nn Oo Pp Qq Rr Ss Tt Uu Vv Ww Xx Yy Zz
0123456789 , . : ; / & ! ? £ $ *

66 BOLD ITALIC

Aa Bb Cc Dd Ee Ff Gg Hh Ii Jj Kk Ll Mm
Nn Oo Pp Qq Rr Ss Tt Uu Vv Ww Xx Yy Zz
*0123456789 , . : ; / & ! ? £ $ **

75 BLACK

Aa Bb Cc Dd Ee Ff Gg Hh Ii Jj Kk Ll
Mm Nn Oo Pp Qq Rr Ss Tt Uu Vv Ww
Xx Yy Zz
0123456789 , . : ; / & ! ? £ $ *

gqt

95 ULTRA BLACK

Aa Bb Cc Dd Ee Ff Gg Hh Ii Jj Kk Ll
Mm Nn Oo Pp Qq Rr Ss Tt Uu Vv Ww
Xx Yy Zz
0123456789 , . : ; / & ! ? £ $ *

gqt

futura

Futura was designed by Paul Renner in 1927 for the Bauer foundry and is a classic example of Modernist typography. Although not directly involved with the Bauhaus, the spirit and ethos of the school is represented in Renner's design. Focusing on geometric shapes, Renner created a relevant typeface to reflect and describe the modern, instead of reviving past type designs. The typeface was an experiment in the new Modernist approach to typography, eliminating decoration and balancing the relationship between type and white space. Its pure and functional nature has ensured its continued success: Volkswagen use it in their advertising, and the commemorative plaque left on the moon by the Apollo 11 astronauts in 1969 is set in Futura. Its success stems from its timeless elegance and simplicity.

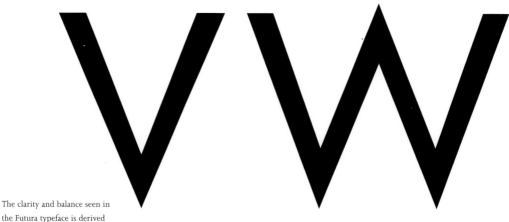

The clarity and balance seen in the Futura typeface is derived from the simple geometric forms upon which Renner based his design. Particularly in upper case, squares, triangles and near-perfect circles can be identified, carrying proportions similar to those of classical roman capitals.

LIGHT

Aa Bb Cc Dd Ee Ff Gg Hh Ii Jj Kk Ll Mm
Nn Oo Pp Qq Rr Ss Tt Uu Vv Ww Xx Yy Zz
0123456789 , . : ; / & ! ? £ $ *

BOOK

Aa Bb Cc Dd Ee Ff Gg Hh Ii Jj Kk Ll Mm
Nn Oo Pp Qq Rr Ss Tt Uu Vv Ww Xx Yy Zz
0123456789 , . : ; / & ! ? £ $ *

BOOK ITALIC

Aa Bb Cc Dd Ee Ff Gg Hh Ii Jj Kk Ll Mm
Nn Oo Pp Qq Rr Ss Tt Uu Vv Ww Xx Yy Zz
0123456789 , . : ; / & ! ? £ $ *

MEDIUM

Aa Bb Cc Dd Ee Ff Gg Hh Ii Jj Kk Ll Mm
Nn Oo Pp Qq Rr Ss Tt Uu Vv Ww Xx Yy Zz
0123456789 , . : ; / & ! ? £ $ *

BOLD

Aa Bb Cc Dd Ee Ff Gg Hh Ii Jj Kk Ll Mm
Nn Oo Pp Qq Rr Ss Tt Uu Vv Ww Xx Yy Zz
0123456789 , . : ; / & ! ? £ $ *

EXTRA BLACK

Aa Bb Cc Dd Ee Ff Gg Hh Ii Jj Kk Ll
Mm Nn Oo Pp Qq Rr Ss Tt Uu Vv Ww
Xx Yy Zz
0123456789 , . : ; / & ! ? £ $ *

LIGHT CONDENSED

Aa Bb Cc Dd Ee Ff Gg Hh Ii Jj Kk Ll
Mm Nn Oo Pp Qq Rr Ss Tt Uu Vv Ww Xx Yy Zz
0123456789 , . : ; / & ! ? £ $ *

garamond

Garamond is a Renaissance roman typeface, derived from the work of Claude Garamond, a highly regarded sixteenth century French typecutter. The venetian type of Aldus Manutius and the handwriting of Angelo Vergecio, a librarian to King Francis I, influenced Garamond's letterforms. In the early twentieth century, type foundries were keen to revive historical typefaces such as Garamond, and ATF, Lanston Monotype and British Monotype used surviving sixteenth century prints of Garamond to create their versions. In 1926, Beatrice Warde discovered that they had accidentally copied work by Garamond's associate Jannon, but by this time the name Garamond had stuck. Jan Tschichold designed Sabon as a historically accurate version of Garamond and named it after Garamond's pupil Jacques Sabon. In 1989, Robert Slimbach designed Adobe Garamond directly from an original set of Garamond's type specimens.

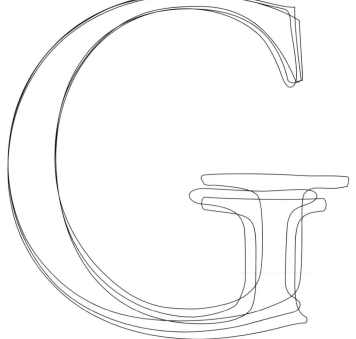

Garamond's roman letterforms convey a sense of fluidity and consistency, as seen in the downward slopes of its long extenders and top serifs. Some of the particular idiosyncrasies include the proportionately small bowl of the a, and the small eye of the e. Shown here is a comparison of form between various cuts (Truetype, Adobe Garamond Pro, and Garamond Premiere Pro).

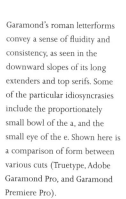

REGULAR

Aa Bb Cc Dd Ee Ff Gg Hh Ii Jj Kk Ll Mm
Nn Oo Pp Qq Rr Ss Tt Uu Vv Ww Xx Yy Zz
0123456789 , . : ; / & ! ? £ $ *

ITALIC

Aa Bb Cc Dd Ee Ff Gg Hh Ii Jj Kk Ll Mm
Nn Oo Pp Qq Rr Ss Tt Uu Vv Ww Xx Yy Zz
*0123456789 , . : ; / & ! ? £ $ **

SEMIBOLD

Aa Bb Cc Dd Ee Ff Gg Hh Ii Jj Kk Ll Mm
Nn Oo Pp Qq Rr Ss Tt Uu Vv Ww Xx Yy Zz
0123456789 , . : ; / & ! ? £ $ *

SEMIBOLD ITALIC

Aa Bb Cc Dd Ee Ff Gg Hh Ii Jj Kk Ll Mm
Nn Oo Pp Qq Rr Ss Tt Uu Vv Ww Xx Yy Zz
0123456789 , . : ; / & ! ? £ $ *

BOLD

Aa Bb Cc Dd Ee Ff Gg Hh Ii Jj Kk Ll Mm
Nn Oo Pp Qq Rr Ss Tt Uu Vv Ww Xx Yy Zz
0123456789 , . : ; / & ! ? £ $ *

BOLD ITALIC

Aa Bb Cc Dd Ee Ff Gg Hh Ii Jj Kk Ll Mm
Nn Oo Pp Qq Rr Ss Tt Uu Vv Ww Xx Yy Zz
0123456789 , . : ; / & ! ? £ $ *

gill

Gill Sans was the first typeface designed by Eric Gill for Monotype. Inspired by Edward Johnston's London Underground typeface, it was designed to compete with Futura and other German sans serifs. Gill Sans was designed with legibility at both large and small sizes in mind, and while German sans serifs have an exaggerated x height to enhance legibility, Gill Sans maintains its legibility with a smaller x height because it is based on roman letterforms, not geometric shapes. Released in 1928, it was immediately successful and is seen as a quintessentially British typeface: it was used extensively by the LNER railway company until nationalisation in 1948, and British Rail then used Gill until 1965. Penguin Books used Gill Sans for the covers of their now classic pocket paperbacks from 1935 onwards, and it has been used for much of the BBC's on-air graphics since 1997.

The capital m of Gill Sans is based on the proportions of a square, with the middle strokes meeting at its centre. With its Carolingian influences, Gill retains the two-storey form in the lower case a and g, unlike realist sans-serifs such as Univers. Its humanist form can also be seen in the vestigal calligraphic tail of the lower case p.

LIGHT

Aa Bb Cc Dd Ee Ff Gg Hh Ii Jj Kk Ll Mm
Nn Oo Pp Qq Rr Ss Tt Uu Vv Ww Xx Yy Zz
0123456789 , . : ; / & ! ? £ $ *

REGULAR

Aa Bb Cc Dd Ee Ff Gg Hh Ii Jj Kk Ll Mm
Nn Oo Pp Qq Rr Ss Tt Uu Vv Ww Xx Yy Zz
0123456789 , . : ; / & ! ? £ $ *

ITALIC

*Aa Bb Cc Dd Ee Ff Gg Hh Ii Jj Kk Ll Mm
Nn Oo Pp Qq Rr Ss Tt Uu Vv Ww Xx Yy Zz
0123456789 , . : ; / & ! ? £ $ **

BOLD

**Aa Bb Cc Dd Ee Ff Gg Hh Ii Jj Kk Ll Mm
Nn Oo Pp Qq Rr Ss Tt Uu Vv Ww Xx Yy Zz
0123456789 , . : ; / & ! ? £ $ ***

EXTRA BOLD

**Aa Bb Cc Dd Ee Ff Gg Hh Ii Jj Kk Ll
Mm Nn Oo Pp Qq Rr Ss Tt Uu Vv Ww
Xx Yy Zz
0123456789 , . : ; / & ! ? £ $ ***

LIGHT SHADOWED

Aa Bb Cc Dd Ee Ff Gg Hh Ii Jj Kk Ll Mm
Nn Oo Pp Qq Rr Ss Tt Uu Vv Ww Xx Yy Zz
0123456789 , . : ; / & ! ? £ $ *

SHADOWED

A B C D E F G H I J K L M N O P Q R S T U V
W X Y Z
0123456789 , . : ; / & ! ? £ $ *

gotham

Hoefler and Frere-Jones designed this typeface in 2000, and it has already become a staple classic for any discerning graphic designer. Inspired by American vernacular lettering, the designers undertook a research project of architectural type. Between the 1930s and 60s and before the era of the graphic designer, many businesses used

engineers or draftsmen to design their signs. For these draftsmen, uniform strokes when laying out type was of utmost importance, paying less attention to style than to consistency. As such, Gotham is a typeface that has a strong geometric base, yet a humanistic quality that comes from its common reference points. It has recently

been used for the cornerstone of the Freedom Tower on the site of the World Trade Centre and for Barack Obama's 2008 presidential campaign in America.

Gotham's generous x height and simple geometric forms make the characters exceptionally legible at small sizes
Gotham's generous x height and simple geometric forms make the characters exceptionally legible at small sizes
Gotham's generous x height and simple geometric forms make the characters exceptionally legible at small sizes
Gotham's generous x height and simple geometric forms make the characters exceptionally legible at small sizes
Gotham's generous x height and simple geometric forms make the characters exceptionally legible at small sizes
Gotham's generous x height and simple geometric forms make the characters exceptionally legible at small sizes
Gotham's generous x height and simple geometric forms make the characters exceptionally legible at small sizes
Gotham's generous x height and simple geometric forms make the characters exceptionally legible at small sizes
Gotham's generous x height and simple geometric forms make the characters exceptionally legible at small sizes
Gotham's generous x height and simple geometric forms make the characters exceptionally legible at small sizes
Gotham's generous x height and simple geometric forms make the characters exceptionally legible at small sizes
Gotham's generous x height and simple geometric forms make the characters exceptionally legible at small sizes
Gotham's generous x height and simple geometric forms make the characters exceptionally legible at small sizes
Gotham's generous x height and simple geometric forms make the characters exceptionally legible at small sizes
Gotham's generous x height and simple geometric forms make the characters exceptionally legible at small sizes
Gotham's generous x height and simple geometric forms make the characters exceptionally legible at small sizes
Gotham's generous x height and simple geometric forms make the characters exceptionally legible at small sizes
Gotham's generous x height and simple geometric forms make the characters exceptionally legible at sma
Gotham's generous x height and simple geometric forms make the characters exceptionally legible at sm
Gotham's generous x height and simple geometric forms make the characters exceptionally leg
Gotham's generous x height and simple geometric forms make the characters exceptionally le
Gotham's generous x height and simple geometric forms make the characters exceptionally l
Gotham's generous x height and simple geometric forms make the characters excepti
Gotham's generous x height and simple geometric forms make the characters excep

Gotham is characterised by unmannered forms and a generous x height, making it exceptionally readable at small sizes. Its geometric foundation means that it transfers well into extra light, italic and condensed forms.

LIGHT

Aa Bb Cc Dd Ee Ff Gg Hh Ii Jj Kk Ll
Mm Nn Oo Pp Qq Rr Ss Tt Uu Vv Ww
Xx Yy Zz
0123456789 , . : ; / & ! ? £ $ *

ITALIC

Aa Bb Cc Dd Ee Ff Gg Hh Ii Jj Kk Ll
Mm Nn Oo Pp Qq Rr Ss Tt Uu Vv Ww
Xx Yy Zz
*0123456789 , . : ; / & ! ? £ $ ***

BOOK

Aa Bb Cc Dd Ee Ff Gg Hh Ii Jj Kk Ll
Mm Nn Oo Pp Qq Rr Ss Tt Uu Vv Ww
Xx Yy Zz
0123456789 , . : ; / & ! ? £ $ *

BOOK ITALIC

Aa Bb Cc Dd Ee Ff Gg Hh Ii Jj Kk Ll
Mm Nn Oo Pp Qq Rr Ss Tt Uu Vv Ww
Xx Yy Zz
*0123456789 , . : ; / & ! ? £ $ ***

MEDIUM

Aa Bb Cc Dd Ee Ff Gg Hh Ii Jj Kk Ll
Mm Nn Oo Pp Qq Rr Ss Tt Uu Vv Ww
Xx Yy Zz
0123456789 , . : ; / & ! ? £ $ *

izes
sizes
ll sizes
all sizes
e at small sizes
le at small sizes
ible at small sizes

BOLD

Aa Bb Cc Dd Ee Ff Gg Hh Ii Jj Kk Ll
Mm Nn Oo Pp Qq Rr Ss Tt Uu Vv Ww
Xx Yy Zz
0123456789 , . : ; / & ! ? £ $ *

helvetica

Helvetica was designed by Max Miedinger and Edouard Hoffmann for the Haas Type Foundry in Münchenstein, Switzerland during 1957. Originally called Neue Haas Grotesk, it was commissioned as a rival to the popular Akzidenz-Grotesk and was based upon Schelter Grotesk, a sans serif by Schelter and Giesecke.

Helvetica's distinctive neutrality and crispness is exemplary of Swiss graphic design which advocated anonymous visual communication and the rationality of grid-structured design. Helvetica's success has continued in the digital age, with use across Apple Inc iPod and iPhone products. Its proliferation within visual culture sees

no sign of slowing; Gary Hustwit's film *Helvetica* explores our love/hate relationship with the worlds most famous typeface and Lars Muller's 2002 book *Helvetica: Homage to a Typeface* explores how often Helvetica is used in public space.

Helvetica is drawn on a rationalist axis, similar to its contemporaries Folio, Swiss 721 and Univers. Other neo-grotesque fonts, such as Arial and Gotham, share similar characteristics. The illustration to the right shows the subtle differences between each font: Arial Regular, Folio Light, Gotham Book, Swiss 721 Light and Helvetica Light.

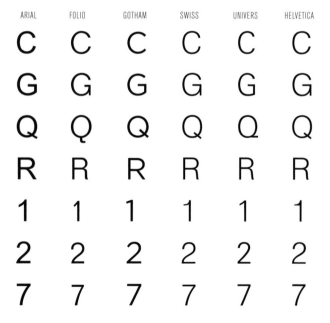

ARIAL	FOLIO	GOTHAM	SWISS	UNIVERS	HELVETICA
C	C	C	C	C	C
G	G	G	G	G	G
Q	Q	Q	Q	Q	Q
R	R	R	R	R	R
1	1	1	1	1	1
2	2	2	2	2	2
7	7	7	7	7	7

LIGHT

Aa Bb Cc Dd Ee Ff Gg Hh Ii Jj Kk Ll Mm
Nn Oo Pp Qq Rr Ss Tt Uu Vv Ww Xx Yy Zz
0123456789 , . : ; / & ! ? £ $ *

MEDIUM

Aa Bb Cc Dd Ee Ff Gg Hh Ii Jj Kk Ll Mm
Nn Oo Pp Qq Rr Ss Tt Uu Vv Ww Xx Yy Zz
0123456789 , . : ; / & ! ? £ $ *

OBLIQUE

*Aa Bb Cc Dd Ee Ff Gg Hh Ii Jj Kk Ll Mm
Nn Oo Pp Qq Rr Ss Tt Uu Vv Ww Xx Yy Zz
0123456789 , . : ; / & ! ? £ $ *

BOLD

**Aa Bb Cc Dd Ee Ff Gg Hh Ii Jj Kk Ll Mm
Nn Oo Pp Qq Rr Ss Tt Uu Vv Ww Xx Yy Zz
0123456789 , . : ; / & ! ? $ % ***

BLACK

**Aa Bb Cc Dd Ee Ff Gg Hh Ii Jj Kk
Ll Mm Nn Oo Pp Qq Rr Ss Tt Uu Vv
Ww Xx Yy Zz
0123456789 , . : ; / & ! ? £ $ ***

LIGHT CONDENSED

Aa Bb Cc Dd Ee Ff Gg Hh Ii Jj Kk Ll Mm
Nn Oo Pp Qq Rr Ss Tt Uu Vv Ww Xx Yy Zz
0123456789 , . : ; / & ! ? £ $ *

MEDIUM CONDENSED

Aa Bb Cc Dd Ee Ff Gg Hh Ii Jj Kk Ll Mm
Nn Oo Pp Qq Rr Ss Tt Uu Vv Ww Xx Yy Zz
0123456789 , . : ; / & ! ? £ $ *

interstate

Interstate was developed by Tobias Frere-Jones between 1993 and 1994 for Font Bureau. It is based on the official signage alphabet Highway Gothic, used for road signs by the United States Federal Highway Administration. Frere-Jones often takes inspiration from his surroundings, preserving the emotive nature of found vernacular type and giving it prolonged life through his designs. Interstate is a sans serif font with a steady and continuous stroke, with open and balanced counters to increase legibility. Unlike Highway Gothic, Interstate can be used for extended text as well as display faces: Frere-Jones adapted the font to conserve space when setting text and to create an even tone when set in a block. With its clean and simple appearance it is frequently used for corporate identity.

STUART HIGHWAY

Alice Springs	**10**
Tennant Creek	**516**
Darwin	**1502**

Interstate was originally conceived as a display face, yet refinements have made it an ideal font for setting extended text. The terminals are short and cut towards the direction of the stroke (see l, p, k) unless on a curve, where they end at a 90 degree angle to the stroke.

LIGHT

Aa Bb Cc Dd Ee Ff Gg Hh Ii Jj Kk Ll Mm
Nn Oo Pp Qq Rr Ss Tt Uu Vv Ww Xx Yy Zz
0123456789 , . : ; / & ! ? £ $ *

REGULAR

Aa Bb Cc Dd Ee Ff Gg Hh Ii Jj Kk Ll Mm
Nn Oo Pp Qq Rr Ss Tt Uu Vv Ww Xx Yy Zz
0123456789 , . : ; / & ! ? £ $ *

BOLD

Aa Bb Cc Dd Ee Ff Gg Hh Ii Jj Kk Ll Mm
Nn Oo Pp Qq Rr Ss Tt Uu Vv Ww Xx Yy Zz
0123456789 , . : ; / & ! ? £ $ *

BLACK

Aa Bb Cc Dd Ee Ff Gg Hh Ii Jj Kk Ll Mm
Nn Oo Pp Qq Rr Ss Tt Uu Vv Ww Xx Yy Zz
0123456789 , . : ; / & ! ? £ $ *

LIGHT CONDENSED

Aa Bb Cc Dd Ee Ff Gg Hh Ii Jj Kk Ll Mm
Nn Oo Pp Qq Rr Ss Tt Uu Vv Ww Xx Yy Zz
0123456789 , . : ; / & ! ? £ $ *

REGULAR CONDENSED

Aa Bb Cc Dd Ee Ff Gg Hh Ii Jj Kk Ll Mm
Nn Oo Pp Qq Rr Ss Tt Uu Vv Ww Xx Yy Zz
0123456789 , . : ; / & ! ? £ $ *

REGULAR CONDENSED ITALIC

*Aa Bb Cc Dd Ee Ff Gg Hh Ii Jj Kk Ll Mm
Nn Oo Pp Qq Rr Ss Tt Uu Vv Ww Xx Yy Zz
0123456789 , . : ; / & ! ? £ $ **

joanna

Joanna was designed in 1930 by Eric Gill and the first cut made by the Caslon foundry in 1931 for hand setting. Originally intended for sole use in Gill's printing shop as a straighforward body-text type, it was not until 1937 that Monotype licensed Joanna and its italic for the first time. A transitional typeface, Joanna combines old style roman letterforms with distinctly modern sharp squared serifs. With calligraphic influences, Joanna retains a humanist axis that reveals a quiet elegance. Gill was inspired by the work of French renaissance typecutter Robert Granjon, a contemporary of Claude Garamond, who was seen as one of the greatest typecutters in history.

The italic of Joanna is distinctively narrower than its roman counterpart and is sloped at only three degrees, appearing almost vertical on the page.

Blue Quartz

The ascenders on Joanna are taller than the cap height, making the typeface elegant yet understated. The serifs are sharp and square, similar to the romantic typeface Bodoni, yet they have a humanist axis showing a calligraphic hand.

REGULAR

Aa Bb Cc Dd Ee Ff Gg Hh Ii Jj Kk Ll Mm
Nn Oo Pp Qq Rr Ss Tt Uu Vv Ww Xx Yy Zz
0123456789 , . : ; / & ! ? £ $ *

ITALIC

Aa Bb Cc Dd Ee Ff Gg Hh Ii Jj Kk Ll Mm
Nn Oo Pp Qq Rr Ss Tt Uu Vv Ww Xx Yy Zz
0123456789 , . : ; / & ! ? £ $ *

SEMI BOLD

Aa Bb Cc Dd Ee Ff Gg Hh Ii Jj Kk Ll Mm
Nn Oo Pp Qq Rr Ss Tt Uu Vv Ww Xx Yy Zz
0123456789 , . : ; / & ! ? £ $ *

SEMIBOLD ITALIC

Aa Bb Cc Dd Ee Ff Gg Hh Ii Jj Kk Ll Mm
Nn Oo Pp Qq Rr Ss Tt Uu Vv Ww Xx Yy Zz
0123456789 , . : ; / & ! ? £ $ *

BOLD

Aa Bb Cc Dd Ee Ff Gg Hh Ii Jj Kk Ll Mm
Nn Oo Pp Qq Rr Ss Tt Uu Vv Ww Xx Yy Zz
0123456789 , . : ; / & ! ? £ $ *

BOLD ITALIC

Aa Bb Cc Dd Ee Ff Gg Hh Ii Jj Kk Ll Mm
Nn Oo Pp Qq Rr Ss Tt Uu Vv Ww Xx Yy Zz
0123456789 , . : ; / & ! ? £ $ *

EXTRA BOLD

Aa Bb Cc Dd Ee Ff Gg Hh Ii Jj Kk Ll Mm
Nn Oo Pp Qq Rr Ss Tt Uu Vv Ww Xx Yy Zz
0123456789 , . : ; / & ! ? £ $ *

johnston

In 1913, London Transport commissioned calligrapher Edward Johnston to design a new typeface for the whole of London's transport network. Johnston drew upon his knowledge of roman square capitals to create easily legible capital letters with a consistent stroke and little contrast. The lower case letters are influenced by humanist minuscule script, the handwriting of scribes in southern Europe in the late 1400s. Punctuation and the dots above i and j are square diamonds, which makes Johnston easily distinguishable from his apprentice Eric Gill's typeface, Gill Sans. Johnston incorporated these elements with a geometric draftmanship, foreshadowing the Modernist typefaces to be produced in Germany in the 1920s. Johnston's Railway Type was issued on all London Transport ephemera from 1916 onwards, with three new weights added in 1979.

A defining feature of Johnson is its diamond shaped tittles used above i, j and for punctuation marks. Edward Johnston was an expert calligrapher and the diamond shaped dots are drawn with a broad nibbed pen, showing his influences and approach to typography. The diamonds are also absent from Gill Sans, created by Johnson's apprentice Eric Gill.

LIGHT

Aa Bb Cc Dd Ee Ff Gg Hh Ii Jj Kk Ll Mm
Nn Oo Pp Qq Rr Ss Tt Uu Vv Ww Xx Yy Zz
0123456789 , . : ; / & ! ? £ $ *

LIGHT ITALIC

*Aa Bb Cc Dd Ee Ff Gg Hh Ii Jj Kk Ll Mm
Nn Oo Pp Qq Rr Ss Tt Uu Vv Ww Xx Yy Zz
0123456789 , . : ; / & ! ? £ $ **

BOOK

Aa Bb Cc Dd Ee Ff Gg Hh Ii Jj Kk Ll Mm
Nn Oo Pp Qq Rr Ss Tt Uu Vv Ww Xx Yy Zz
0123456789 , . : ; / & ! ? £ $*

BOOK ITALIC

*Aa Bb Cc Dd Ee Ff Gg Hh Ii Jj Kk Ll Mm
Nn Oo Pp Qq Rr Ss Tt Uu Vv Ww Xx Yy Zz
0123456789 , . : ; / & ! ? £ $ **

MEDIUM

**Aa Bb Cc Dd Ee Ff Gg Hh Ii Jj Kk Ll Mm
Nn Oo Pp Qq Rr Ss Tt Uu Vv Ww Xx Yy Zz
0123456789 , . : ; / & ! ? £ $ ***

MEDIUM ITALIC

***Aa Bb Cc Dd Ee Ff Gg Hh Ii Jj Kk Ll Mm
Nn Oo Pp Qq Rr Ss Tt Uu Vv Ww Xx Yy Zz
0123456789 , . : ; / & ! ? £ $ ****

BOLD

**Aa Bb Cc Dd Ee Ff Gg Hh Ii Jj Kk Ll Mm
Nn Oo Pp Qq Rr Ss Tt Uu Vv Ww Xx Yy Zz
0123456789 , . : ; / & ! ? £ $ ***

knockout

The 1994 Knockout is a huge type family, consisting of 32 sans serifs in nine widths and four weights. Designers Jonathan Hoefler and Tobias Frere-Jones took their inspiration from late eighteenth century American vernacular typefaces designed before the introduction of the American Type Founders Company (ATF). At this time, sans serifs were produced in a makeshift manner in order to fulfill specific needs, with woodcuts created anonymously. It was the Modernist typographers who introduced the type 'family', where roman, italics, boldfaces and ornaments all relate to one another. Knockout combines these two ideologies: it appears to be a well organised family, yet each weight and width has its own particularities. Knockout has many separate voices within a single set, which leads to a much larger variety of possible designs and combinations.

KA-POWWWW

Knockout has the appearance of traditional woodcut letterforms, referring to America's own history of type and printing. By mixing the different widths and weights of Knockout you can create a unique voice and appearance on the page. The unusual idiosyncrasies of each letterform are also present in the lower case forms.

46 FLYWEIGHT

Aa Bb Cc Dd Ee Ff Gg Hh Ii Jj Kk Ll Mm
Nn Oo Pp Qq Rr Ss Tt Uu Vv Ww Xx Yy Zz
0123456789 , . : ; / & ! ? £ $ *

47 BANTAMWEIGHT

Aa Bb Cc Dd Ee Ff Gg Hh Ii Jj Kk Ll Mm
Nn Oo Pp Qq Rr Ss Tt Uu Vv Ww Xx Yy Zz
0123456789 , . : ; / & ! ? £ $ *

48 FEATHERWEIGHT

Aa Bb Cc Dd Ee Ff Gg Hh Ii Jj Kk Ll Mm
Nn Oo Pp Qq Rr Ss Tt Uu Vv Ww Xx Yy Zz
0123456789 , . : ; / & ! ? £ $ *

49 LITEWEIGHT

Aa Bb Cc Dd Ee Ff Gg Hh Ii Jj Kk Ll Mm
Nn Oo Pp Qq Rr Ss Tt Uu Vv Ww Xx Yy Zz
0123456789 , . : ; / & ! ? £ $ *

50 WELTERWEIGHT

Aa Bb Cc Dd Ee Ff Gg Hh Ii Jj Kk Ll Mm
Nn Oo Pp Qq Rr Ss Tt Uu Vv Ww Xx Yy Zz
0123456789 , . : ; / & ! ? £ $ *

72 FULL CRUISERWEIGHT

Aa Bb Cc Dd Ee Ff Gg Hh Ii Jj Kk Ll Mm
Nn Oo Pp Qq Rr Ss Tt Uu Vv Ww Xx Yy Zz
0123456789 , . : ; / & ! ? £ $ *

94 ULTIMATE SUMO

Aa Bb Cc Dd Ee Ff Gg Hh Ii Jj Kk Ll
Mm Nn Oo Pp Qq Rr Ss Tt Uu Vv
Ww Xx Yy Zz
0123456789 , . : ; / & ! ? £ $ *

lucida

Lucida Sans is part of the extended Lucida type family designed by Charles Bigelow and Kris Holmes in 1985. It is a humanist sans serif, influenced by traditional roman letterforms. With strong clear strokes and generous proportions, it is highly legible at small sizes. Lucida Sans has a calligraphic element, looking almost hand-drawn, which gives it a relaxed rhythm. It has a large x height and open spacing creating a harmonious look on the page. What Lucida Sans lacks in character it makes up for in readability, making it a sucessful screen-based font.

Lucida has an extended type family designed specifically for screen display and low-resolution laser printers.

Opposite from the top:

Lucida Sans Demibold Roman, Lucida Blackletter, Lucida Bright, Lucida Handwriting, Lucida Calligraphy, Lucida Sans Typewriter, Lucida Fax.

a
ab
abc
abcd
abcde
abcdef
abcdefg
abcdefgh

REGULAR

Aa Bb Cc Dd Ee Ff Gg Hh Ii Jj Kk Ll Mm
Nn Oo Pp Qq Rr Ss Tt Uu Vv Ww Xx Yy Zz
0123456789 , . : ; / & ! ? £ $ *

ITALIC

*Aa Bb Cc Dd Ee Ff Gg Hh Ii Jj Kk Ll Mm
Nn Oo Pp Qq Rr Ss Tt Uu Vv Ww Xx Yy Zz
0123456789 , . : ; / & ! ? £ $ **

DEMIBOLD ROMAN

**Aa Bb Cc Dd Ee Ff Gg Hh Ii Jj Kk Ll
Mm Nn Oo Pp Qq Rr Ss Tt Uu Vv Ww
Xx Yy Zz
0123456789 , . : ; / & ! ? £ $ ***

DEMIBOLD ITALIC

***Aa Bb Cc Dd Ee Ff Gg Hh Ii Jj Kk Ll
Mm Nn Oo Pp Qq Rr Ss Tt Uu Vv Ww
Xx Yy Zz
0123456789 , . : ; / & ! ? £ $ ****

LUCIDA FAX

Aa Bb Cc Dd Ee Ff Gg Hh Ii Jj Kk Ll Mm
Nn Oo Pp Qq Rr Ss Tt Uu Vv Ww Xx Yy Zz
0123456789 , . : ; / & ! ? £ $ *

LUCIDA BRIGHT

Aa Bb Cc Dd Ee Ff Gg Hh Ii Jj Kk Ll Mm
Nn Oo Pp Qq Rr Ss Tt Uu Vv Ww Xx Yy Zz
0123456789 , . : ; / & ! ? £ $ *

LUCIDA BLACKLETTER

Aa Bb Cc Dd Ee Ff Gg Hh Ii Jj Kk Ll Mm Nn
Oo Pp Qq Rr Ss Tt Uu Vv Ww Xx Yy
Zz 0123456789 , . : ; / & ! ? £ $ *

matrix

Designed in 1984 by Zuzana Licko at the Emigre foundry, Matrix has become one of the most successful typefaces of recent times. Borne out of the restrictions imposed by the slow processing speeds of the earliest Macintosh computers, Licko created a typeface with the utmost simplicity of form, in order that it could withstand low-resolution printing. Licko's letterforms were therefore constructed from the fewest defining points possible, giving Matrix its distinctive geometric structure, including its unique triangular serifs. Its success as a headline and display face resulted from the fact that it retains its integrity even when stretched or obliqued. In 1992, it featured on the *Batman Returns* film merchandising, raising the profile of the typeface considerably. Since this first prominent unveiling, Matrix has been used in the corporate branding of several large multi-national corporations.

45 degree serifs require fewer points to define shapes, making economic use of memory space and resulting in faster printing.

forty
five

BOOK

Aa Bb Cc Dd Ee Ff Gg Hh Ii Jj Kk Ll Mm
Nn Oo Pp Qq Rr Ss Tt Uu Vv Ww Xx Yy Zz
0123456789 , . : ; / & ! ? £ $ *

REGULAR

Aa Bb Cc Dd Ee Ff Gg Hh Ii Jj Kk Ll Mm
Nn Oo Pp Qq Rr Ss Tt Uu Vv Ww Xx Yy Zz
0123456789 , . : ; / & ! ? £ $ *

REGULAR SCRIPT

*Aa Bb Cc Dd Ee Ff Gg Hh Ii Jj Kk Ll Mm
Nn Oo Pp Qq Rr Ss Tt Uu Vv Ww Xx Yy Zz
0123456789 , . : ; / & ! ? £ $ *

BOLD

**Aa Bb Cc Dd Ee Ff Gg Hh Ii Jj Kk Ll Mm
Nn Oo Pp Qq Rr Ss Tt Uu Vv Ww Xx Yy Zz
0123456789 , . : ; / & ! ? £ $ ***

EXTRA BOLD

**Aa Bb Cc Dd Ee Ff Gg Hh Ii Jj Kk Ll Mm
Nn Oo Pp Qq Rr Ss Tt Uu Vv Ww Xx Yy Zz
0123456789 , . : ; / & ! ? £ $ ***

EXTRA BOLD INLINE

**Aa Bb Cc Dd Ee Ff Gg Hh Ii Jj Kk Ll Mm Nn Oo Pp
Qq Rr Ss Tt Uu Vv Ww Xx Yy Zz
0123456789 , . : ; / & ! ? £ $ ***

REGULAR SMALL CAPS

Aa Bb Cc Dd Ee Ff Gg Hh Ii Jj Kk Ll Mm
Nn Oo Pp Qq Rr Ss Tt Uu Vv Ww Xx Yy Zz
0123456789 , . : ; / & ! ? 3 $

meta

The German graphic designer and founder of the FontShop Erik Spiekermann created Meta in 1984. It was intended to be the corporate typeface for Deutsche Bundespost but the face was not accepted and the entire project was cancelled. In 1989, it was resurrected by Just van Rossum, giving the typeface three digitised styles. Because it was meant to be easily read from any angle and in smaller point sizes, Meta has a humanist appearance and a sans serif typeface. This gives the overall structure a more organic effect. The typeface has been extremely popular, and has been appropriated by a wide variety of young designers, which is why Meta is often described as the font of the 1990s.

1984

Meta is designed for legibility, with large x heights and a clean, crisp even stroke. The ascenders are curved at the terminals to suggest further height. Meta is a sans serif but has a humanist appearance—as seen here on the number 8 where the stroke follows the pattern of brush.

NORMAL ROMAN

Aa Bb Cc Dd Ee Ff Gg Hh Ii Jj Kk Ll Mm
Nn Oo Pp Qq Rr Ss Tt Uu Vv Ww Xx Yy Zz
0123456789 , . : ; / & ! ? £ $ *

NORMAL ITALIC

Aa Bb Cc Dd Ee Ff Gg Hh Ii Jj Kk Ll Mm
Nn Oo Pp Qq Rr Ss Tt Uu Vv Ww Xx Yy Zz
*0123456789 , . : ; / & ! ? £ $ **

NORMAL CAPS

Aa Bb Cc Dd Ee Ff Gg Hh Ii Jj Kk Ll Mm
Nn Oo Pp Qq Rr Ss Tt Uu Vv Ww Xx Yy Zz
0123456789 , . : ; / & ! ? £ $ *

BOLD ROMAN

Aa Bb Cc Dd Ee Ff Gg Hh Ii Jj Kk Ll Mm
Nn Oo Pp Qq Rr Ss Tt Uu Vv Ww Xx Yy Zz
0123456789 , . : ; / & ! ? £ $ *

BOLD ITALIC

Aa Bb Cc Dd Ee Ff Gg Hh Ii Jj Kk Ll Mm
Nn Oo Pp Qq Rr Ss Tt Uu Vv Ww Xx Yy Zz
0123456789 , . : ; / & ! ? £ $ *

BOLD CAPS

Aa Bb Cc Dd Ee Ff Gg Hh Ii Jj Kk Ll Mm
Nn Oo Pp Qq Rr Ss Tt Uu Vv Ww Xx Yy Zz
0123456789 , . : ; / & ! ? £ $ *

BLACK ROMAN

Aa Bb Cc Dd Ee Ff Gg Hh Ii Jj Kk Ll Mm
Nn Oo Pp Qq Rr Ss Tt Uu Vv Ww Xx Yy Zz
0123456789 , . : ; / & ! ? £ $ *

mrs eaves

The Mrs Eaves typeface was designed by Zuzana Licko in 1996. A revival of the Baskerville typeface, Mrs Eaves can be seen as a transitional face, straddling traditional and contemporary styles. It is an homage to the forgotten women of typography, named after Sarah Ruston Eaves, who was initially John Baskerville's housekeeper, then lover and eventually wife, and who would often help with his work. Although Licko's Mrs Eaves was less academic than other revivals, it was based on contemporary methods of reproduction: it tries to imitate the unpredictability of form found in letterpress text. Licko wanted to retain the sense of openness and lightness seen in Baskerville whilst at the same time giving her own character to the letterforms. Mrs Eaves was used extensively for the first time in Issue 38 of *Emigre Magazine*.

five *fleckered* frogs

Like Baskerville, Mrs Eaves has a near vertical stress, departing from the old style model. Among its identifying characters is the lower case g with its open lower counter and swashlike ear, and the flowing swashlike tail of the roman and italic upper case q.

ROMAN

Aa Bb Cc Dd Ee Ff Gg Hh Ii Jj Kk Ll Mm
Nn Oo Pp Qq Rr Ss Tt Uu Vv Ww Xx Yy Zz
0123456789 , . : ; / & ! ? £ $ *

ITALIC

Aa Bb Cc Dd Ee Ff Gg Hh Ii Jj Kk Ll Mm
Nn Oo Pp Qq Rr Ss Tt Uu Vv Ww Xx Yy Zz
0123456789 , . : ; / & ! ? £ $ *

BOLD

Aa Bb Cc Dd Ee Ff Gg Hh Ii Jj Kk Ll Mm
Nn Oo Pp Qq Rr Ss Tt Uu Vv Ww Xx Yy Zz
0123456789 , . : ; / & ! ? £ $ *

SMALL CAPS

Aa Bb Cc Dd Ee Ff Gg Hh Ii Jj Kk Ll Mm
Nn Oo Pp Qq Rr Ss Tt Uu Vv Ww Xx Yy Zz
0123456789 , . : ; / & ! ? $ *

PETITE CAPS

Aa Bb Cc Dd Ee Ff Gg Hh Ii Jj Kk Ll Mm
Nn Oo Pp Qq Rr Ss Tt Uu Vv Ww Xx Yy Zz
0123456789 , . : ; / & ! ? $ *

FRACTIONS

↢↣A ↤B ©C ‡D ⚡E ↦F ¼G ½H ¾I ⅛J ⅜K ⅝L ⅞M
⅓N ⅔O ℗P ❄Q ®R ☼S ❋T ⇡U ffv fiw flx ffiy fflz
0123456789 , . : ; / ?

news gothic

Designed by Morris Fuller Benton in 1908, News Gothic is a realist sans-serif typeface manufactured by American Type Founders. The original design was essentially a lighter version of Franklin Gothic, also designed by Benton. Heavier versions were produced in later decades along with some condensed weights. In the late 1940s, after a decline in popularity due to the success of European sans serifs (including Gill Sans, Futura and Kabel), American Gothic typefaces made a comeback. It was during this time that more versions of News Gothic were designed, including News Gothic Bold, which Intertype released in 1955. Like Franklin Gothic, News Gothic is commonly used in advertising, packaging but also newspaper and magazine publishing.

Where Helvetica and Univers strive for geometric precision, News Gothic compromises to improve legibility by adding more humanistic features, such as letting the stroke taper on the curves and incorporating a calligraphic loop in the lower case g. News Gothic has a strong even stroke, designed to be robust under the stresses of high speed newspaper printing.

HIGH SP

REGULAR

Aa Bb Cc Dd Ee Ff Gg Hh Ii Jj Kk Ll Mm
Nn Oo Pp Qq Rr Ss Tt Uu Vv Ww Xx Yy Zz
0123456789 , . : ; / & ! ? £ $ *

OBLIQUE

Aa Bb Cc Dd Ee Ff Gg Hh Ii Jj Kk Ll Mm
Nn Oo Pp Qq Rr Ss Tt Uu Vv Ww Xx Yy Zz
*0123456789 , . : ; / & ! ? £ $ *

BOLD

Aa Bb Cc Dd Ee Ff Gg Hh Ii Jj Kk Ll Mm
Nn Oo Pp Qq Rr Ss Tt Uu Vv Ww Xx Yy Zz
0123456789 , . : ; / & ! ? £ $ *

BOLD OBLIQUE

Aa Bb Cc Dd Ee Ff Gg Hh Ii Jj Kk Ll Mm
Nn Oo Pp Qq Rr Ss Tt Uu Vv Ww Xx Yy Zz
***0123456789 , . : ; / & ! ? £ $ ***

officina

Officina Serif is a geometric postmodern face, seen in its artificial, asymmetrical form. Erik Spiekermann and Just van Rossum designed Officina Serif for the International Typeface Corporation in 1990. It was meant to convey the step from typewriter type to more contemporary typographic design. The plain, narrow, yet robust appearance of

Officina Serif is not only able to cope with rough printing conditions, it is designed to improve considerably along with increased mechanical standards. In practical terms, this means that the typeface is not easily distorted. The idea was to create a typeface for the digital office printer that evoked the immediacy of the strike-on effect of the

traditional typewriter face. Spiekermann is also the designer of the Meta family.

Designed as an alternative typewriter font to Courier, Officina is seen as a more contemporary and relevant typeface than its predecessor. It has a heavier stroke, reminiscent of the strike-on typewriter, yet it was designed for the digital office printer. The heavy oversized dots and tight contrast between strokes makes Officina highly legible at small sizes, while also functioning as a dynamic display face at larger sizes.

BOOK

Aa Bb Cc Dd Ee Ff Gg Hh Ii Jj Kk Ll Mm
Nn Oo Pp Qq Rr Ss Tt Uu Vv Ww Xx Yy Zz
0123456789 , . : ; / & ! ? £ $ *

BOOK ITALIC

Aa Bb Cc Dd Ee Ff Gg Hh Ii Jj Kk Ll Mm
Nn Oo Pp Qq Rr Ss Tt Uu Vv Ww Xx Yy Zz
*0123456789 , . : ; / & ! ? £ $ ***

BOLD

Aa Bb Cc Dd Ee Ff Gg Hh Ii Jj Kk Ll Mm
Nn Oo Pp Qq Rr Ss Tt Uu Vv Ww Xx Yy Zz
0123456789 , . : ; / & ! ? £ $ *

BOLD ITALIC

Aa Bb Cc Dd Ee Ff Gg Hh Ii Jj Kk Ll Mm
Nn Oo Pp Qq Rr Ss Tt Uu Vv Ww Xx Yy Zz
***0123456789 , . : ; / & ! ? £ $ ***

SANS BOOK

Aa Bb Cc Dd Ee Ff Gg Hh Ii Jj Kk Ll Mm
Nn Oo Pp Qq Rr Ss Tt Uu Vv Ww Xx Yy Zz
0123456789 , . : ; / & ! ? £ $ *

SANS BOOK BOLD

Aa Bb Cc Dd Ee Ff Gg Hh Ii Jj Kk Ll Mm
Nn Oo Pp Qq Rr Ss Tt Uu Vv Ww Xx Yy Zz
0123456789 , . : ; / & ! ? £ $ *

SANS BOOK ITALIC

Aa Bb Cc Dd Ee Ff Gg Hh Ii Jj Kk Ll Mm
Nn Oo Pp Qq Rr Ss Tt Uu Vv Ww Xx Yy Zz
*0123456789 , . : ; / & ! ? £ $ ***

optima

Released in 1958 by the D Stempel AG foundry in Frankfurt and designed by Hermann Zapf, Optima has remained a classic, contemporary-looking font since its creation 50 years ago. It can generally be described as a humanist sans serif, although its italic variant is more typical of a realist face such as Helvetica, as it is in essence a sloped roman rather than true italic. Unusually again for a sans serif, Zapf's design includes classic Imperial Roman-style capital letterforms. Optima has enjoyed widespread success, particularly for signage purposes, as it remains highly effective at larger sizes. Its simple lines and even weighting make it an attractive choice for applications that favour functionality over aesthetics. For example, Optima was used to engrave the names on the Vietnam Veterans Memorial, in Washington, DC

As a humanist typeface, Optima has a fine brushstroke quality with a moderated stroke which tapers outwards at the terminals instead of having a serif. Similar in its construction to many humanist sans serifs, Optima bridges the gap between serif and sans serif as its defined moderated stroke is unusual for a sans serif typeface.

optima's *fine*

REGULAR

Aa Bb Cc Dd Ee Ff Gg Hh Ii Jj Kk Ll Mm
Nn Oo Pp Qq Rr Ss Tt Uu Vv Ww Xx Yy Zz
0123456789 , . : ; / & ! ? £ $ *

ITALIC

*Aa Bb Cc Dd Ee Ff Gg Hh Ii Jj Kk Ll Mm
Nn Oo Pp Qq Rr Ss Tt Uu Vv Ww Xx Yy Zz
0123456789 , . : ; / & ! ? £ $ **

BOLD

**Aa Bb Cc Dd Ee Ff Gg Hh Ii Jj Kk Ll Mm
Nn Oo Pp Qq Rr Ss Tt Uu Vv Ww Xx Yy Zz
0123456789 , . : ; / & ! ? £ $ ***

BOLD ITALIC

***Aa Bb Cc Dd Ee Ff Gg Hh Ii Jj Kk Ll Mm
Nn Oo Pp Qq Rr Ss Tt Uu Vv Ww Xx Yy Zz
0123456789 , . : ; / & ! ? £ $ ****

EXTRA BLACK

**Aa Bb Cc Dd Ee Ff Gg Hh Ii Jj Kk Ll
Mm Nn Oo Pp Qq Rr Ss Tt Uu Vv Ww
Xx Yy Zz
0123456789 , . : ; / & ! ? £ $ ***

brushstrokes

perpetua

Perpetua is a serif typeface designed by Eric Gill and issued by the Monotype foundry in 1925.

Though not designed in the same era as Baskerville, Perpetua can be classified alongside transitional typefaces because of its visual characteristics such as high stroke contrast and bracketed serifs, and reflects the distinct personality of Eric Gill's letterforms. It was developed based on some of the classic proportions and characteristics of the Trajan column. The miniscule letters of the face were designed to be in complete harmony with the majuscule Trajan influenced forms.

In 1929, Perpetua was used in a limited edition of the book *The Passion of Perpetua and Felicity*, and it is also used in the Artemis Fowl series of children's books.

The italic of Perpetua has a strong calligraphic stroke, particularly evident on the upper case b, d, p and r and the tail of q. The lower case g is reminiscent of an upside down majuscule b. The upper case letterforms are based upon the capitalis monumentalis found on Trajan's column in Rome, appearing as well-proportioned square capitals.

REGULAR

Aa Bb Cc Dd Ee Ff Gg Hh Ii Jj Kk Ll Mm
Nn Oo Pp Qq Rr Ss Tt Uu Vv Ww Xx Yy Zz
0123456789 , . : ; / & ! ? £ $ *

ITALIC

Aa Bb Cc Dd Ee Ff Gg Hh Ii Jj Kk Ll Mm
Nn Oo Pp Qq Rr Ss Tt Uu Vv Ww Xx Yy Zz
*0123456789 , . : ; / & ! ? £ $ **

BOLD

Aa Bb Cc Dd Ee Ff Gg Hh Ii Jj Kk Ll Mm
Nn Oo Pp Qq Rr Ss Tt Uu Vv Ww Xx Yy Zz
0123456789 , . : ; / & ! ? £ $ *

BOLD ITALIC

Aa Bb Cc Dd Ee Ff Gg Hh Ii Jj Kk Ll Mm
Nn Oo Pp Qq Rr Ss Tt Uu Vv Ww Xx Yy Zz
0123456789 , . : ; / & ! ? £ $ *

TITLING LIGHT

A B C D E F G H I J K L M N O P
Q R S T U V W X Y Z
0123456789 , . : ; / & ! ? £ $ *

TITLING BOLD

A B C D E F G H I J K L M N O P
Q R S T U V W X Y Z
0123456789 , . : ; / & ! ? £ $ *

quadraat

Dutch designer Fred Smeijers designed FF Quadraat in 1992, and named the typeface after the Quadraat studio design group in Arnhem, which Smeijers co-founded in 1985. Licensed by the FontShop International's FontFont type library, Quadraat was Smiejer's first released typeface and was created without historical model or precedent.

An original serif typeface, Smeijers later followed the design with a sans variant, and expanded Quadraat with compatible sans and serif sub-families. Smeijers established the OurType type publishing label in 2002, releasing several other notable fonts, including OurType Arnhem and OurType Fresco.

Quadraat has a strong calligraphic quality, similar to Renaissance Italian humanistic script, which is particularly evident on the lower case e and top serifs on b and d. On the other hand, the italic has curves that are slightly angular, referencing its digital means of production.

abcdefi

abcdefi

koqrtwy

koqrtwy

REGULAR

Aa Bb Cc Dd Ee Ff Gg Hh Ii Jj Kk Ll Mm
Nn Oo Pp Qq Rr Ss Tt Uu Vv Ww Xx Yy Zz
0123456789 , . : ; / & ! ? £ $ *

ITALIC

Aa Bb Cc Dd Ee Ff Gg Hh Ii Jj Kk Ll Mm
Nn Oo Pp Qq Rr Ss Tt Uu Vv Ww Xx Yy Zz
0123456789 , . : ; / & ! ? £ $ *

BOLD

**Aa Bb Cc Dd Ee Ff Gg Hh Ii Jj Kk Ll Mm
Nn Oo Pp Qq Rr Ss Tt Uu Vv Ww Xx Yy Zz
0123456789 , . : ; / & ! ? £ $ ★**

SMALL CAPS

Aa Bb Cc Dd Ee Ff Gg Hh Ii Jj Kk Ll Mm
Nn Oo Pp Qq Rr Ss Tt Uu Vv Ww Xx Yy Zz
0123456789 , . : ; / & ! ? £ $ *

SANS REGULAR

Aa Bb Cc Dd Ee Ff Gg Hh Ii Jj Kk Ll Mm
Nn Oo Pp Qq Rr Ss Tt Uu Vv Ww Xx Yy Zz
0123456789 , . : ; / & ! ? £ $ *

SANS ITALIC

Aa Bb Cc Dd Ee Ff Gg Hh Ii Jj Kk Ll Mm
Nn Oo Pp Qq Rr Ss Tt Uu Vv Ww Xx Yy Zz
0123456789 , . : ; / & ! ? £ $ *

rockwell

Rockwell is a twentieth century slab serif typeface that was designed at the Monotype foundry studio in 1934, under the supervision of Frank Hinman Pierpont. An earlier face, Litho Antique, served as the foundation for the Rockwell design, which also bears a resemblance to realist sans serifs such as Akzidenz Grotesk or Franklin Gothic. Rockwell is geometric, its upper and lower case o more of a circle than an ellipse, and has a distinct serif at the apex of upper case a.

Rockwell's bold form makes it particularly appropriate for advertising and headline texts, rather than block texts. It was used by *The Guinness World Records* in some of their early 1990s editions, and is now used throughout the fast food chain Burger King's advertisements and in-store products.

Rockwell is a slab serif typeface drawn with a strong geometric presence, as shown by the almost perfectly circular lower case o. The double story lower case a is reminiscent of Akzidenz Grotesk, while the upper case a has a heavy slab serif at the apex—a recognisable feature of Rockwell.

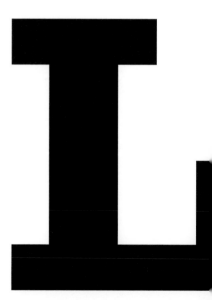

REGULAR

Aa Bb Cc Dd Ee Ff Gg Hh Ii Jj Kk Ll Mm
Nn Oo Pp Qq Rr Ss Tt Uu Vv Ww Xx Yy Zz
0123456789 , . : ; / & ! ? £ $ *

ITALIC

Aa Bb Cc Dd Ee Ff Gg Hh Ii Jj Kk Ll Mm
Nn Oo Pp Qq Rr Ss Tt Uu Vv Ww Xx Yy Zz
*0123456789 , . : ; / & ! ? £ $ **

BOLD

Aa Bb Cc Dd Ee Ff Gg Hh Ii Jj Kk Ll Mm
Nn Oo Pp Qq Rr Ss Tt Uu Vv Ww Xx Yy Zz
0123456789 , . : ; / & ! ? £ $ *

BOLD ITALIC

Aa Bb Cc Dd Ee Ff Gg Hh Ii Jj Kk Ll Mm
Nn Oo Pp Qq Rr Ss Tt Uu Vv Ww Xx Yy Zz
0123456789 , . : ; / & ! ? £ $ *

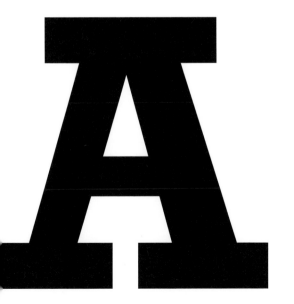
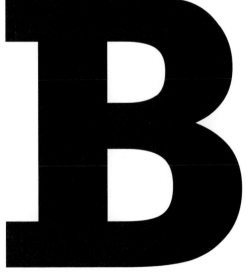

ROSEWOOD

Released in 1994, Rosewood is an ornate display face, inspired by woodcut type from the era of the Industrial Revolution. This was the dawn of advertising and ephemeral media—display faces were designed to grab attention and sell products, and these elaborate woodcut designs were usually printed in a variety of colours. When designing Rosewood, Kim Buker Chanster, Carl Crossgrove and Carol Twombly made this feature an integral part of the design. Instead of weights, Rosewood is available in Regular and Fill. The Fill of the typeface is very similar in construction to Clarendon with its truncated serifs and is to be printed first. Regular Rosewood is larger than the Fill and is printed on top, to recreate the ornate styles of yesteryear.

Rosewood is at its best when printed in two colours. The Fill (shown on the opposite page) is printed first with the regular font printed on top. It is reminiscent of Victorian display faces and is currently very popular when used to advertise music festivals.

REGULAR

ABCDEFGHIJKLMNOPQRSTUVWXYZ
0123456789 ,.:;/ &!?£$*

FILL

ABCDEFGHIJKLMNOPQRSTUVWXYZ
0123456789 ,.:;/ &!?£$*

ABCDEFG
HIJKLMN
OPQRSTU
VWXYZ
0123456789
,.:;/ &!?£$*

scala

In 1993, the Vredenburg Music Center in Utrecht, the Netherlands, commissioned the designer Martin Majoor to create a sans serif typeface to stand alongside his previous serif face, FF Scala. Majoor's new typeface retained signs of serif old style faces, and, unusually, also kept some of the humanism of FF Scala. As mentioned by Majoor himself, similarities can be seen between the upper and lower cases of his sans serif and typefaces such as Gill Sans and Syntax. FF Scala Sans is an unusually complete sans serif, in that it includes true small capitals, lining and non-lining (old style figures) and a variety of ligatures. The Scala family has been used worldwide in corporate identity such as KLM Royal Dutch Airlines and the Taschen Verlag publishing house.

Scala has large ascenders that reach above cap height and long descenders to aid the legibility of the typeface. The counters are a unique feature of Scala as they are angular and not perfectly curved, like many geometric faces, giving the face a quiet contemporary look.

REGULAR

Aa Bb Cc Dd Ee Ff Gg Hh Ii Jj Kk Ll Mm
Nn Oo Pp Qq Rr Ss Tt Uu Vv Ww Xx Yy Zz
0123456789 , . : ; / & ! ? £ $ *

ITALIC

Aa Bb Cc Dd Ee Ff Gg Hh Ii Jj Kk Ll Mm
Nn Oo Pp Qq Rr Ss Tt Uu Vv Ww Xx Yy Zz
0123456789 , . : ; / & ! ? £ $ *

BOLD

Aa Bb Cc Dd Ee Ff Gg Hh Ii Jj Kk Ll Mm
Nn Oo Pp Qq Rr Ss Tt Uu Vv Ww Xx Yy Zz
0123456789 , . : ; / & ! ? £ $ *

SERIF REGULAR

Aa Bb Cc Dd Ee Ff Gg Hh Ii Jj Kk Ll Mm
Nn Oo Pp Qq Rr Ss Tt Uu Vv Ww Xx Yy Zz
0123456789 , . : ; / & ! ? £ $ *

SERIF ITALIC

Aa Bb Cc Dd Ee Ff Gg Hh Ii Jj Kk Ll Mm
Nn Oo Pp Qq Rr Ss Tt Uu Vv Ww Xx Yy Zz
0123456789 , . : ; / & ! ? £ $

SERIF BOLD

Aa Bb Cc Dd Ee Ff Gg Hh Ii Jj Kk Ll Mm
Nn Oo Pp Qq Rr Ss Tt Uu Vv Ww Xx Yy Zz
0123456789 , . : ; / & ! ? £ $ *

souvenir

Souvenir was designed by Morris Fuller Benton for the American Type Founders company in 1914, and first shown as a single-weight design with no italic complement. After a brief initial success, and a later ineffective 1923 promotion, its popularity declined for over four decades; it was not until the late 1960s and the advent of photocomposition that the face became popular again. Formed in 1971, ITC launched ITC Souvenir as one of its initial typeface families. Designed by Ed Benguiat, and released in four weights with complimentary italic design, the font soon became one of ITC's most popular offerings. Although in recent years its popularity has somehow declined, it remains one of the milestones of twentieth century type, particularly for its soft design, that is, its lack of sharp edges and right angles.

Souvenir is a soft typeface, far removed from the geometric style of Futura or Helvetica. Curves are pronounced and the letterforms seem to flow with the ease of handwriting, particularly in the ligatures. This Art Nouveau-inspired typeface was particularly popular with phototypesetting, becoming a font synonymous with the 1970s and a benchmark for twentieth century type.

LIGHT

Aa Bb Cc Dd Ee Ff Gg Hh Ii Jj Kk Ll Mm
Nn Oo Pp Qq Rr Ss Tt Uu Vv Ww Xx Yy Zz
0123456789 , . : ; / & ! ? £ $ *

LIGHT ITALIC

Aa Bb Cc Dd Ee Ff Gg Hh Ii Jj Kk Ll Mm
Nn Oo Pp Qq Rr Ss Tt Uu Vv Ww Xx Yy Zz
0123456789 , . : ; / & ! ? £ $ *

MEDIUM

Aa Bb Cc Dd Ee Ff Gg Hh Ii Jj Kk Ll Mm
Nn Oo Pp Qq Rr Ss Tt Uu Vv Ww Xx Yy Zz
0123456789 , . : ; / & ! ? £ $ *

MEDIUM ITALIC

Aa Bb Cc Dd Ee Ff Gg Hh Ii Jj Kk Ll
Mm Nn Oo Pp Qq Rr Ss Tt Uu Vv Ww
Xx Yy Zz
0123456789 , . : ; / & ! ? £ $ *

DEMI

Aa Bb Cc Dd Ee Ff Gg Hh Ii Jj Kk Ll
Mm Nn Oo Pp Qq Rr Ss Tt Uu Vv Ww
Xx Yy Zz
0123456789 , . : ; / & ! ? £ $ *

BOLD

Aa Bb Cc Dd Ee Ff Gg Hh Ii Jj Kk Ll
Mm Nn Oo Pp Qq Rr Ss Tt Uu Vv Ww
Xx Yy Zz
0123456789 , . : ; / & ! ? £ $ *

stone

Designed by Sumner Stone at his Stone Type Foundry, ITC Stone is an original family of typefaces intended to be suitable to an essentially limitless range of applications. Stone performs well in a range of publications, from small-size business communication and extended text, to advertising, large-scale layouts and corporate identities. The strength of Stone's design is the ability for its typefaces to stand alone, with clear individual characteristics, but also to form a unified and distinctly modelled family. The sans serif design, ITC Stone Sans, combines the influence of prominent letterforms such as Gill Sans with the slightly condensed proportions of Stone Serif. Stone's informal sub-family retains an amount of dynamic personality and references to handwriting, whilst remaining an appropriate formal typographic font across a variety of applications.

The Stone type family, consisting of serif, sans, humanist and informal styles, gives the designer a multitude of voices within one design. With a transitional approach, it is reminiscent of Gill Sans and as the stroke changes in width as it reaches the curves it demonstrates a handwritten quality.

A mad b

a quick,

in the bo

SEMI

Aa Bb Cc Dd Ee Ff Gg Hh Ii Jj Kk Ll Mm
Nn Oo Pp Qq Rr Ss Tt Uu Vv Ww Xx Yy Zz
0123456789 , . : ; / & ! ? £ $ *

SEMI ITALIC

*Aa Bb Cc Dd Ee Ff Gg Hh Ii Jj Kk Ll Mm
Nn Oo Pp Qq Rr Ss Tt Uu Vv Ww Xx Yy Zz
0123456789 , . : ; / & ! ? £ $ **

oxer shot

gloved jab

k

syntax

In 1969, the Linotype type foundry released Syntax, a sans serif typeface designed the previous year by Hans Eduard Meier. Described by Meier as modelled on Renaissance serif typefaces (such as Bembo) Syntax has humanist forms that can be seen, for example, where the terminals do not sit parallel to the baseline. Unconventionally perhaps, Linotype's italic variant merges humanist italics with realist oblique forms; the lower case a in the italic variant has two storeys, unlike those seen in similar typefaces such as FF Scala Sans by Martin Majoor. Size 10 Syntax is generally used as the default typeface of Oberon operating systems, with whom Meijer designed a hand-optimised bitmap version of Syntax and its variants.

	ROMAN	ITALIC	ROMAN	ITALIC
SYNTAX	a	a	g	q
GILL	a	a	g	q
HUMANIST 521	a	a	g	q

Syntax's lower case a and g follow the old style model of having two stories. The italics are a combination of humanist italic forms, seen in the lower case italic q, and realist obliques, seen in the lower case italic a, which retains two stories, unlike other humanist sans serif typefaces.

ROMAN

Aa Bb Cc Dd Ee Ff Gg Hh Ii Jj Kk Ll Mm
Nn Oo Pp Qq Rr Ss Tt Uu Vv Ww Xx Yy Zz
0123456789 , . : ; / & ! ? £ $ *

ITALIC

Aa Bb Cc Dd Ee Ff Gg Hh Ii Jj Kk Ll Mm
Nn Oo Pp Qq Rr Ss Tt Uu Vv Ww Xx Yy Zz
*0123456789 , . : ; / & ! ? £ $ **

BOLD

Aa Bb Cc Dd Ee Ff Gg Hh Ii Jj Kk Ll Mm
Nn Oo Pp Qq Rr Ss Tt Uu Vv Ww Xx Yy Zz
0123456789 , . : ; / & ! ? £ $ *

BLACK

Aa Bb Cc Dd Ee Ff Gg Hh Ii Jj Kk Ll
Mm Nn Oo Pp Qq Rr Ss Tt Uu Vv Ww
Xx Yy Zz
0123456789 , . : ; / & ! ? £ $ *

ULTRA BLACK

Aa Bb Cc Dd Ee Ff Gg Hh Ii Jj Kk Ll
Mm Nn Oo Pp Qq Rr Ss Tt Uu Vv Ww
Xx Yy Zz
0123456789 , . : ; / & ! ? £ $ *

thesis

Dutch type designer Lucas de Groot (also known as Luc(as) de Groot) developed the Thesis typeface between 1994 and 1999. An extensive family of type variants including a sans serif (TheSans), a monospace (TheSansMono), and a mixed typeface (TheMix), Thesis began as an original design. De Groot intended to create a contemporary humanistic typeface that would be suitable for authoritative applications. Recent variants include TheAntiqua, and de Groot has also designed the Corpid and Calibri families. Thesis has become increasingly popular since its original release.

THESIS MONO PLAIN

Aa Bb Cc Dd Ee Ff
Gg Hh Ii Jj Kk Ll
Mm Nn Oo Pp Qq Rr
Ss Tt Uu Vv Ww Xx
Yy Zz

COURIER REGULAR

Aa Bb Cc Dd Ee Ff
Gg Hh Ii Jj Kk Ll
Mm Nn Oo Pp Qq Rr
Ss Tt Uu Vv Ww Xx
Yy Zz

Thesis is a large typeface family designed by Lucas de Groot. The font family includes a sans-serif typeface, a serif typeface, a monospace typeface and a mixed typeface.

EXTRA LIGHT PLAIN

Aa Bb Cc Dd Ee Ff Gg Hh Ii Jj Kk Ll Mm
Nn Oo Pp Qq Rr Ss Tt Uu Vv Ww Xx Yy Zz
0123456789 , . : ; / & ! ? £ $ *

LIGHT PLAIN

Aa Bb Cc Dd Ee Ff Gg Hh Ii Jj Kk Ll Mm
Nn Oo Pp Qq Rr Ss Tt Uu Vv Ww Xx Yy Zz
0123456789 , . : ; / & ! ? £ $ *

LIGHT ITALIC

Aa Bb Cc Dd Ee Ff Gg Hh Ii Jj Kk Ll Mm
Nn Oo Pp Qq Rr Ss Tt Uu Vv Ww Xx Yy Zz
*0123456789 , . : ; / & ! ? £ $ **

LIGHT CAPS

Aa Bb Cc Dd Ee Ff Gg Hh Ii Jj Kk Ll Mm
Nn Oo Pp Qq Rr Ss Tt Uu Vv Ww Xx Zz
0123456789 , . : ; / & ! ? £ $ *

BOLD PLAIN

Aa Bb Cc Dd Ee Ff Gg Hh Ii Jj Kk Ll Mm
Nn Oo Pp Qq Rr Ss Tt Uu Vv Ww Xx Yy Zz
0123456789 , . : ; / & ! ? £ $ *

BOLD ITALIC

Aa Bb Cc Dd Ee Ff Gg Hh Ii Jj Kk Ll Mm
Nn Oo Pp Qq Rr Ss Tt Uu Vv Ww Xx Yy Zz
0123456789 , . : ; / & ! ? £ $ *

MONO PLAIN

Aa Bb Cc Dd Ee Ff Gg Hh Ii Jj Kk
Ll Mm Nn Oo Pp Qq Rr Ss Tt Uu Vv
Ww Xx Yy Zz
0123456789 , . : ; / & ! ? £ $ *

times new roman

Stanley Morison was commissioned by the *The Times* newspaper to design a new typeface after he criticised the quality and relevance of their typesetting and printing in 1931. That year, he and Victor Lardent set to work at the British branch of the Monotype foundry. The Plantin and Perpetua fonts formed the basis of his design, and were re-worked to create a typeface that was clearly legible and economic with the space provided. Morison and Lardent produced a crisp, clean serif typeface, and while it has many old-style characteristics, it has now become one of the most successful typefaces in history. Despite no longer being used by *The Times*, it is bundled with every Microsoft Windows package and widely used as a serve-all typeface for desktop publishing.

Moon men return to earth upside down but safe

Times New Roman's features include large x heights, flat, straight serifs and tilted Os. Shown here is a headline from *The Times* newspaper, July 25, 1969.

REGULAR

Aa Bb Cc Dd Ee Ff Gg Hh Ii Jj Kk Ll Mm
Nn Oo Pp Qq Rr Ss Tt Uu Vv Ww Xx Yy Zz
0123456789 , . : ; / & ! ? £ $ *

ITALIC

Aa Bb Cc Dd Ee Ff Gg Hh Ii Jj Kk Ll Mm
Nn Oo Pp Qq Rr Ss Tt Uu Vv Ww Xx Yy Zz
*0123456789 , . : ; / & ! ? £ $ **

BOLD

Aa Bb Cc Dd Ee Ff Gg Hh Ii Jj Kk Ll Mm
Nn Oo Pp Qq Rr Ss Tt Uu Vv Ww Xx Yy Zz
0123456789 , . : ; / & ! ? £ $ *

BOLD ITALIC

Aa Bb Cc Dd Ee Ff Gg Hh Ii Jj Kk Ll Mm
Nn Oo Pp Qq Rr Ss Tt Uu Vv Ww Xx Yy Zz
0123456789 , . : ; / & ! ? £ $ *

Aa Bb Cc Dd
Ee Ff Gg Hh Ii Jj
Kk Ll Mm Nn Oo
Pp Qq Rr Ss Tt Uu
Vv Ww Xx Yy Zz

trade gothic

Trade Gothic is the name given to the neo-grotesque typeface family designed by Jackson Burke. Similar in form to the News Gothic variant released by Bitstream, Burke's design follows the tradition of grotesque sans serifs created in the nineteenth century. The first cut of Trade Gothic was released in 1948 through Linotype, and Burke continued to create a further 13 weight combinations and stylistic variants until 1960. Although the Trade Gothic family has perhaps a less conventional or cohesive relationship between its individual faces, its success might be derived precisely from the naturalistic sensibility that this produces. Trade Gothic has a relatively narrow form and condensed proportions, and as such has become a popular typeface for setting newspaper headlines. It is also often used in multimedia applications, where its hand-worked appearance can be combined with roman or antiqua typefaces.

SixBig Devils

Trade Gothic's essential features are its large x height and fairly narrow proportions, making it ideal for setting headlines in newspapers.

LIGHT

Aa Bb Cc Dd Ee Ff Gg Hh Ii Jj Kk Ll Mm
Nn Oo Pp Qq Rr Ss Tt Uu Vv Ww Xx Yy Zz
0123456789 , . : ; / & ! ? £ $ *

MEDIUM

Aa Bb Cc Dd Ee Ff Gg Hh Ii Jj Kk Ll Mm
Nn Oo Pp Qq Rr Ss Tt Uu Vv Ww Xx Yy Zz
0123456789 , . : ; / & ! ? £ $ *

OBLIQUE

Aa Bb Cc Dd Ee Ff Gg Hh Ii Jj Kk Ll Mm
Nn Oo Pp Qq Rr Ss Tt Uu Vv Ww Xx Yy Zz
*0123456789 , . : ; / & ! ? £ $ **

BOLD

Aa Bb Cc Dd Ee Ff Gg Hh Ii Jj Kk Ll Mm
Nn Oo Pp Qq Rr Ss Tt Uu Vv Ww Xx Yy Zz
0123456789 , . : ; / & ! ? £ $ *

BOLD OBLIQUE

Aa Bb Cc Dd Ee Ff Gg Hh Ii Jj Kk Ll Mm
Nn Oo Pp Qq Rr Ss Tt Uu Vv Ww Xx Yy Zz
0123456789 , . : ; / & ! ? £ $ *

CONDENSED NUMBER 18

Aa Bb Cc Dd Ee Ff Gg Hh Ii Jj Kk Ll Mm
Nn Oo Pp Qq Rr Ss Tt Uu Vv Ww Xx Yy Zz
0123456789 , . : ; / & ! ? £ $ *

BOLD CONDENSED NUMBER 20

Aa Bb Cc Dd Ee Ff Gg Hh Ii Jj Kk Ll Mm
Nn Oo Pp Qq Rr Ss Tt Uu Vv Ww Xx Yy Zz
0123456789 , . : ; / & ! ? £ $ *

TRAJAN

Trajan is an old style serif typeface designed in 1989 by Carol Twombly and licensed in digital form by Adobe Systems. It is one of several prominent letterforms based on the inscription at the base of Trajan's Column in Rome. Carved in 113 AD, it is regarded as one of the best uses of roman square capitals, or capitalis monumentalis, and most distinguished remaining examples of the Imperial Roman alphabet. Alternative derivative typefaces include Frederic Goudy's Goudy Trajan, and Warren Chappell's Trajanus. However, Twombly's cut has become the best known of all of these variations, and her digitalisation of the inscriptional lettering has been widely used in American film and television, although its overuse has been somewhat criticised. Trajan is constructed solely of small capitals, as lower case did not yet exist during the Roman period.

Inspired by the inscription on Trajan's column, erected AD 106–113 by the Roman Emperor Trajan and seen as one of the finest examples of roman monumental type. Consisting of only square capitals, or capitalis monumentalis, Trajan is a classic and elegant typeface, the letterforms replicating the carving tools of Ancient Rome with its strong stroke and crisp serifs.

SENATVS·PO

IMP·CAESARI·

TRAIANO·AVG·

MAXIMO·TRIB·P(

AD·DECLARANDV

MONS·ET·LOCVS·TAI

REGULAR

Aa Bb Cc Dd Ee Ff Gg Hh Ii Jj Kk
Ll Mm Nn Oo Pp Qq Rr Ss Tt Uu Vv
Ww Xx Yy Zz
0123456789 , . : ; / & ! ? £ $ *

BOLD

Aa Bb Cc Dd Ee Ff Gg Hh Ii Jj Kk
Ll Mm Nn Oo Pp Qq Rr Ss Tt Uu Vv
Ww Xx Yy Zz
0123456789 , . : ; / & !? £ $ *

LVSQVE·ROMANVS

VI·NERVAE·F·NERVAE

RM·DACICO·PONTIF

XVII·IMP·VI·COS·VI·P·P

QVANTAE·ALTITVDINIS

IS·OPER>IBVS·SIT·EGESTVS

triplex

Triplex is part of the Emigre font family, and was created as a substitute for Helvetica in 1990. The type designer, Zuzana Licko, had wanted Triplex to be a geometrical and rational typeface, although it evolved to be one of Licko's most intuitive typefaces. The design finds its origins in the first Macintosh computers of 1984: Emigre sought to establish new typeface appropriate to the low-resolution output of Macintosh computers. Triplex was Licko's first sans serif typeface, evolved from Citizen, a text typeface that had only straight lines—inspired by the low resolution restrictions of the early Macintosh computers. Triplex progresses from these restrictions because it is notably more traditional and less modular. Many questioned the legibility of the Triplex, but it gradually became accepted as a new way of approaching text type, despite its idiosyncracities.

triplex is derived from citizen, a typeface of straight lines

CITIZEN LIGHT

Zuzana Licko designed Triplex based on Citizen, a typeface almost wholly composed of straight lines. Triplex was originally criticised for its lack of legibility, but has become increasingly popular in recent years.

triplex is derived from citizen, a typeface of straight lines

TRIPLEX LIGHT

LIGHT

Aa Bb Cc Dd Ee Ff Gg Hh Ii Jj Kk Ll Mm
Nn Oo Pp Qq Rr Ss Tt Uu Vv Ww Xx Yy Zz
0123456789 , . : ; / & ! ? £ $ *

LIGHT ITALIC

Aa Bb Cc Dd Ee Ff Gg Hh Ii Jj Kk Ll Mm
Nn Oo Pp Qq Rr Ss Tt Uu Vv Ww Xx Yy Zz
0123456789 , . : ; / & ! ? £ $ *

BOLD

Aa Bb Cc Dd Ee Ff Gg Hh Ii Jj Kk Ll Mm
Nn Oo Pp Qq Rr Ss Tt Uu Vv Ww Xx Yy Zz
0123456789 , . : ; / & ! ? £ $ *

BOLD ITALIC

Aa Bb Cc Dd Ee Ff Gg Hh Ii Jj Kk Ll Mm
Nn Oo Pp Qq Rr Ss Tt Uu Vv Ww Xx Yy Zz
0123456789 , . : ; / & ! ? £ $ *

EXTRA BOLD

Aa Bb Cc Dd Ee Ff Gg Hh Ii Jj Kk Ll Mm
Nn Oo Pp Qq Rr Ss Tt Uu Vv Ww Xx Yy Zz
0123456789 , . : ; / & ! ? £ $ *

SERIF LIGHT

Aa Bb Cc Dd Ee Ff Gg Hh Ii Jj Kk Ll Mm
Nn Oo Pp Qq Rr Ss Tt Uu Vv Ww Xx Yy Zz
0123456789 , . : ; / & ! ? £ $ *

SERIF BOLD

Aa Bb Cc Dd Ee Ff Gg Hh Ii Jj Kk Ll Mm
Nn Oo Pp Qq Rr Ss Tt Uu Vv Ww Xx Yy Zz
0123456789 , . : ; / & ! ? £ $ *

univers

Univers is a neo-grotesque sans serif, designed by Adrian Frutiger in 1956 and released by the type foundry Deberny et Piegnot in 1957. Frutiger had been asked to design a linear sans serif in several weights for setting extended text—an exciting challenge in 1956, as sans serifs were generally used only as display faces. Frutiger was reluctant to adapt an existing font to create his new typeface, instead finding inspiration in his old sketches from his studies at Kunstgewerbeschule (school of applied arts) in Zürich. Univers is an example of great Swiss design, one that projects an air of neutrality and cool elegance. It is widely used for corporate branding to express rationality and clarity, and its highly legible nature means that it is frequently used for signage.

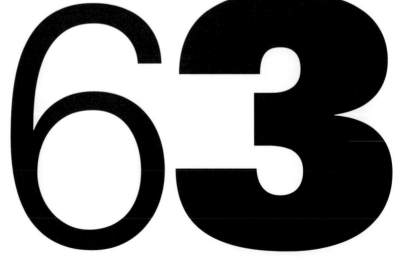

Univers was the first typeface designed with its own numbering system, so that each weight, width and style could easily be found. The multitude of combinations within Univers means that it is suitable for almost any purpose and it works impressively well when different weights are used together.

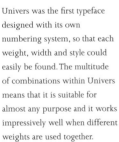

45 LIGHT

Aa Bb Cc Dd Ee Ff Gg Hh Ii Jj Kk Ll Mm
Nn Oo Pp Qq Rr Ss Tt Uu Vv Ww Xx Yy Zz
0123456789 , . : ; / & ! ? £ $ *

55 ROMAN

Aa Bb Cc Dd Ee Ff Gg Hh Ii Jj Kk Ll Mm
Nn Oo Pp Qq Rr Ss Tt Uu Vv Ww Xx Yy Zz
0123456789 , . : ; / & ! ? £ $ *

55 OBLIQUE

*Aa Bb Cc Dd Ee Ff Gg Hh Ii Jj Kk Ll Mm
Nn Oo Pp Qq Rr Ss Tt Uu Vv Ww Xx Yy Zz
0123456789 , . : ; / & ! ? £ $ **

65 BOLD

**Aa Bb Cc Dd Ee Ff Gg Hh Ii Jj Kk Ll Mm
Nn Oo Pp Qq Rr Ss Tt Uu Vv Ww Xx Yy Zz
0123456789 , . : ; / & ! ? £ $ ***

75 BLACK

**Aa Bb Cc Dd Ee Ff Gg Hh Ii Jj Kk Ll
Mm Nn Oo Pp Qq Rr Ss Tt Uu Vv Ww
Xx Yy Zz
0123456789 , . : ; / & ! ? £ $ ***

47 LIGHT CONDENSED

Aa Bb Cc Dd Ee Ff Gg Hh Ii Jj Kk Ll Mm Nn Oo Pp Qq Rr
Ss Tt Uu Vv Ww Xx Yy Zz
0123456789 , . : ; / & ! ? £ $ *

53 EXTENDED

Aa Bb Cc Dd Ee Ff Gg Hh Ii Jj Kk Ll
Mm Nn Oo Pp Qq Rr Ss Tt Uu Vv
Ww Xx Yy Zz
0123456789 , . : ; / & ! ? £ $ *

walbaum

Walbaum is a romantic typeface, similar to Didot and Bodoni, created by Justus Erich Walbaum at the turn of the nineteenth century. It has a rationalist axis and appears drawn instead of written, with a high contrast between thick and thin strokes. This contrast is less exaggerated than that of Didot or Bodoni, which increases its legibility, making Walbaum more appropriate for setting extended text. Berthold acquired the matrices a century later in 1903, and in 1976, Walbaum was redrawn for photosetting by Gunter Gerhard Lange. Digital versions are faithful to the original, although versions by Monotype differ to the original Berthold slightly as they were drawn from the smaller letters instead of the larger versions used by Berthold himself.

the five boxing wizards jump quickly

WALBAUM BOOK REGULAR

Walbaum is similar to the Romantic typeface Bodoni in that they are both drawn on a rationalist axis, yet Walbaum differs as its contrast between strokes is not as strong and it has a more calligraphic feel. The ascenders are not as tall and instead of ball terminals Walbaum has lachrymal, or teardrop, terminals.

BODONI BOOK

the five boxing wizards jump quickly

BOOK REGULAR

Aa Bb Cc Dd Ee Ff Gg Hh Ii Jj Kk Ll Mm
Nn Oo Pp Qq Rr Ss Tt Uu Vv Ww Xx Yy Zz
0123456789 , . : ; / & ! ? £ $ *

BOOK ITALIC

Aa Bb Cc Dd Ee Ff Gg Hh Ii Jj Kk Ll Mm
Nn Oo Pp Qq Rr Ss Tt Uu Vv Ww Xx Yy Zz
*0123456789 , . : ; / & ! ? £ $ ***

BOOK MEDIUM

Aa Bb Cc Dd Ee Ff Gg Hh Ii Jj Kk Ll Mm
Nn Oo Pp Qq Rr Ss Tt Uu Vv Ww Xx Yy Zz
0123456789 , . : ; / & ! ? £ $ *

BOOK MEDIUM ITALIC

Aa Bb Cc Dd Ee Ff Gg Hh Ii Jj Kk Ll Mm
Nn Oo Pp Qq Rr Ss Tt Uu Vv Ww Xx Yy Zz
***0123456789 , . : ; / & ! ? £ $ ***

BOOK BOLD

Aa Bb Cc Dd Ee Ff Gg Hh Ii Jj Kk Ll
Mm Nn Oo Pp Qq Rr Ss Tt Uu Vv Ww
Xx Yy Zz
0123456789 , . : ; / & ! ? £ $ *

BOOK BOLD ITALIC

Aa Bb Cc Dd Ee Ff Gg Hh Ii Jj Kk Ll
Mm Nn Oo Pp Qq Rr Ss Tt Uu Vv Ww
Xx Yy Zz
***0123456789 , . : ; / & ! ? £ $ ***

BOOK ROMAN SMALL CAPS
& OLDSTYLE FIGURES

Aa Bb Cc Dd Ee Ff Gg Hh Ii Jj Kk Ll Mm
Nn Oo Pp Qq Rr Ss Tt Uu Vv Ww Xx Yy Zz
0123456789 , . : ; / & ! ? £ $ *

Zapfino is an ornate, calligraphic typeface designed by Hermann Zapf in 1998. Zapf wanted to create a font that could reflect the flexibility and freedom of handwriting and first began working on his idea in 1944. In 1948, the Stempel foundry approached Zapf to create a calligraphic typeface but his idea was not achievable using metal type. However, the digital era meant that Zapf's idea could now be possible, and upon release in 1998 it had four alphabets, ornaments, flourishes and dingbats. In 2003 Zapf redesigned Zapfino with Akira Kobayashi, exploiting Open Type technology to create a typeface that could automatically substitute glyphs. These substitutions enable the typeface to flourish and have the flexibility of handwriting, creating a perfect combination of artistic and technical ability.

twenty s

Zapfino is a complex font, used on the computer for creating calligraphic script layout designs. OpenType allows the typographer to select from many alternative characters and ligatures, allowing a unique flexibility that mirrors a handwritten style. Zapfino is commonly used as a display face, exploiting the delicacy of the intricate letterforms.

Aa Bb Cc Dd Ee Ff Gg Hh Ii
Jj Kk Ll Mm Nn Oo Pp Qq
Rr Ss Tt Uu Vv Ww Xx Yy Zz
0123456789
, . : ; / @ !? £ $ *

x letters

NOTES

THE DEVELOPMENT OF WRITING

[1] Diringer, David. *The Alphabet*, London, 1968.

[2] Diringer, David. *The Book Before Printing: Ancient, Medieval, Oriental*, Dover Publications, 1982, p 109.

[3] Lucas, Christopher J. "The Scibal Tablet House in Ancient Mesopotamia", in *History of Education Quarterly*, vol 19, no 3 (Autumn, 1979), pp 305–332.

[4] Diringer, David. *The Book Before Printing: Ancient, Medieval, Oriental*, Dover Publications, 1982, p 263.

[5] Trinity College, Dublin.

[6] Pierpont Morgan Library, M871.

I DAVID PEARSON
Penguin Books—Great Ideas

[1] There are two standard book sizes within the paperback industry: A format: the original Penguin size (181 x 111 mm). B format: used widely since the mid 1980s sparking a significant rise in the price of paperback books (198 x 129 mm). Individual copies were priced at £3.99.

[2] Most major publishing houses stage weekly jacket meetings, attended by representatives of editorial, marketing, publicity and sales departments.

[3] Proofed covers are important aids to the sales team as the trade will often only buy into a title if they believe it's cover will sell it.

[4] Free from protective, ultraviolet laminates.

[5] Until the mid-1960s, Penguin's covers relied heavily on a series specific colour-coding system: orange for fiction, green for mystery and crime, pink for travel and adventure and so on.

[6] Printing one color over another, instead of 'knocking out' the background color.

PRINTING AND PROCESS

[1] An inventory of the all the books held by Cambridge University in 1424 recoded only 122 volumes.

[3] See: Dirck Volckertszoon Coornhert's preface to a translation of Cicero, *Officia Ciceronis, leerende wat yeghelijck in allen staten behoort te doen*, 1561, in which he claims Haarlem as the birthplace of printing. Other early sources can be found in: Samuel Ampzing *Beschrijvingh ende lof van Haerlem*, Haarlem, 1628 and Van Oosten de Bruyn *De Stad Haarlem*, 1765.

[4] Moxon, Joseph. *Mechanick Exercises: Or, the Doctrine of Handy-Works Applied to the Art of Printing*, London, Printed for Joseph Moxon, 1683, p 102, pp 134–135.

[5] Schöffer is listed as being amongst Fust's witnesses in the Helmasperger Instrument, a legal document dated 6 November 1455, in which Fust sought from Gutenberg repayment of 2,020 gulden, representing two loans of 880 gulden each together with the accumulated interest.

[6] Ing, Janet. *Johann Gutenberg and His Bible: a Historical Study*, The Typofiles, New York, 1988, p 76.

[7] See, Paul Schwenke, *Untersuchungen zur Geschichte des ersten Buchdrucks*, Berlin, 1900.

[8] Johnson, John. *Typographia, or the Printers' Instructor*, Longmans, 1824, vol 2, p 648.

[9] Moran, James. *Printing Presses History & Development from the Fifteenth Century to Modern Times*, University of California Press, 1973, pp 35–36.

[10] Timperley, C H. *The Printers' Manual*, H Johnson, 1838, p 12.

[11] Luckombe, P. *The History and Art of Printing*, London, printed by W Adlard, 1771, p 369.

[12] Ibid, p 370.

[13] Ing, Janet. *Johann Gutenberg and His Bible A Historical Study*, The Typofiles, New York, 1988, p 79.

[14] *Princeton Weekly Bulletin*, 12 February 2001, vol 90, no 16.

[15] In *Kunst-und-Werk-Schul*, Nuremberg, 1690.

LETTERS

[2] Reproduced in: Daniel Berkley Updike, *Printing Types Their History, Forms and Use*, Cambridge, 1937, vol 2, p 118.

[3] Timperley, CH. *The Printer's Manual*, London, H Johnson, 1838, p 56.

[4] Timperley, CH. *The Printer's Manual*, London, H Johnson, 1838, p 58.

[5] Ibid, p 63.

[6] Ibid, p 63.

[7] Ibid, p 63.

[8] Foucault, Michel. *The Order of Things: An Archaeology of the Human Sciences*, London: Routledge, 1991, p xv.

[9] Ibid, p xv.

[10] Loxley, Simon. *Type: The Secret History of Letters*, London: IB Tauris, 2004, p 27.

[11] Emery Walker's Cambridge Sandars lecture.

[12] Timperley, CH. *The Printer's Manual*, London, H Johnson, 1838, p 63.

[13] Ibid, p 63.

[14] See, GK Schauer, *Klassifikation Bemühungen um eine Ordnung im Druckschriften-bestand*, Darmstadt, 1975. Quoted in Rurai McLean *The Thames and Hudson Manual of Typography*, London, 1980, p 63.

[15] Nesbitt, A. *Lettering*, New York, 1950.

[16] Ibid.

3 WILL HILL
Old Forms, New Ideas: Typographic Revival and the Uses of History

This essay draws substantially upon my dissertation *Historical Reference and Revival in Twentieth-Century Type Design*, published by MBP Academic.

MOVE TO THE MODERN

[1] See Stanley Morison *John Fell*, 1967 which is hand-set in Fell type.

[2] As recounted by Talbot Baines Reed in *A History of Old English Letter Foundries*, London, 1952.

[3] *Ward & Price's Birmingham Directory*, Birmingham, 1823, p 66.

[4] John Milton, *Paradise Lost*, Birmingham, 1758, preface.

[5] Pierre Simon Fournier, *Modèles des Caractères de l'imprimerie*, 1742.

MECHANISATION

[1] Johnson, John. *Typographia, or the Printers' Instructor*, London, 1824, vol 2, p 536.

[3] Timmins, Samuel. *The Industrial History of Birmingham*, London, 1866.

[4] Johnson, John. *Typographia, or the Printers' Instructor*, London, 1824, vol 2, p 532.

[5] See British Library collection, which dates the scroll to 868, 587 years before

Gutenberg printed his 42-line Bible.

[6] Twyman, Michael. *The Brtish Library Guide to Printing History and Techniques*, London: The British Library, 1998, p 47.

[7] Updike, DB. *Printing Types*, Cambridge, 1937, vol 2, p 199.

[8] McLean, R. *Victorian Book Design and Colour Printing*, London, 1972, p 70.

6 TEAL TRIGGS
Great Women Typographers: Where are They?
Teal Triggs asks Sibylle Hagmann

Sibylle Hagmann began her career in Switzerland after earning a BFA from the Basel School of Design in 1989. She explored her passion for typography and type design while completing her MFA at the California Institute of the Arts in 1996. Her work has been featured in numerous publications and recognised by the Type Directors Club of New York. Hagmann founded her Houston-based design studio Kontour in 2000, where her clients include the CORE Program, The Museum of Fine Arts, Houston; The Menil Collection, Houston; Dallas Museum of Art; and the University of Southern California (USC), Los Angeles. She teaches at the University of Houston in the graphic communications program.

[1] Dargis, M. (2008) "Is There a Real Woman in This Multiplex?" *The New York Times*, pp 3, 32. Bibliography: Drucker, J and McVarish, E. *Graphic Design History: A Critical Guide*, New Jersey: Pearson Prentice Hall, 2009; Eskilson, S *Graphic Design: a New History*, London: Laurence King, 2007; Hagmann, S "Non-existent Design: Women and the Creation of Type", in Triggs, T. (ed), *The New Typography*, a special issue of *Visual Communication* 4 (2), 2005. pp 186–194; Kinross, R. "Modern Typography: An Essay in Critical History". London, Hyphen Press, 1992, 2004; Lupton, E. "Women Graphic Designers: Women Designers in the USA, 1900–2000" in Kirkham, P (ed), New Haven: Yale University Press, 2000; Makela, L. and Lupton, E. "Underground Matriarchy", *Eye*14 (4),1994, pp 42–47; Meggs, P. *A History of Graphic Design*. New York, Van Nostrand Reinhold, 1983; Nochlin, L. "Why Have There Been No Great Women Artists?" *ARTnews* January,1971, pp 22–39, 67–71; Scotford, M. "Messy History vs Neat History: Toward an Expended View of Women in Graphic Design", in Blauvelt, A (ed), *New Perspectives: Critical Histories of Graphic Design*, a special issue of *Visible Language*, 28.4,1994, pp 367-87; Triggs, T. "Chapter 7: Graphic Design", in Carson, F. and Pajaczkowska, C. (eds), *Feminist Visual Culture* Edinburgh, Edinburgh University Press, 2000, pp 147–170; Walters, J and various "Lust and Likeability", *Eye*67, Spring, 2008, pp 26–Ⳃ33.

ART AND STYLE

[1] Herbert Percy Horne and A H Mackmurdo, *The Century Guild Hobby Horse*, London, Chiswick Press, 1884-1892. Crafted with generous margins, close-set type, deckled edges and deeply-inked woodcut decorations, the journal is widely seen as having anticipated the private press' preoccupations with traditional methods of printing.

[2] See William S Peterson, *Type Designs of William Morris*, Printing Historical Society Journal, nos 19 and 20, 1985–1987.

[3] See LM Newman *Edward Gordon Craig Black Figures*, Wellingborough Christopher Skelton, 1989.

[4] Extracted from: *Looking Closer 3: Classic Writings on Graphic Design*, Michael Bierut, Jessica Helfand, Steven Heller, and Rick Poynor (ed), New York, Allworth Press, 1999, p 10.

[5] From: *1919 Bauhaus 1928* Herbert Bayer, Walter Gropius and Ise Gropius (ed), New York The Museum of Modern Art, 1938, p 149.

[6] Tschichold, Jan. *The New Typography*, Translated by Ruari McLean, 1928.

[7] Bielenson, Peter. *The Story of Frederic W Goudy*, Mt Vernon, 1939 and 1965, quoted in Simon Loxley, *The Secret History of Type*, London, 2006, p 93.

[8] Continuing in a long tradition of setting nameplates in grotesques. The LNWR used a face akin to Stevens Shank's Royal Gothic in the nameplate of their locomotive Hardwicke, now preserved in the National Railway Museum, York.

[9] Bartram, Alan. *Typeforms: a History*, The British Library, 2007, p 97.

THE DIGITAL AGE

[1] T Montague, N. *The Art and Practice of Printing Lithography, Photo-Lithography Offset, Bronzing and Allied Process*, London, Pitman, 1933, p 76.

[2] Jeffrey, Keedy. "Graphic Design in the Postmodern Era", *Émigré* 47, 1998.

FIRST THINGS FIRST 1964

Manifesto published jointly by 33 signatories in: *Adbusters*, the *AIGA Journal*, *Blueprint, Emigre, Eye, Form, Items*, Fall 1999 / Spring 2000. Foreword by Chris Dixon, *Adbusters*, Introduction by Rick Poynor, reaction by Jouke Kleerebezem, discussion Info Design Cafe mailinglist, miscellaneous reactions Max Bruinsma.

FIRST THINGS FIRST 2000

Manifesto published jointly by 33 signatories in: *Adbusters*, the *AIGA Journal*, *Blueprint, Emigre, Eye, Form, Items*, Fall 1999 / Spring 2000. Foreword by Chris Dixon, *Adbusters*, Introduction by Rick Poynor, reaction by Jouke Kleerebezem, discussion Info Design Cafe mailinglist, miscellaneous reactions Max Bruinsma.

INDEX

ACKNOWLEDGEMENTS

Nadine Monem
Editor

I would like to thank Emma Gibson for her enthusiasm, encouragement and constant hard work. Thank you to all who contributed to the book, especially Bruce Tice, Peter Bil'ak, Will Hill, Teal Triggs, David Pearson, Danny, Marieke and Erwin at Experimental Jetset, Ed Fella, Stefan Sagmeister, Ben James and Domenic Lippa at Pentagram, Dave Lane and Sam Mallett. A special thank you to the design team at Black Dog Publishing—Matthew Pull, Josh Baker, Julia Trudeau Rivest, Rachel Pfleger and Ana Estrougo for all of their good counsel, support and expertise. To Nigel Roche and everyone at St Bride Library for their vast knowledge, saint-like tolerance and good humour. And finally, a big thank you to Emily Chicken for designing what may well be the most beautiful book I have ever had the pleasure to work on.

Emma Gibson
Creative Consultant

Whilst echoing the above thanks to all the contributors to this book, a special thank you to Bruce Tice for his writings, Emily Chicken for her great design work, Dave Lane for contributing at the last possible minute and Luke Waller for his help and illustrations. To Jerry Kotomski and Matt Pull for photographic expertise and Nigel and his team at St Bride Library for amazing patience and skill. I would also like to say thank you to fellow creatives at Studio 69a for constant support and a good eye, the Gibson Family for endless offerings and knowledge, and The Home For Lost Girls and all it's visitors.

And especially Enid Nomen.

Text By: Bruce Tice, Nadine Monem, David Pearson, Alexander W White, Will Hill, Domenic Lippa, Ed Fella, Teal Triggs, Sybille Hagmann, Peter Bil'ak, Danny Marieke and Erwin at Experimental Jetset, Sam Winston, Charlotte Jane Lord, Muriel Moukawem and Aimee Selby.

Black Dog Publishing Limited
10A Acton Street
London WC1X 9NG
info@blackdogonline.com

Editor: Nadine Käthe Monem
Assistant Editor: Nikolaos Kotsopoulos
Designer: Emily Chicken
Creative Consultant: Emma Gibson www.egibson.co.uk

All opinions expressed within this publication are those of the authors and not necessarily of the publisher.

British Library Cataloguing-in-Publication Data. A CIP record for this book is available from the British Library
ISBN 978 1 906155 414

Black Dog Publishing Limited, London, UK, is an environmentally responsible company. *Font. The Sourcebook* is set in Akzidenz Grotesque and Joanna and is printed on Munken Arctic Volume 115gsm, an FSC certified paper.

architecture art design
fashion history photography
theory and things

black dog
publishing

www.blackdogonline.com london uk